THE ULTIMATE BOOK OF
VEGAN COOKING

THE ULTIMATE BOOK OF
VEGAN COOKING

Everything you need to know about going vegan, from choosing
the best ingredients to practical advice on health and nutrition

Tony and Yvonne Bishop-Weston

LORENZ BOOKS

This edition is published by
Lorenz Books, an imprint of
Anness Publishing Ltd,
Blaby Road, Wigston,
Leicestershire LE18 4SE

Email: info@anness.com
Web: www.lorenzbooks.com;
www.annesspublishing.com

If you like the images in this book and
would like to investigate using them
for publishing, promotions or advertising,
please visit our website
www.practicalpictures.com for more
information.

Publisher: Joanna Lorenz
Editors: Elizabeth Woodland and
  Kate Eddison
Copy Editor: Jay Thundercliffe
Design: Nigel Partridge
Production Manager: Claire Rae

Main front cover image shows Avocado
and Grapefruit Salad – for recipe, see
page 143

PUBLISHER'S NOTE
Although the advice and information in this
book are believed to be accurate and true
at the time of going to press, neither the
authors nor the publisher can accept any
legal responsibility or liability for any errors
or omissions that may be made nor for any
inaccuracies nor for any loss, harm or
injury that comes about from following
instructions or advice in this book.

**641.
563**

NOTES
• Bracketed terms are intended for
American readers.
• For all recipes, quantities are given in
both metric and imperial measures
and, where appropriate, in standard
cups and spoons.
• Follow one set of measures, but not
a mixture, because they are not
interchangeable.
• Standard spoon and cup measures
are level. 1 tsp = 5ml, 1 tbsp = 15ml,
1 cup = 250ml/8fl oz.
• Australian standard tablespoons
are 20ml.
• Australian readers should use 3 tsp
in place of 1 tbsp for measuring small
quantities.
• American pints are 16fl oz/2 cups.
American readers should use 20fl oz/
2.5 cups in place of 1 pint when
measuring liquids.
• Electric oven temperatures in this book
are for conventional ovens. When using
a fan oven, the temperature will probably
need to be reduced by about 10–20°C/
20–40°F. Since ovens vary, you should
check with your manufacturer's
instruction book for guidance.
• The nutritional analysis given for each
recipe is calculated per portion (i.e.
serving or item), unless otherwise stated.
• If the recipe gives a range, such as
Serves 4–6, then the nutritional
analysis will be for the smaller portion
size, i.e. 6 servings.
• Measurements for sodium do not
include salt added to taste.
• Medium (US large) eggs are used
unless otherwise stated.

ETHICAL TRADING POLICY
At Anness Publishing we believe that
business should be conducted in an
ethical and ecologically sustainable way,
with respect for the environment and a
proper regard to the replacement of the
natural resources we employ.

As a publisher, we use a lot of wood
pulp to make high-quality paper for
printing, and that wood commonly
comes from spruce trees. We are
therefore currently growing more than
750,000 trees in three Scottish forest
plantations: Berrymoss (130 hectares/
320 acres), West Touxhill (125 hectares/
305 acres) and Deveron Forest
(75 hectares/185 acres). The forests we
manage contain more than 3.5 times
the number of trees employed each
year in making paper for the books we
manufacture.

Because of this ongoing ecological
investment programme, you, as our
customer, can have the pleasure and
reassurance of knowing that a tree is
being cultivated on your behalf to
naturally replace the materials used
to make the book you are holding.

Our forestry programme is run in
accordance with the UK Woodland
Assurance Scheme (UKWAS) and will
be certified by the internationally
recognized Forest Stewardship Council
(FSC). The FSC is a non-government
organization dedicated to promoting
responsible management of the world's
forests. Certification ensures forests are
managed in an environmentally
sustainable and socially responsible
way. For further information about this
scheme, go to
www.annesspublishing.com/trees

Contents

Introduction

Veganism is much more than simply a particular diet to be followed. There is a wide and varied philosophy and lifestyle behind it that incorporates many of the issues which are becoming growing concerns in the modern world. For example, animal welfare and environmental issues have long been vital components of veganism and these are reflected in today's headlines, dominated by the quest to reduce our carbon emissions, both on a personal level and within industries such as livestock farming.

People are now increasingly looking for a way of life to counteract many of the global issues and problems that face us. One of the most appropriate of those lifestyles is veganism.

What is veganism?

In the most basic terms a vegan is someone who avoids consuming or utilizing any product that is, or was once, part of an animal or is sourced from an animal.

Humans are one of the most complex and adaptable species on the planet and can survive in many extremes and on a vast range of diets. Vegans believe that a varied plant-based diet produces the

Below: Vegans can enjoy a nutritious and diverse diet which is completely free from animal-derived products.

Above: Vegans believe that a varied plant-based diet is the key to physical and mental wellbeing.

optimal state of physical and mental being, and that the principles of veganism are kinder to people, animals and the environment. The vegan line is drawn somewhere between algae being from the plant kingdom, which is acceptable on the diet, and plankton from the animal kingdom, which is not acceptable.

The Vegan Society, the first-ever vegan organization, which was founded in the UK in 1944, defines a vegan as a person who, "excludes all forms of exploitation of, and cruelty to, animals for food, clothing or any other purpose". The definitions of veganism in the many other vegan organizations around the world are fundamentally similar to that

of the Vegan Society. Therefore, any vegan seeks to lead a lifestyle, where practically possible, that is completely free from animal products for the benefit of all people, animals and the environment.

Fundamentally, it is the risk of the exploitation and harm of a living creature and causing it suffering that is an important part of veganism – not just

THE VEGAN SOCIETY DEFINITION OF VEGANISM

"The word 'veganism' denotes a philosophy and way of living which seeks to exclude – as far as is possible and practical – all forms of exploitation of, and cruelty to, animals for food, clothing or any other purpose; and by extension, promotes the development and use of animal-free alternatives for the benefit of humans, animals and the environment. In dietary terms it denotes the practice of dispensing with all products derived wholly or partly from animals."

avoiding the direct responsibility of causing an animal's death, as is the case with vegetarianism.

Vegetarians may use and consume products that committed vegans avoid, because the products are made without actually killing an animal. Dairy products, such as milk and cheese, other animal-derived foods, such as honey, and materials derived in some way from animals, such as wool and silk, are available to the vegetarian because the animals are not killed in the process. Vegans, on the other hand, will avoid such products due to the exploitation and harm done to the animals merely by farming them for our benefit. Vegans use plant-based alternatives to milk, cheese and eggs, such as soya, and agave or maple syrup instead of honey. Vegans also use cotton, linen, hemp and synthetic fibres instead of silk, leather, wool and other items that are made from animals.

The minute details of how a product is made will have a big impact on whether it is acceptable to vegans. For example, beers and wines are often made with isinglass (made from the bladder of a fish) or gelatine, so vegans choose filtered alternatives or products fined with betonite (a mineral) or seaweed extracts. Vegan wines and beers are now widely available thanks to an interest in natural produce and a growing trend to avoid unnecessary additives.

Products that have been tested on animals are also avoided by vegans because of the harm they cause. Vegans prefer to use cosmetics and toiletries that are tested on humans or cells in a dish rather than cause suffering to animals.

The father of veganism, Donald Watson, who founded the Vegan Society in 1944, was a conscientious objector who believed that humans would always struggle to be kinder to fellow human beings if they failed to show compassion to voiceless and helpless animals. He argued that true civilization depended on accepting the responsibilities we have that come with our human advantages of choice.

Rather than constantly having to argue and make decisions about an acceptable level of animal cruelty or discomfort, Watson insisted that vegans should simply opt out of exploitation of another sentient being's life and use the many ethical, practical and sustainable alternatives that nature provides us with.

Using this book

The biggest hurdle that many people have to overcome when following a vegan diet is to have plenty of exciting, healthy and delicious recipes to cook. The following chapters will help to answer the question that many vegans get asked: 'What do you eat?' Even to

Left: Vegans use plant-based alternatives to dairy and meat products, such as soya milk and yogurt, tofu and tempeh.

those people who are contemplating a vegan lifestyle, the prospect of a wholly plant-based diet can be daunting. The recipe section in this book is brimming with ideas demonstrating the options that are available to vegans.

However, this is more than just a guide to cooking. Veganism is a complex philosophy that impacts on every aspect of life, from the shoes we wear to the shampoo we use and the medications we take. The first chapter, The Vegan Life, examines and answers many of the issues affecting vegans, from the reasons for choosing the lifestyle and the essential nutrients needed, to shopping, medicine and advice for pregnancy.

The second chapter, The Vegan Kitchen, is a detailed guide to the vital foods that are an important part of any vegan pantry. It covers a vast range of foods, from fruits and vegetables, to beans, peas and lentils.

The main section of the book comprises a compilation of tempting recipes, which are split into convenient chapters to help you find the perfect dish for any occasion, from everyday nutritious breakfasts to dinner party specialities.

Below: There is no reason why vegans cannot enjoy an exciting diet of mouthwatering, healthy meals.

the
vegan
life

Although becoming a vegan can be an intimidating
prospect, it can also be an exciting and fulfilling adventure.
This chapter looks at the many issues around veganism,
such as the history of the movement and reasons for
choosing the lifestyle. There is also a wealth of essential
information on nutrition, health and pregnancy, as well as
a guide to ethical shopping, entertaining and eating out.

The history of veganism

Veganism is a logical progression from vegetarianism – the exclusion of meat and some other animal-derived products from the diet – which has a long and varied history around the world. As a concept and practice, vegetarianism has been recorded as early as the 6th century BC in communities in ancient India and the classical Greek world. The reasons for abstaining from meat were mainly religious and concerned the idea of non-violence toward animals, which was termed *ahimsa* in Sanskrit, the ancient Indian language. Pythagoras (*c.*582–507BC), the Greek philosopher and mathematician, abstained from eggs and the flesh of animals, as part of an ascetic and philosophical way of life. In fact, until the formation of the Vegetarian Society in the UK in 1847, which popularized the term 'vegetarian', those who did not consume meat or fish were known as 'Pythagoreans'. The formation of the Vegetarian Society reflected the growing popularity of an animal-free diet.

Below: Donald Watson, who coined the word 'vegan' and founded the Vegan Society in November 1944.

Above: Vegetarian foods were popular choices at banquets and feasts in ancient Greece.

The birth of veganism

It was not long before vegetarians were concerned about the practices of the dairy industry and its relationship to the meat industry. At a meeting in London in November 1944, a handful of members of the Vegetarian Society, led by Donald Watson (1910–2005), a teacher who largely practised a non-dairy vegetarianism, decided to form a new society that would address their beliefs. They needed a new word to describe themselves, and Watson coined the word 'vegan' to describe the new philosophy, using the first and last letters from 'vegetarian'. He described the new concept as 'the beginning and end of vegetarian'.

Another leading pioneer in the very early days of the movement was Arthur Ling, who founded the company Plamil (whose name came about by contracting 'plant milk'). His dedication to the vegan cause helped bring soya milk to the UK and he went on to perfect other vegan products, like chocolate and mayonnaise.

Veganism in the USA

American veganism owes thanks to a man called H. Jay Dinshah, a lifelong vegetarian born in Malaga, New Jersey. His father was a Parsi from Bombay in India and his mother was an American

THE VEGAN NEWS, 1944
Below is the introduction to the first Vegan Society newsletter:

"The use of dairy produce has revealed very strong evidence to show that the production of these foods involves much cruel exploitation and slaughter of highly sentient life. The excuse that it is not necessary to kill in order to obtain dairy produce is untenable for those with a knowledge of livestock farming methods.

For years many of us accepted that the flesh-food industry and the dairy produce industry were related, and that in some ways they subsidised one another. We accepted, therefore, that the case on ethical grounds for the disuse of these foods was exceptionally strong, and we hoped that sooner or later a crisis in our conscience would set us free.

That freedom has now come to us. The unquestionable cruelty associated with the production of dairy produce has made it clear that lacto-vegetarianism is but a halfway house between flesh-eating and a truly humane, civilised diet, and we think, therefore, that during our life on earth we should try to evolve sufficiently to make the 'full journey'."

of German descent. He founded the American Vegan Society in 1960. There had been a regional vegan society in California for just over 10 years, but it was Jay Dinshah, with his wife Freya, who carried the vegan flag nationwide in a series of lectures across the USA and into Canada. They wrote books, published a regular magazine called *Ahimsa* and hosted conventions around the USA which spawned and inspired other groups, in particular a group of doctors calling themselves PCRM (Physicians Committee for Responsible Medicine), who advocate a vegan diet.

Members of the Seventh-day Adventist Church were also very influential in the spread of veganism in the USA. They achieved this partly by practical example in proving how healthy the vegan diet can be, but mainly by inspiring and supporting a network of health-food stores and restaurants. The Farm (a community in Tennessee) has also supported veganism, publishing books on vegan cooking and nutrition. These enterprises have provided the opportunity for people to sample veganism and have made vegan foods more accessible.

Below: A dedicated vegan, Arthur Ling founded the company Plamil and brought soya milk to the UK.

Growing popularity

Veganism really started to come to the attention of the general public during the 1960s, as vegetarianism moved into the mainstream. Cranks, a chain of wholefood vegetarian restaurants, opened on London's trendy Carnaby Street in 1961. Celebrity customers, including The Beatles and The Rolling Stones, brought the ideology of vegetarianism, and with it, veganism, to a whole new audience.

Below: H. Jay Dinshah founded the American Vegan Society in 1960 and brought veganism to the USA.

Above: Health-food stores offer a huge choice of fresh foods suitable for those following a vegan diet.

There are now many vegan societies and organizations spread across the world, and a vegan diet is promoted by many other groups and societies. These include international organizations such as the US-based animal-rights group PETA (People for the Ethical Treatment of Animals), which has nearly two million members. The International Vegetarian Union, set up in 1908 to promote vegetarianism, now always has a strictly vegan menu at its annual congress. These groups are never short of a vegan celebrity to add weight to their cause and catch the media's eye while promoting campaigns.

The Vegan Society's Diamond Jubilee in 2004 welcomed a new dawn for veganism with a new breed of vegan entrepreneurs launching their products. Mainstream businesses have recognized the importance of the growing vegan demographic with a range of food and drink, clothing and cosmetics available to vegans in mainstream outlets.

As more and more people have become vegan, the diet and lifestyle have got easier to follow. An increasing number of choices are now available to vegans, from the food they buy and the restaurants they can eat in, to the clothes they wear and the household products they use.

Why go vegan?

The decision to become a vegan is a very personal one, and there is a huge variety of reasons why people choose to adopt a vegan way of life. The health benefits of a vegan diet are a big attraction to many people. Others are initially impressed by the vegan philosophy of an ethical and moral life. Some, on the other hand, wish to follow a more environmentally friendly and ecological way of life. Spiritual factors also come into play in helping some people decide to opt for a vegan lifestyle.

A nutritious vegan diet

Most people are aware of the importance of eating a healthy diet. The question is whether cutting out all animal-derived foods and following a vegan diet will actually have any beneficial impact on our physical and mental wellbeing.

Studies such as the EPIC-Oxford Study and other research on Seventh-day Adventists have shown that a varied and properly balanced plant-based diet can provide an optimum mix of nutrients for a healthy body.

A well-balanced vegan diet is naturally lower in saturated fats, higher in essential fats, higher in fibre and

Below: Studies have shown that a vegan diet can have a beneficial effect on health.

Above: Meat and dairy products have been linked to a variety of illnesses.

antioxidants and potentially lower in toxins due to eating lower down the food chain. Eating meat and dairy has been linked to various cancers, digestive disorders, deteriorating heart health, Alzheimer's, osteoporosis, stroke and inflammatory conditions, such as arthritis, diabetes and high blood pressure, though results of studies are inconclusive.

Proven health benefits One of the biggest studies on the vegan population, the EPIC-Oxford Study, showed that vegans were at least as

Above: Vegans can still enjoy luxurious puddings like these chocolate brownies.

healthy as the healthiest of the meat-eaters, i.e. those who had a healthy diet with a reduction in meat consumption and a higher than average amount of fruit and vegetables. Other positive findings of the study include the fact that vegetarians, and especially vegans, have a lower prevalence of hypertension and lower blood pressure than meat-eaters.

EPIC

The European Prospective Investigation into Cancer and Nutrition (EPIC) was initiated in 1992 and is the largest detailed study of diet and health ever undertaken. It involves over 500,000 people in ten European countries and is co-ordinated by the World Health Organization.

The EPIC-Oxford Study group recruited people between 1993 and 1999, and targeted vegetarians and vegans. The results are of great scientific value because the diets of vegetarians, and especially vegans, differ substantially from those of meat-eaters and so it is easier to detect links between nutrition and health.

Right: A balanced vegan diet could lead to increased health and vitality.

The EPIC findings show that if vegans took more care to make sure their plant-based diet is varied, well-balanced and heathy, they could be enjoying an extra ten years of healthy living. By eating more fruit and dark green leafy vegetables and taking care to ensure adequate intake of essential fats, B vitamins, vitamin D and antioxidants from berries, vegans have the opportunity to prove that a vegan diet is the healthiest on the planet.

A common concern among those tempted by a vegan diet is that they may be missing out on some vital component of a human diet. However, there is no essential nutrient that you cannot get from vegan sources. Even vitamin B12, which is unfortunately rarely found in non-animal products, has now been shown to be abundantly available in algae.

Vegan foods healthier Many vegan food manufacturers have begun reformulating their products to be even healthier than before. Many non-vegans choose soya products over dairy

Below: Dark green leafy vegetables are a great source of iron and calcium.

products, and vegan sausages and burgers, for example, over traditional meat. Having realized that the majority of their customers are not necessarily vegans but simply healthy eaters wanting healthier options, many vegetarian food manufacturers are reducing the amount of saturated fats and increasing the protein levels in their foods.

Reduced risk of poisoning Eating vegan can also lessen the risk of food poisoning. Although reheated rice can be very dangerous, most of the worst

Below: Berries are a rich and tasty source of antioxidents.

cases of food poisoning are from animal foods, such as red meat, pork, chicken, fish, eggs, cheese and milk-based foods.

Eggs, dairy, meat and fish are also common allergens. It is thought that most people in the world are actually lactose intolerant. It is most common in non-dairy consuming societies. Lactose tolerance is, in fact, a mutation allowing people to produce lactase after childhood and be able to digest dairy products.

Nutritional knowledge There is still a great deal of ignorance about human nutrition. Family doctors and general medical practitioners often claim that vegan diets lack key nutrients, such as iron, vitamin B12, essential fats, calcium, zinc and essential amino acids. Ironically these nutrients are often deficient in their meat-eating patients too – the solution is not to eat more nutrient-depleted meat but to eat a better, more varied, plant-based diet. The problems may lie with convenient food choices, rather than with veganism itself.

By arming yourself with the nutritional facts and information contained in this book, you can easily dispel general concerns that you are missing out on any key nutrient. In fact, you will discover how to eat one of the healthiest diets available.

Ethical veganism

There are vegans who have chosen their lifestyle for ethical, moral or religious reasons. For many, one of the essential aspects of adopting a vegan diet is the basic belief that harming a living creature is wrong.

Religious ethics The spiritual basis for a vegan diet can be traced back many thousands of years and is seen in the doctrines of various ancient religions. In India, Hindus, who hold vegetarianism as an ideal, and Jains, for whom vegetarianism is mandatory, avoid eggs and regard cows as sacred, giving them more legal rights than many people. Jain monks follow a strict vegan lifestyle and even brush the path in front of them and wear masks to avoid harming insects and bugs. Buddhism, which prohibits killing, has varying attitudes toward vegetarianism and veganism throughout the world.

The Essenes, a reclusive Jewish sect in the 2nd century BC, who claimed to be the source of early Christianity, were also virtually vegan on religious grounds. The first chapter in the Bible speaks of plants, seeds and fruit as food for all life and calls for respect and responsibility for all living things. Many Seventh-day Adventists and Quakers are vegan, and veganism is increasingly popular in Humanist and Scientology circles too.

Below: Animals are the centre of ethical and religious concerns for some vegans.

The Rastafari tradition of *ital*, meaning the foods that are approved, is based on dietary laws of the Old Testament. Interpretation of the laws varies but the general principle is that food should be natural, or pure, and from the earth. Therefore chemically modified foods or those with artificial additives are avoided, and foods produced with chemicals such as pesticides are often not considered *ital*. In common with religions such as Judaism, Islam and Ethiopian Christianity, *ital* prohibits the eating of pork, and most Rastas do not eat red meat or shellfish. There are many, however, who restrict what is *ital* to the extent that they are on a vegan diet, and many more are vegetarians.

Philosophical ethics The non-religious debate regarding the moral right or wrong of consuming meat has been around for thousands of years as well. Greek philosophers, such as Pythagoras, the father of mathematics, and Hippocrates, the father of modern medicine, preached the virtues of eating a diet which does not cause suffering to an animal.

Many vegans, along with animal rights supporters and a lot of vegetarians, hold the basic philosophical position that animals possess certain rights – or that humans have particular responsibilities – which means that we have a duty to avoid inflicting any unnecessary pain on them or cause them any suffering.

Above: Harm caused to animals in the dairy industry can be a primary reason for choosing a vegan diet.

Many vegans and other vegetarians maintain that harming a living animal is as wrong as harming a human. This is because animals and humans share certain qualities, such as the instinct to survive and the capacity to feel happiness and pleasure as well as fear and pain. They believe that no animal should suffer harm or death unnecessarily and since we can follow a plant-based diet without detriment, killing and consuming an animal is not justifiable. In essence, the good that we get from the meat does not outweigh the bad done to the animal.

The argument against killing for food is extended by vegans to include the use of animals for any human purpose. The rights of animals, it is said, are still infringed whether they are in a dairy farm or on a sheep farm producing wool.

Active committed vegans often go beyond just food and clothing, challenging both the pharmaceutical and cosmetics industries. They argue that companies frivolously and repeatedly choose animal testing without any true benefit to mankind. They believe it is often to human detriment, and certainly to the detriment of many animals.

Environmental veganism

Many people choose to adopt a vegan lifestyle because they believe that it is better for the environment. They hold the view that a vegan diet uses far fewer resources and causes much less damage to the planet than an animal-based diet.

Although arguments about the unsustainability of meat and dairy production were around before Donald Watson's first editorial in the *Vegan News* in 1944, it is only relatively recently that it has begun to filter into governmental thinking.

In 2006, the United Nations published a 400-page report called *Livestock's Long Shadow*, in an attempt to "assess the full impact of the livestock sector on environmental problems". It was provoked by growing concerns about global warming and carbon emissions along with other environmental problems. The report confirmed that livestock production is responsible for land degradation, climate change, air pollution, water shortage, water pollution and loss of biodiversity. It was deduced from the report that by raising animals for food, livestock farmers produce more climate change gases than all the motor vehicles in the world. Steak from a grain-fed cow requires 35 calories of fossil fuel for every 1 calorie of consumable meat.

Below: The Amazon rainforest is being deforested for livestock pasture.

Above: Many vegans are concerned about the destructive impact of overfishing on marine ecosystems.

In response to the *Livestock's Long Shadow* report, the International Water Institute in Stockholm concluded that unless we change our reliance on animal-derived foods, we will undoubtedly run out of water. They claim that 1kg/2¼lb of wheat takes 120 litres/32 gallons of water to produce, while an equal amount of beef requires 3,700 litres/978 gallons.

Vegans maintain that feeding grain to animals to produce protein for humans is both inefficient and a waste of precious resources. Up to ten times as many people could be fed on a plant-based diet compared to a diet of beef.

Seventy per cent of the Amazon deforestation is attributable to livestock production. It is often argued that soya, an essential component of many vegan diets, is partly responsible for rainforest devastation. However, it is important to remember that 90 per cent of the world's soya is used for feeding animals, not humans.

The planet's marine ecosystems are being adversely affected due to overfishing, not just for food but also for oil which is used in both cosmetic and pharmaceutical products. Biologists worry that it is the largest fish that are most scarce, and it is these larger game fish that guide the smaller fish to spawning grounds. With the important discovery of complex omega-3 oils in sustainably grown algae, fishing policies need to be subjected to an urgent review.

In today's society, when people are concerned about carbon emissions and their own 'carbon footprint', a University of Chicago study in 2006 is enlightening. It found that switching from an average American diet to a plant-based vegan one would reduce each person's carbon dioxide emissions by 1,485kg/3,275lb a year – a significant difference bearing in mind that the average car generates about 3,000kg/6,600lb per year.

The essentials of nutrition

A balanced vegan diet is naturally and abundantly rich in the nutrients that are essential to a healthy diet. Nutrients such as fibre, essential fats and antioxidants are necessary for our wellbeing and in the prevention of chronic disease. Along with water, there are six essential dietary components we need for good health. If we consume the correct type of these nutrients in the right proportions, we will provide our body with sustained energy and an optimal balance of nutrients. These six components are complex carbohydrates, soluble fibre, amino acids from protein, essential fats, vitamins and minerals – all of which are abundantly available in plant foods.

Carbohydrates

For simplicity, carbohydrate-rich foods can be divided into three groups.
• Unrefined complex carbohydrates – wholegrain cereals, wholemeal (wholewheat) bread or pasta, and brown rice.
• Refined complex carbohydrates – white bread, white pasta and white rice.
• Simple carbohydrates – also known as sugars – includes fruit and vegetables, and foods with added sugars, such as cakes and biscuits.

Below: Ensure there is a bit of natural colour in your carbohydrates. Refined carbohydrates are stripped of nutrients.

Above: Carbohydrate-rich vegetables, such as potatoes and plantains, provide slow-release energy.

Carbohydrates are the body's major source of energy and they supply a substantial amount of protein, vitamins, minerals and fibre, with very little fat.

About half the food we eat should be fruit and vegetables. Nutritionists recommend at least five portions of fresh vegetables and three portions of fruit per day. One portion is roughly the size of a heaped pile in the palm of your hand.

Generally a quarter of your diet should be complex carbohydrates – often referred to as starchy foods – such as wholegrain cereals, wholemeal bread and pasta, brown rice and beans. These foods are broken down slowly by the body and provide a steady supply of energy. Try to opt for unrefined carbohydrates such as

wholemeal, wholegrain versions of food as the refined versions, such as white flour, bread, pasta, rice and sugar, are stripped of nutrients such as vitamins, minerals and fibre.

Simple carbohydrates – also known as sugars – include fruit and vegetables, which contain natural sugars, and refined simple carbohydrates with added sugars such as biscuits, cakes and fizzy drinks.

These refined simple carbohydrates could leave you depleted of key nutrients because they will need to 'steal' from your body's reserves of vitamins and minerals in order to convert the sugar into energy. It is these foods with added sugars which should be avoided or cut down on. They are quickly absorbed into the bloodstream and give only a short-term energy boost. The resulting peaks and troughs in the blood sugar level means that you have subseqently less stable energy levels in the body. They are more likely to be stored as fat if the energy is not used up and can also cause tooth decay.

Fibre

Adequate fibre is not usually a problem in a vegan diet as plant foods (fruits, vegetables, grains, legumes, nuts and seeds) are full of dietry fibre, unlike meat and dairy that have no fibre and are mainly saturated fat. There are two types of fibre: insoluble and soluble.

• Insoluble fibre, which is found in whole wheat, brown rice, bran and nuts, provides bulk to the diet and helps to facilitate a smooth exit for your food once your body has extracted all the nutrients out of it.

• Soluble fibre, found in legumes, oats and vegetables, binds with toxins in the gut and promotes their excretion, and also helps to reduce blood cholesterol.

Both types of fibre-rich foods reduce the risk of bowel disorders, including diverticulitis, colon and rectal cancer, and irritable bowel syndrome. Fibre also provides a better environment for good gut bacteria to flourish.

Few people get enough fibre. On average we eat about 12 grams of fibre a day, but we should be consuming at least 18 grams. People who wish to lose weight will find that eating more high-fibre foods is beneficial as it provides bulk and naturally reduces cravings for nutrient-depleted, high-calorie foods.

Below: Peanut butter is a great source of protein for vegans. Combined with bread, it provides essential amino acids.

Above: Brown rice, lentils, peas, beans and nuts all provide fibre, which is essential for a healthy digestive system.

Protein and amino acids

Although cases of protein deficiency are generally very rare, it is important not to overlook this macro-nutrient – it is essential for the maintenance and repair of every cell in the human body. The role that each type of protein plays in the body depends entirely on its composition.

Protein is made up of amino acids of which there are 20 in total, and about 8–10 of these need to be supplied by diet – these are known as essential amino acids. Shortages of these key amino acids have been implicated in a number of health issues, such as infertility, weight problems and depression. A food containing all eight amino acids is known as a 'complete' or high-quality protein. For those on a vegan diet, these include foods such as hemp seeds, quinoa, amaranth, buckwheat and soya products.

Protein derived from plant sources, such as nuts, pasta, potatoes, legumes, cereals and rice, does not usually contain all eight amino acids and is regarded as an 'incomplete' or low-quality protein. It is no longer thought that you must eat a combination of different protein plant foods in each meal. Providing you eat a varied diet it is hard to avoid combining protein groups to ensure consuming the essential amino acids and therefore high-quality protein. However, there are many simple vegan meals which provide complete protein, such as baked beans on toast, mushrooms and rice, lentils and rice, beans and rice, peanut butter sandwiches and hummus served in pitta breads. Every day, you should aim for approximately 25 per cent or one quarter of your dinner plate to consist of protein-rich food.

It is necessary to eat protein every day as the human body is not able to store it. However, it is thought that consuming too much protein can be more detrimental to the body than too little. High-protein foods, such as dairy products, have been found to leach calcium from the body, which can increase the risk of osteoporosis. Very high protein diets are also thought to play a part in contributing to conditions such as arthritis and diabetes. Interestingly, American footballers, who are renowned for their diets that are high in animal-derived protein, have a dramatically lower life expectancy than that of the average American.

Fats

Avoiding fat can be dangerous. Some polyunsaturated fats, omega-3 and omega-6 essential fats are vital for good health. Fat not only provides vitamins A, D and E and essential fatty acids that cannot be made in the body, but also contributes greatly to the taste, texture and palatability of food. Fat is highly calorific which is why it is all the more crucial to have the right types of fat and avoid wasting calories on fats that will only encourage weight gain without contributing to optimal health.

Saturated animal fat has been associated with an increased risk of cancer and coronary heart disease. Eating too much saturated fat can raise blood cholesterol levels and lead to narrowed arteries.

Unsaturated fats, including both polyunsaturated and monounsaturated, can help to reduce harmful LDL (low density lipoprotein) cholesterol – the type that furs up arteries – and, importantly, increase the beneficial HDL (high density lipoprotein) cholesterol, which is thought to reduce the cholesterol levels in the body.

Monounsaturated fats, such as olive oil, which is rich in omega-9, sesame oil and rapeseed (canola) oil are less vulnerable to oxidation than polyunsaturated fats, are more stable

Above: A rainbow of colours in your regular daily diet helps to maximize your intake of vitamins.

and thus better for cooking purposes. Polyunsaturated fats provide the essential fatty acids, omega-3 and omega-6, which are called essential because they cannot be made in the body, and therefore must be part of the diet. Omega-3, which is found in walnuts, soya beans, hemp and rapeseed oil, has been found to reduce the risk of heart disease, while omega-6 (linoleic acid), which is found in nuts, seeds and oils, is thought to reduce blood cholesterol.

The ideal ratio for these essential fats is often argued about but generally regarded to be around 4:1 (omega-6: omega-3). A healthy person can then process the basic omega-3 fats into the brain-building and brain-fuelling fatty acids DHA (docosahexanoic acid) and EPA (eicosapentaenoic acid). Lack of nutrients, digestive imbalances, liver problems and stress can all thwart the body's ability to do this. In this instance you may consider pure EPA and DHA derived from special strains of algae, otherwise a daily tablespoon of hemp oil is a good balanced way to boost your levels of omega-6, omega-3 and omega-9.

Vitamins

These nutrients are vital for good health and the functioning of our bodies, and with a few exceptions must be supplied by diet. The levels required by our bodies vary depending on health, lifestyle and age. Contrary to popular belief, vitamins and minerals do not provide energy but assist in the release of energy provided by carbohydrates, fat and protein.

Vitamins are either water-soluble or fat-soluble. Fat-soluble vitamins A, D, E and K are stored in the liver for some time. Water-soluble vitamins, B complex and C, cannot be stored by our bodies and therefore must be replaced on a daily basis. Drinking alcohol and smoking will increase your body's need for vitamin B- and C-rich foods as your body tries to cope with these toxins. In addition to protecting the nervous system, vitamin B12 is now realized to be also vitally important for a healthy heart by moderating homocystein, which is a powerful risk factor for cardiovascular disease.

Vitamin D is now claimed to be even more important than vitamin C in boosting your immune system and fighting disease. It is thought to protect against skin cancer, which is slightly ironic since the body makes it from exposure to sunshine.

Below: Nuts and seeds provide the essential fatty acids omega-3 and omega-6 in a vegan diet.

Above: Leafy green vegetables such as broccoli, kale and spinach are a great source of iron for vegans.

Minerals

There are 16 essential minerals. Some, such as calcium, are required in relatively large amounts, while trace elements such as selenium and magnesium are needed in tiny quantities. Minerals have various functions but predominantly regulate and balance the body and maintain a healthy immune system. A deficiency of iron affects one-fifth of the world's population, so make a point of eating iron-rich foods.

Water

The importance of water is often taken for granted, yet it is vital to all animal life. Although it is possible for a human to survive for weeks without food, we can live for only a few days without taking in water.

Water plays a vital role in the body. It transports nutrients, regulates the body temperature, transports waste via the kidneys, and also acts as a lubricating fluid. Most people do not drink enough water: it is thought that an adult requires up to 2.5 litres/4 pints per day, and this should be increased in hot weather or after exercise. A shortage of water can provoke headaches, tiredness and loss of concentration. Carbonated drinks, alcohol, tea and coffee can all act as diuretics and speed up the loss of water and cause dehydration.

How to preserve nutrients

The nutrients in food, particularly fruits and vegetables, are unstable and are diminished by time, preparation methods and cooking. If a piece of cut fruit or a sliced potato is left exposed to air or soaked in water, its vitamin and mineral levels will plummet. Old, wilted or damaged produce also has reduced levels of vitamins and minerals. The following tips will ensure you get the most from your fruit and vegetables:

Below: Water is vital for survival but is often taken for granted; aim to drink 2.5 litres/4 pints each day.

• Buy fruits and vegetables that are as fresh as possible in order to provide maximum nutrients.
• Avoid fruits and vegetables that have been stored under fluorescent light, as this can set off a chemical reaction that depletes nutrients.
• Buy loose fresh produce where possible, as it is much easier to check for quality than pre-packed foods.
• Buy fruits and vegetables in small quantities and do not keep them for too long.
• Remove fruits and vegetables from plastic bags as soon as possible.
• Depending on the type of fruit or vegetable, store in a cool larder or in the bottom of the refrigerator.
• Avoid peeling fruits and vegetables, if possible, and do not prepare them too far in advance of cooking, as nutrients, for example vitamin C, will be destroyed.
• Where possible, eat fruits and vegetables raw, when they are at their most nutritious.
• Avoid boiling vegetables. This method of cooking destroys water-soluble vitamins, such as thiamine and vitamins B and C. If you must boil vegetables, use as little water as possible and do not overcook them. The cooking water can also be kept and used as stock for soup.

Below: Avoid peeling and boiling fruits and vegetables, which are at their most nutritious when raw.

Minerals and vitamins

All people need a range of minerals and vitamins in the right amounts to be healthy. Choosing a wide variety of foods should ensure that all our requirements are met. The vegan diet avoids certain foods that are common providers of these minerals and vitamins in other peoples' diets, so you need to be sure of obtaining an adequate intake of vital nutrients from other plant-based sources.

In a non-vegan diet, animal products are seen as a key source of protein, but they are also providers of iron, zinc and vitamin B12. Dairy products are seen as the key source of calcium. There are, however, plenty of alternative non-animal derived foods which will povide these minerals and vitamins.

Above: Dried fruits are a nutritious source of iron and calcium for vegans.

Calcium

Milk and dairy products are the main source of calcium in the diet, so when these foods are avoided while following a vegan diet, it is important to ensure that calcium is supplied by other food sources. The mineral calcium is essential for building and strengthening bones and teeth. An adequate intake from infancy and throughout life can help to prevent fractures and the brittle bone disease, osteoporosis, which mainly affects post-menopausal women.

Calcium is also needed in the body for normal blood clotting, muscle contraction (including regulating heartbeat) and nerve impulse transmission, as well as for certain digestive processes. Vitamin D, which is produced by the action of sunlight on the skin, is also needed for the absorbtion of calcium from food into the body.

Vegan sources of calcium are plentiful. Dark green leafy vegetables, such as kale, spring greens (collards) and Chinese leaves (Chinese cabbage), are one of the key sources. A 100g/3³⁄₄oz serving of these vegetables provides a similar quantity of retained calcium as a cup of cow's milk.

If you are not getting enough of those dark green vegetables then you can supplement your diet with the many other sources of calcium available to vegans. Two cups of fortified soya milk, for example, would be adequate, providing you with about 300 milligrams of calcium per cup.

Nuts and seeds, tofu and dried fruits are all good sources of calcium for those following a vegan diet.

Non-vegan sources Milk and other dairy products, canned sardines and pilchards with bones.

Vegan sources Dark green leafy vegetables (kale, spring greens, Chinese leaves, spinach, broccoli), beans, peas, lentils, nuts (especially almonds and brazil nuts), sesame and sunflower seeds, dried figs and fortified soya products.

Left: Fortified soya yogurt is a healthy and low-fat source of calcium.

Iron

This mineral is needed to help the body convert food into energy and to make haemoglobin, which is the pigment in red blood cells that carries oxygen around the body in the blood. It is also essential for many other functions, including keeping your immune system in good order. Iron requirements vary depending on your age and sex, and menstruating women in particular should be sure they are getting enough. There are two types of iron in food: haem iron that comes from meat and non-haem iron from plants and grains. Haem iron is better absorbed by the body, but absorption of non-haem iron can be boosted by eating a food or drink rich in vitamin C at the same time as the food containing the non-haem iron. Iron deficiency is the most common cause of anaemia in women of child-bearing age.

Non-vegan sources Red meat and offal, sardines and egg yolks.

Vegan sources Fortified breakfast cereals, oatmeal, beans, peas, lentils, dried fruits, nuts and dark green leafy vegetables, such as Savoy cabbage, spinach, spring greens (collards), chard and kale.

Zinc

This trace mineral is involved in the metabolism of carbohydrates, proteins and fats, as well as the basic processes of cell reproduction, tissue growth and damage healing. A deficiency in zinc is characterized by slow wound healing, impaired growth and a loss of taste.

Non-vegan sources Oysters, lean meat and cheese.

Vegan sources Most nuts, tofu, wholegrains, pumpkin seeds, sesame seeds and tahini, beans and lentils.

Left: Try to eat a range of vegetables every day to obtain a sufficient amount of vital nutrients.

Folate (folic acid)

This B vitamin is essential for the production of red blood cells and is particularly important for women who are pregnant or trying to conceive, to help protect against spina bifida.

Non-vegan sources Eggs

Vegan sources Green leafy vegetables, beetroot (beets), beans, peas, lentils, whole grains, citrus fruits, bananas and nuts. It is used to fortify some breakfast cereals and yeast extract.

Vitamin B12

There are eight vitamins in the B complex group and they all perform similar functions in the body. These include the conversion of food into energy, the maintainance of healthy skin, nerves and heart function, the formation of red blood cells and growth and development in children. Very low quantities of this vitamin can cause anaemia and damage to the nervous system. Symptoms of anaemia include excessive tiredness, breathlessness and poor resistance to infection.

Unfortunately, the vitamin B12 is only found in useful quantities in foods of animal origin, such as red meat, offal and dairy products. Therefore vegans need to include foods that are fortified with vitamin B12 in their diets. Foods such as breakfast cereals, yeast extract and non-dairy milk alternatives are often fortified with vitamin B12. Alternatively, you could take a regular supplement.

Non-vegan sources Meat, poultry, fish, eggs and dairy products.

Vegan sources Foods fortified with vitamin B12, such as soya milk, yeast extract and breakfast cereals.

Below: As well as providing good levels of protein, beans and peas also provide lots of other essential nutrients.

Table of minerals and vitamins

Regular intake of a wide range of minerals and vitamins is essential for general good health, and the vast majority can be found in many different types of plant-based foods. By eating enough of the correct foods, including five portions of vegetables and three portions of fruit and every day, most vegans will find that they are getting plenty of these essential vitamins and minerals to maintain their wellbeing. Try to ensure that you eat a variety of different types and colours of produce, in particular brightly coloured and dark green fruit and vegetables, to ensure that you are obtaining as wide a range of nutrients and beneficial compounds as possible. This handy chart describes which foods are the richest sources of each nutrient, the role the mineral or vitamin plays in maintaining good health, and the signs that may suggest that you have a deficiency of one of these in your diet.

Mineral	Best Sources	Role in Health	Deficiency
Calcium	Green leafy vegetables, orange juice, sesame seeds and tahini, fortified soya milk, almonds, dried figs and brazil nuts.	Essential for building and maintaining strong bones and teeth, muscle function and the nervous system.	Deficiency is characterized by soft and brittle bones, osteoporosis, fractures and muscle weakness.
Chloride	Nuts, wholegrains, beans, peas, lentils, tofu and black tea.	Regulates and maintains the balance of fluids in the body.	Deficiency is rare.
Iodine	Seaweed and iodized salt.	Aids the production of hormones released by the thyroid gland.	Deficiency can lead to sluggish metabolism, and dry skin and hair.
Iron	Fortified cereals, green leafy vegetables, dried fruit, nuts, seeds, beans, peas and tofu.	Essential for healthy blood and muscles.	Deficiency is characterized by anaemia, fatigue and low resistance to infection.
Magnesium	Nuts, seeds, wholegrains, beans, peas, lentils, tofu, dried figs and apricots, and green vegetables.	Essential for healthy muscles, bones and teeth, normal growth, and nerves.	Deficiency is characterized by lethargy, weak bones and muscles, depression and irritability.
Manganese	Nuts, wholegrains, beans, lentils, brown rice, tofu and black tea.	Essential component of enzymes involved in energy production.	Deficiency is not characterized by any specific symptoms.
Phosphorus	Found in many foods, especially wholegrains, lentils, beans, peas, peanuts and nuts.	Essential for healthy bones and teeth, energy production and the absorption of many nutrients.	Deficiency is rare.
Potassium	Bananas, beans, peas, lentils, brazil nuts, seeds, wholegrains, potatoes and root vegetables.	Essential for water balance, regulating blood pressure, and nerve transmission.	Deficiency is characterized by weakness, thirst, fatigue, mental confusion and raised blood pressure.
Selenium	Citrus fruits, avocados, lentils, brazil nuts, wholegrains, yeast extract, chickpeas and seaweed.	Essential for protecting against free radical damage and may protect against cancer – an antioxidant.	Deficiency is characterized by reduced antioxidant protection.
Sodium	Found in most foods, but comes mainly from processed foods.	Essential for nerve and muscle function and body fluid regulation.	Deficiency is unlikely but can lead to dehydration and cramps.
Zinc	Most nuts, wholegrains, tofu, pumpkin seeds, sesame seeds and tahini, beans and lentils.	Essential for a healthy immune system, normal growth, wound healing and reproduction.	Deficiency is characterized by impaired growth, slow wound healing and loss of taste.

Vitamin	Best Sources	Role in Health	Deficiency
A (beta carotene)	Carrots, dried fruit, red and orange (bell) peppers, broccoli, green leafy vegetables, tomatoes, mangoes, sweet potatoes and squash.	Essential for vision, bone growth, and skin and tissue repair. Beta carotene acts as an antioxidant and protects the immune system.	Deficiency is characterized by poor night vision, dry skin and lower resistance to infection, especially respiratory disorders.
B1 (thiamin)	Wholegrain and fortified bread and cereals, fortified yeast extract, potatoes, nuts, beans, peas, lentils and sunflower seeds.	Essential for energy production, the nervous system, muscles and heart. Promotes growth and boosts mental ability.	Deficiency is characterized by depression, irritability, nervous disorders, loss of memory. Common among alcoholics.
B2 (riboflavin)	Fortified bread and cereals, yeast extract, dried prunes, mushrooms, almonds and avocados.	Essential for energy production and for the functioning of vitamin B6 and niacin, as well as tissue repair.	Deficiency is characterized by lack of energy, dry cracked lips, numbness and itchy eyes.
Niacin (nicotinic acid, also called B3)	Beans, peas, lentils, potatoes, fortified breakfast cereals, yeast extract, wheatgerm, nuts, peas, mushrooms, green leafy vegetables, figs and prunes.	Essential for a healthy digestive system, skin and circulation. It is also needed for the release of energy.	Deficiency is unusual, but characterized by lack of energy, depression and scaly skin.
B6 (piridoxine)	Wholegrain cereals, brown rice, hazelnuts, bananas and cruciferous vegetables, such as broccoli, cabbage and cauliflower.	Essential for assimilating protein and fat, for making red blood cells and maintaining a healthy immune system.	Deficiency is characterized by anaemia, dermatitis and depression.
B12 (cyano-cobalamin)	Fortified breakfast cereals, yeast extract, fortified soya milk and fortified margarine.	Essential for growth, formation of red blood cells and maintaining a healthy nervous system.	Deficiency is characterized by fatigue, increased risk of infection, and anaemia.
Folate (folic acid)	Dark green leafy vegetables, wholegrain and fortified breakfast cereals, bread, nuts, beans, peas, lentils, bananas and yeast extract.	Essential for cell division; especially needed before conception and during pregnancy.	Deficiency is characterized by anaemia and appetite loss. Linked with neural defects in babies.
C (ascorbic acid)	Citrus fruit, melons, strawberries, tomatoes, broccoli, potatoes, (bell) peppers and green vegetables.	Essential for the absorption of iron, healthy skin, teeth and bones. Strengthens the immune system and helps to fight infection.	Deficiency is characterized by increased susceptibility to infection, fatigue, poor sleep and depression.
D (calciferol)	Mainly exposure to sunlight. Also fortified breakfast cereals, fortified soya milk and margarine.	Essential for bone and tooth formation; helps the body to absorb calcium and phosphorus.	Deficiency is characterized by softening of the bones, muscle weakness and anaemia. Shortage in children can cause rickets.
E (tocopherols)	Seeds, nuts, vegetable oils, wholemeal (whole-wheat) bread, green leafy vegtables, avocados and spinach.	Essential for healthy skin, circulation and maintaining cells – an antioxidant.	Deficiency is characterized by increased risk of heart attack, strokes and certain cancers.

Food as medicine

Causes of health problems and disease are numerous. Diet and lifestyle are both known to influence your health. There may be hereditary, genetic and environmental factors, and sometimes causes are not known. However, there are many preventative nutritional measures you can take on a vegan diet to help reduce the risk of common diseases and to manage health conditions. Always seek medical attention for any health problems.

A varied vegan diet is often naturally higher in a number of beneficial nutritional elements:
• Antioxidants – to help boost the immune system.
• Soluble fibre – to aid the body's detoxifying process and the support of probiotics.
• Essential fats – to assist in repairing cells and to protect the heart and brain.
• Minerals – for protecting bones.

A vegan diet also cuts out some of the foods, such as meat and dairy, that have been linked to an increased risk of inflammatory conditions such as arthritis and some cancers.

Below: Smoothies are a simple and tasty way to get a variety of different nutrients into your diet.

If there is a history of a particular disease in your family then visit a nutritionist to test for any early signs and discuss a vegan strategy to reduce the risks of hereditary suffering.

Irritable bowel syndrome (IBS)

This is the most common bowel disorder in the Western world and affects women more often than men. Symptoms are constipation and/or diarrhoea, combined with a stomach-ache, bloating and wind. IBS may be triggered by stress, gut infections, nutrient deficiencies or an intolerance to foods, such as wheat, corn or oats.

Prevention tips
• Seek out a recommendation for a qualified nutritional therapist to review your diet.
• Test for food intolerance.
• Test for gut and parasitical infections.
• Test for correct gut bacteria balance.
• Manage stress effectively.

High blood pressure

This means that the pressure of blood in your arteries (blood vessels) is too high. High blood pressure usually causes no symptoms, but if left untreated may damage some arteries and put a strain on the heart. High blood pressure increases the risk of developing heart disease, stroke, dementia and kidney damage.

Prevention tips
• Lose weight if you are overweight.
• Eat healthily – aim for five portions of different fresh vegetables and three portions of fruit a day.
• Eat less salt and cut down on processed foods.
• Exercise for at least 30 minutes, on five or more days a week.
• Cut down on alcohol.
• Give up smoking.

Diabetes

This is a lifelong condition in which there is too much glucose in the blood. Diabetes develops because the body

Above: Regular exercise can help to prevent high blood pressure, osteoporosis, arthritis and cancer.

does not produce enough insulin, a hormone, which allows the body to use glucose – mainly from starches and sugars – for fuel.
• Type 1 diabetes is when little or no insulin is produced.
• Type 2 diabetes is when the body produces some insulin, but not enough for its needs, or when the insulin is not properly used by the body.

Type 2 is the most common form of diabetes and usually affects people over 40 years of age. Typical symptoms include increased thirst, passing large amounts of urine, extreme tiredness, weight loss and blurred vision.

Cause and control
The causes of diabetes are still debated – meat, dairy, sugar, too many simple carbohydrates and insufficient intake of fruit and vegetables have all been said to exacerbate the onset of the disease. There is some evidence to suggest that people who follow a vegan diet have less incidence of diabetes. Control of the condition requires a healthy, varied diet, which helps to keep blood sugar levels steady, regular exercise and maintaining an ideal weight.

Osteoporosis

A condition where bone material is lost so the bones become gradually more fragile and likely to break. Bones are at their strongest in the late twenties, then gradually begin to lose their density with increasing age. This process speeds up in women in the ten years after the menopause because the ovaries stop producing the female sex hormone oestrogen, one of the substances that can help to keep the bones strong.

Prevention tips

• Eat a healthy diet, featuring foods that are high in calcium, such as green leafy vegetables, tofu, tahini, sesame seeds, almonds, brazil nuts and dried figs.
• Keep physically active and increase weight-bearing exercise, such as walking or jogging.
• Don't drink too much alcohol, which reduces the body's ability to form bone.
• Avoid smoking. Tobacco lowers the oestrogen level in women and may cause early menopause – which is another risk factor.
• Choose plant-milks that are fortified with calcium.
• Ensure you get enough vitamins and minerals that support bone formation, such as vitamin D and magnesium.

Arthritis

This causes inflammation and swelling in the joints. The most common type is osteoarthritis, which mainly affects weight-bearing joints such as the hips, knees and spine. It is a degenerative disease caused by the breaking down of cartilage around joints. The bones become thicker and the fluid-filled space becomes smaller. The bones rub together causing inflammation and pain, and the shape of the joint often changes.

Rheumatoid arthritis is an inflammatory disorder involving the immune system, which for unknown reasons starts to attack the joints. It can strike at any age, but mostly starts between the ages of 30 and 50. People with this form suffer painful flare-ups, with the joints becoming stiff and swollen. Both forms of arthritis are more common in women than in men.

Prevention tips

• Avoid becoming overweight as obesity increases the risk of developing osteoarthritis by putting undue stress on the joints. Weight control is also vital to minimize stress, reduce pain and optimize mobility, when osteoarthritis has already developed.
• Avoid saturated fats.
• Take regular exercise to strengthen the muscles that protect the joints and help prevent stiffness.
• A food allergy or intolerance may be linked with rheumatoid arthritis. Seek specialist advice for an exclusion diet.
• Omega-3 oils can be helpful for their anti-inflammatory effect on arthritic joints.

Cancer

The sequence of events that leads to a cancer is complex and varied. Most cancers begin when the body is exposed to a carcinogen – a cancer-causing substance in the environment. Carcinogens can be found in tobacco, food, industrial compounds or a virus. Even the rays of the sun can be carcinogenic. Usually the body's natural defence system is able to destroy these harmful substances before they cause permanent damage to cells, but sometimes the carcinogen escapes and succeeds in changing a cell's structure, thus creating a potentially cancerous cell, which may, over a period of time, multiply and develop into a cluster of abnormal cells, known as a tumour.

There are many different types of cancer and all have different causes. However, it is thought that a considerable percentage of all cancers could be prevented by making relatively simple changes to both your diet and lifestyle.

Prevention tips

• Avoid being overweight.
• Eat plenty of fruit and vegetables, as they contain antioxidants and phytochemicals that help to counteract the damaging effects of free radicals in the body.
• Be sure to include plenty of high-fibre foods in your diet, such as wholegrains, beans, peas and lentils, to ensure healthy digestion, prevent constipation and allow the speedy removal of toxic waste products.
• Cut down on fatty foods.
• Avoid charred food.
• Restrict high-salt foods.
• Moderate your alcohol consumption.
• Be physically active.
• Don't smoke.
• Reduce your skin's exposure to the sun and cover up with clothing and high factor sunscreen.

Below: Plenty of fruit in your daily diet can have a positive effect on your health and may help to prevent some cancers.

Herbs and spices for health

Using a variety of herbs and spices is an excellent way of enlivening a vegan diet. They can transform a plain, simple dish into a delicious eating experience of lively and refreshing flavours that excite the taste buds. They reduce the need for adding salt as a seasoning, can help ease digestion and may also offer natural, curative properties for various common ailments. The medicinal and cosmetic uses of herbs and spices have a long history, and herbs have been used in these ways throughout the world for thousands of years, as well as for decorative and aromatic purposes. Today, herbs are enjoying a revival, and eaten in abundance, many varieties can supply a small, yet valuable source of many vitamins and minerals. Use them in cooking and for herbal drinks, according to your preferences. Use fresh varieties whenever possible, as they impart the best flavour and beneficial qualities.

Herb/Spice	Good for	Use in
Basil	Aiding digestion and calming nervous system.	Herbal tea, salads, soups, pasta sauces.
Bay	Stimulating the appetite and aiding digestion.	Soups, stews, stocks and marinades.
Black pepper	Stimulating digestive juices, promoting appetite and relieving constipation. Also improves circulation.	Complements all savoury dishes.
Borage	Rheumatism and respiratory infections.	Hot and cold drinks and salads.
Caraway	Stimulating appetite and digestion and relieving wind. May help relieve menstrual pain.	Cabbage, potato, onion, carrot and bean dishes, casseroles, bread and cakes.
Cardamom	Relieving indigestion and sweetening breath (if chewed). Good for coughs and colds.	Curries, rice and fruit dishes.
Chamomile	Relieving anxiety and promoting sound sleep.	Hot herbal tea.
Chillies	Relieving congestion and clearing mucus.	Curries, stir-fries and marinades.
Chives	Cleansing blood, aiding digestion, clearing catarrh, protecting against colds.	Salads, soups and dips. Complements a variety of potato dishes.
Cinnamon	Indigestion and colds, as a nasal decongestant.	Casseroles and curries, sweet and savoury rice dishes, stewed fruits, mulled wine.
Coriander leaf (cilantro)	Stimulating digestion. Both seeds and leaves may help strengthen the urinary tract.	Add to salads, salsas, soups, stews, curries and rice dishes.
Coriander seed	(as above)	Casseroles, curries and chutneys. Complements vegetable and lentil dishes and stewed fruit.
Cumin seed	Helping to relieve indigestion and wind.	Curries and spicy dishes using peas, beans or lentils. Complements beans, lentils, vegetables and rice dishes.
Dandelion leaf	Fluid retention, blood cleansing and skin disorders, such as eczema.	Salads and herbal teas.
Dill	Wind, hiccups, stomach-ache.	Soups and salads. Complements a variety of vegetable dishes.
Fennel (seed or leaf)	Aiding digestion, and helping to relieve wind, bloating, stomach-ache, nausea, fluid retention and insomnia. The seeds makes an effective breath freshener.	Salads, soups and vegetable dishes. It also complements rice, potatoes and apple dishes. Use for herbal tea.

Herb/Spice	Good for	Use in
Fenugreek seeds	Stimulating digestion, relieving wind and relieving coughing.	Curries and chutneys.
Garlic	Colds, poor circulation, sinusitis. Highly antiseptic and good for purifying and thinning the blood.	Complements rice, pulse and vegetable dishes.
Ginger	Aiding digestion and stimulating the liver to remove toxins from the bloodstream. Helps to relieve colds.	Curries, stews and stir-fries. Good for herbal tea.
Horseradish	Stimulating digestion.	Young leaves in salads, grated root in sauces.
Lavender	Soothing headaches, calming nerves and aiding sleep.	The flowers and leaves can be used fresh or dried in herbal teas, salads or to add flavour to cakes and desserts.
Lemon balm	Relief from chronic bronchial catarrh, feverish colds and headaches.	Herbal teas, cold drinks and savoury or fruit salads.
Marjoram	Aiding digestion, colds and headaches and as a relaxant.	Salads and vegetable dishes. Also good infused as a herbal tea.
Mint	Digestion, upset stomach, colds, influenza and headaches.	Teas and cold drinks, salads, dips and dressings. Complements many vegetables, especially peas, tomatoes and new potatoes.
Nutmeg (and mace)	Helping to alleviate nausea, wind and diarrhoea.	Sweet and savoury dishes including pasta sauces, cakes and puddings.
Oregano	Coughs, nervous headaches and irritability.	Infuse as a relaxing tea and use in the same way as for marjoram.
Parsley and chervil	Stimulating digestion, as a breath freshener and for healthy skin. Good source of vitamin C and iron.	Soups, salads, sauces and casseroles. Complements all kinds of savoury dishes. Chew parsley after eating garlic.
Rosemary	Stimulating circulation and aids in the digestion of fats.	Marinades and a variety of vegetable dishes, stews and casseroles. Also good when infused to make a herbal tea.
Sage	Aiding digestion of rich food and relieves indigestion. Also antiseptic and antifungal, and can help ease anxiety.	As a flavouring for stuffing, good with vegetable stews and casseroles. Also good when infused to make a herbal tea.
Tarragon	Stimulating appetite and digestion and good general tonic.	Soups, salads and vegetable stews and casseroles. Also good with a variety of raw or cooked tomato-based dishes.
Thyme	Aiding digestion and can help relieve coughs, colds and sore throats.	Use to make bouquet garni with parsley and bay. Add to stocks, marinades, soups and casseroles. Good with a variety of vegetable dishes. Also good infused as a tea.
Turmeric	Relieving digestive problems, improves circulation and has antibacterial properties.	Curries, vegetable and rice dishes.

Vegan and ethical shopping

There are many factors to take into consideration when shopping as a vegan, which go far beyond the plant-based diet. From the clothes on your back to the shoes on your feet and the cleaning products you use, the ethos of veganism in excluding all forms of exploitation or cruelty to animals should dictate which products you buy.

Beyond this, the wider philosophy of veganism aims to promote the welfare of people, animals and the environment, which will also affect what products you buy and the way you buy them. It could be argued that vegans are failing to live up to their basic vegan principles if, for example, they buy non-leather shoes made by sweat-shop child labour, or use bio-fuel made from a crop responsible for devastating the rainforests.

There are a number of schemes designed to help vegan and other environmentally concerned shoppers to choose more ethically but caution is often advised. Something labelled 'carbon neutral' could still contain chemicals that harm the environment, or a fair-trade product may be fairer for people but involve cruelty to animals.

Below: Join a box scheme run by a local farm to get fresh, seasonal produce without the packaging.

If you cannot find what you are looking for in your local stores then the Internet is an excellent resource. There are dedicated on-line retailers selling everything from vegan marshmallows to vegan condoms. Up-to-date lists of products are also published by a number of organizations. In the UK, the *Animal Free Shopper* is an excellent resource and is published every couple of years by The Vegan Society. For vegans in the USA, PETA publish a cruelty-free shopping guide to help consumers find products that are not tested on animals. Vegetarian and vegan magazines also have a useful classified section in the back.

Food

The vegan diet and the plant-based alternatives available will be looked at in detail in the following pages. However, many vegans have a number of other concerns about the origin, processing and transportation of the food they buy, as well as the basic need to seek out some of the essential ingredients they need in their diet.

Organic farming This is a system of agriculture in which organic products and techniques are used, such as when the soil is treated with manure rather than with chemical fertilizers, or when

Above: Buy your fruit and vegetables directly from the grower at local farmers' markets.

plant pests are eliminated by introducing insects that prey on them rather than by spraying chemical insecticides. The market for organic produce has increased hugely in the last ten years as consumers recognize the environmental damage caused by some methods used in conventional farming as well as the nutritional value of organic produce.

Stock-free farming This system, also known as vegan-organic growing, avoids all artificial chemical products (synthetic fertilizer, pesticides, growth regulators), genetically modified organisms, animal manures and slaughterhouse by-products (blood, fish meal, bone meal, etc).

Advocates of stock-free farming argue it is more natural to use crop rotation, composting, soil replenishment crops and mulching as a synergistic means of managing the soil quality. It is suggested that manure and other waste products such as feathers not only support factory farming but compromise health and contamination concerns.

Fair trade There are various fair trade or equal exchange schemes. The idea is that the organization tries to bring producers closer to their market, cutting out the middle-men, so that they get a bigger share of the price of the final product. This was extremely successful with commodities such as

tea and coffee where, despite their high final price, only a tiny fraction of the profits was going to the farmers who grew the product. Fair trade schemes have helped many communities climb out of poverty and inspired a slightly more responsible attitude among the giant international food manufacturers.

Co-ops These are customer- or producer-owned schemes where all profits are shared out or ploughed back into the business to allow more ethical practices and decisions unmotivated by profit. They tend to be very community minded. Many retail co-operative societies have an honest labelling policy and have pioneered new fair trade categories. Many label products such as wine and beer with the true ingredients,

---

ENVIRONMENTAL CONCERNS WHEN FOOD SHOPPING

Vegans try to act in a way that is beneficial to the environment. Think about these factors when buying your food:

- **Production** – How is the food you eat grown? Is it organically produced? Or is it from a farm using synthetic fertilizers, chemicals and pesticides?
- **Transportation** – How far has the food you are buying had to travel? Can it be bought nearer home? Do you really need it?
- **Producers** – Are the people who grow and harvest your food free from exploitation and receiving a fair price for their work? Can you buy the same product in a fair trade system? Can you buy the same thing directly from your local farmer?
- **Packaging** – Is it necessary to wrap the food you buy in plastic? Choose loose fruit and vegetables or join a box scheme. Take reusable bags to the store instead of using the plastic bags provided.
- **Recycling** – Is the packaging you use able to be recycled locally? If not, try and avoid it.

including production aids, such as gelatine. They are an excellent example of a retailer labelling vegan products.

Vegetable box schemes These schemes were introduced in an attempt to support organic, local farming. Consumers order seasonal produce directly from the local farmers and growers, and this is delivered to their homes or picked up, often within a matter of hours after harvesting. As well as supplying the consumer with fresh, seasonal produce these schemes have a number of other benefits: they support the local economy; cut out some of the excessive profits made by supermarkets; reduce transportation of food and decrease unnecessary packaging.

Community supported agriculture Often referred to as CSAs, these are systems of buying local produce that are popular in the USA. Like the box scheme, this is a direct relationship between the consumer and the farmer. The particular way this system works may vary but the arrangement is usually based on the farmer taking a 'subscription' or offering 'shares' in their crops. After harvesting, the subscribers or shareholders receive fresh, seasonal produce.

Farmers' markets Also called greenmarkets, these are public markets where farmers and other vendors can sell their products directly to the consumer. These markets are frequently held in the open air and are becoming increasingly popular in many countries

Above: Fair trade schemes aim to ensure that farmers and workers receive a fair price for their produce.

around the world. It is another way of buying fresh, seasonal produce directly from the grower, and many of the farmers will be using organic methods.

Health-food stores The local independent health-food store is a great resource for buying vegan products that supermarkets do not think viable. They are also a good source of advice, as well as support in obtaining an item even if it is not already stocked.

Below: Try to buy your food in a way that is good for the producers, yourself and the environment.

Above: Clothing made from non-animal derived products, such as hemp, is widely available for the vegan shopper.

Footwear

Vegetarian and vegan shoes have been available to the animal-free shopper for a long time, though they were not always the most tasteful or practical option. However, the variety available to the modern vegan means that there is a comfortable and stylish shoe suitable for any occasion. From workboots and hiking shoes to running shoes and fashionable footwear for nights out, there is now no design, style or type of shoe for which there is not a vegan equivalent.

Artificial leather, often made from a textile treated with an oil-based coating, has been used by vegan shoemakers for many years. Modern advances in 'pleather' (a slang term for 'plastic leather') means that the comfort and durability of animal-free shoes is just as good as leather. There are now a number of top designers creating smart shoes in pleather and other fabrics so that vegans need never feel they are missing out on the latest stylish footwear.

Clothing

There is a huge variety of animal-free clothing available in mainstream stores, which means that avoiding animal-derived clothing, such as leather, silk, wool and fur, should not cause you any serious problems. Cotton, linen and man-made fibres are available in normal clothing outlets, and the variety of specialist vegan stores, on-line and through mail order, sell clothing made from hemp, bamboo and organic cotton.

Although cotton clothing is widely accessible, vegans may be concerned with the ethics of its manufacture, including chemical production methods and exploitation of workforce. For these reasons, organic and fairtrade cotton is becoming increasingly popular.

The image of vegan clothing being unstylish is no longer true. A range of fashionable and functional clothing is now available. Linen suits can make a good alternative to wool suits, and are often preferable in warmer climates. A range of suits made from versatile, hardwearing and breathable fabrics, such as cotton corduroy and hemp, is challenging the dominance of the old-fashioned wool suit. They can both look suitably smart for many purposes.

Photography

Digital photography has been a lifesaver for vegans. The light-sensitive films and papers used in traditional photography are coated in an emulsion coating that contains gelatine. Digital photography means vegans can bypass these products and print out their own pictures. Be cautious which paper you buy to print out on as some of the inkjet papers that use a high gloss finish for printing photos also contain gelatine.

Cosmetics and toiletries

The cosmetic industry has been criticized and protested against by animal rights campaigners for many years. In addition to the testing of products on animals, there are many animal-based ingredients that are used in a wide variety of cosmetic products to look out for when shopping. Everyday cosmetic products and toiletries, such as soaps, perfumes, lipsticks, moisturizers and nail varnishes (polishes), can all contain animal products, including lanolin (a fatty substance obtained from wool), horse urine, marine oil from clubbed seals, whale oil, fish scales and pig's brains.

International companies such as The Body Shop and Lush Cosmetics pioneered the idea of cosmetics and bathroom products using fairly traded natural ingredients that are not tested on animals. Many smaller companies followed their lead and today there is a wide variety of cruelty-free options.

Below: Animal-based products are used in many cosmetics, which are often tested on animals as well.

SOME ANIMAL PRODUCTS USED IN COSMETICS

Below are listed a few ingredients to watch out for when buying cosmetics and toiletries:

- Tallow (hard animal fat) – soaps.
- Lanolin (a fatty substance derived from wool) or beeswax – lipsticks.
- Shellac (resin secreted by insects) – nail varnish.
- Castoreum (secretion from gland of the beaver) – perfume.
- Musk (from gland of male musk deer) – perfume.
- Keratin (protein from hair, horn, hoof and feathers) – shampoos, conditioners and some skin care products.
- Civet (from anal pouch of civet cat) – perfume.
- Gelatine (from animal bones, skin and hide) – general use.
- Propolis (tree sap used as a glue by bees) – general use.
- Chitin (hard substance from insects and crustaceans) – general use.
- Squalene (derived from shark liver) – skin moisturizers.

Pharmaceuticals and supplements

As within the cosmetics industry, animal-based ingredients are used by pharmaceutical manufacturers, such as bile from the stomach of calves. Pharmaceutical companies are usually secretive about their product ingredients and many medicines will have been tested on animals. Many vegans find a solution to this dilemma by seeking out alternative therapy, such as homeopathy. Ensure that your medical practitioner is aware of your vegan lifestyle and discuss your options with them.

For many years vegetarians had to squeeze medications and supplements from their capsules as they contained gelatine. Many companies are now using animal-free versions such as plant cellulose or vegetable starch capsules for their medicinal products.

There are numerous vitamins that can be derived from animals. Vitamin D3, for example, often contains lanolin, a substance derived from the fat in sheep's wool, and although it can be extracted from algae, this option is rare. Other dietary supplements are animal-derived, such as royal jelly, which is a secretion from honeybees. Always check the ingredients in any supplement.

Household goods and cleaning products

Most mainstream household chemicals and cleaning products are in some way linked to animal testing. Even well-known eco-friendly brands, who make products rich in natural ingredients, test on animals in order to establish that their products are safer than others for marine life.

There are, however, many companies who go the extra mile to make products that are not only effective but are not tested on animals and so are suitable for vegans. Many of these companies can be found on-line or in vegan literature and shopping guides.

There is a surprisingly large amount of household products to avoid, so always ensure you check what the item contains before buying it. Household paints frequently contain shellac, and gardening products often contain manure or other animal products such as bone meal and blood. Even matches use gelatine in the explosive bit on the end.

Consumer power

One of the aspects of veganism that has the greatest impact is the power that you wield as a consumer. By simply refusing to buy a product due to its animal-based or environmentally unfriendly status you send a loud, clear message to companies that they are losing profits to their more ethical and conscientious competitors.

You may consider there is no ethical or economic impact to be made from throwing out a perfectly good leather, feather or animal-derived product just because it is not vegan. You may even feel it is a bit of an insult to the animal.

Above: Read the labels to avoid cleaning products that cause harm to animals or the environment.

It is certainly not very environmentally friendly and perhaps you should use it until it needs replacing, or give it away. These are decisions to be made by individuals, and vegans will vary on what they do.

The important thing is to avoid supporting or encouraging, either morally or financially, those who thrive or profit from harmful practices to animals, people or the environment.

Below: Many medicines are tested on animals and the coating of capsules is often made using gelatine.

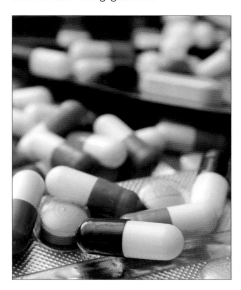

The daily vegan diet

A vegan diet often seems like an impossible task to those who eat meat and dairy products. Even to recently converted vegans, a trip to the supermarket or the need to feed a family can seem like a daunting task. However, a few pieces of essential advice, a little knowledge about the foods you eat and some tempting ideas, and the world of vegan food opens up. Eating a plant-based diet will then become a pleasure rather than a chore and, as an added bonus, it will be good for your health as well.

Plan your daily menus

If you are thinking of following a vegan diet or are still adjusting to one, then it is a good idea to plan out your menus for the day in advance. Once you are a seasoned vegan, a daily menu will still be a great way to explore and experiment with new dishes and to ensure that you are getting all the nutrients you need.

Breakfasts

Always start the day with a balanced breakfast, including at least one piece of fruit. Stick to one or two regular weekday cereals if that is easy and healthy – home-made muesli or porridge with seeds and berries is perfect. Check out the ingredients lists on cereal packets as many seemingly healthy products contain large amounts of sugar.

• Wholemeal (whole-wheat) toast is good as long as you include some protein-rich nut butter, or a sprinkle of seeds.

• Rolled oats are good raw or cooked. Mix them with dried fruit and flaked (sliced) almonds or chopped nuts.

• Try all the dairy-free milks until you find a sugar-free one that you like. If you have an uncompromising sweet tooth, try the apple-sweetened varieties.

• Add diced fresh fruit, berries, dried fruit, nuts and seeds to live soya yogurt.

• Try scrambled tofu with parsley and spring onions (scallions) on a field (portabello) mushroom sprinkled with hemp seeds.

• If you have lots of ripe tomatoes, chop them in half and roast in the oven before adding to chunky slices of toasted wholemeal bread.

• In an emergency when you are short of time, try a fruit smoothie with some hemp protein added or with a handful of seeds.

Lunches and light meals

Satisfying small meals and lunches make a positive contribution in a balanced vegan diet. The lunchtime meal at work is fast becoming a sandwich at the desk or food grabbed on the go. It is vital to take time out of your working day and avoid buying a sandwich as much as possible – make your own instead.

When catering for children who need packed lunches to take to school, ensure that you fill their lunchboxes with plenty of nutritious foods. Also try to make their choices as interesting as possible so that they wil not feel they are missing out on the foods that their friends are eating.

• Have lots of wholemeal pitta pockets, or split multigrain wholemeal rolls ready in the freezer for quick, nutritious lunches. The bread keeps the filling cool and fresh, and will have thawed out by lunchtime. Spread it with vegetable pâté, hummus or tahini, include lots of vegetables and make it a doorstep sandwich for slow-release energy and lots of vitamin value.

Above: The zesty flavours in tabbouleh and guacamole tortilla wraps make a healthy and refreshing lunch.

• Baked potatoes and sweet potatoes with baked beans, a little grated carrot and a sprinkle of seeds is a good lunch. Fibre and protein from the beans help to slow down the carbohydrate absorption from the potato. Use hemp, walnut, sesame or pumpkin seed oil.

• Tofu sandwich with grated courgette (zucchini) and spring onions (scallions), and soya mayonnaise. Use toasted wholemeal bread and marinated tofu.

Below: Pack children's lunchboxes with nutritious and wholesome foods to provide them with the energy they need.

Above: A simple baked potato can be easily transformed into an ideal light lunch or dinner.

• Scrambled tofu with various vegetables. For low-fat but really creamy scrambled tofu, cook the tofu in oat milk. Stir in some parboiled asparagus tips and peas, serve with multigrain bread, toasted one side, then brushed lightly with olive oil and garlic before toasting the second side.

• Make a tasty pizza crumpet. Toast a wholemeal crumpet on both sides and top with tomato salsa, thin slivers of mushrooms, and finally a covering layer of a spoonful of seasoned soya yogurt mixed with yeast extract and tomato ketchup. Grill (broil) until crisp and golden. Good with lots of cherry tomatoes and salad leaves on the side.

Main meals

When planning your main meal, you may find it easier to start with a core base ingredient. A high-protein complex carbohydrate makes an excellent nutritious base, such as buckwheat pasta, quinoa, barley, basmati rice, mung bean noodles, beansprouts or a wholemeal pancake.

Once you have decided what you want to make up the base and bulk of the meal, you can consider the vegetable element to accompany it, and there is a huge range of options available, including:

• Roasted mixed vegetables: onions, (bell) peppers and aubergines (eggplants)
• Baked pumpkin or squash
• Stir-fried sugarsnap peas, green beans and baby corn
• Stir-fried white cabbage, carrots, onions and apples
• Lightly steamed cauliflower and broad (fava) beans, plus cherry tomatoes
• Diced cooked beetroot (beet), shredded red cabbage and chopped red onion
• Stir-fried celery, carrots, Chinese leaves (Chinese cabbage) and baby spinach

Once you have your vegetables, then consider adding a protein element to your meal. Options include:
• Meat alternatives such as soya
• Baked tempeh
• Marinated and grilled tofu
• Seitan
• Pine nuts, chopped nuts or seeds
• Falafel
• Nut roast
• Bean burgers
• Bean salad

Snacks

Dried fruit, seeds and nuts are far better than confectionery or processed snacks. Make up your own mix of lightly roasted cashew nuts, walnuts,

Below: A fruit salad is fantastic for breakfasts, snacks and desserts, and will keep in the refrigerator for two days.

brazil nuts and hazelnuts, with quartered dried apricots and raisins. Roast the nuts gently and slowly in the oven, then allow them to cool completely before storing with the fruit in an airtight jar.

For a savoury snack, finely chop a garlic clove and add to the nuts with a sprinkling of ground coriander, several sprigs of thyme and a couple of bay leaves. Mix well, cover and leave to stand for 30 minutes before roasting. Discard the bay leaves and thyme sprigs before storing the nuts.

Fruit salads

At any time of day, fruit salad is real feel-good food. Make a huge bowlful every couple of days and have it with porridge, soya yogurt or cereal for breakfast. It is great for healthy snacking, as a quick lunch with lots of nuts and seeds, and good for dessert, of course.

A basic salad, with lemon added, will keep well for two days, covered, in the refrigerator. Diced apple, diced orange and canned pineapple or peaches in fruit juice (not syrup) make a basic mix. Select a thin-skinned lemon, scrub it well and chop it, skin and all, then add it to the salad. This prevents discoloration and gives the salad a delicious zingy flavour.

• Berries do not keep for more than a day before softening – try using frozen berries. Add them about 30 minutes before serving, leaving enough time for them to soften and chill the salad.
• Pears should be added to a salad on the same day, bananas and kiwi fruit at the last minute.
• Peeled and finely chopped fresh root ginger is fabulous in fruit salad, especially with grapes, mango or pear.
• Chopped dried ready-to-eat apricots or raisins and grated orange rind add lots of flavour to a salad of apples, pears and banana. This is very good stirred into soya yogurt.
• Cook peeled, sliced or diced pears in apple juice with a little chopped lemon and fresh root ginger (if you like), cool, chill and use as a delicious base for making more fruit salad.

Parties and special occasions

Many of the important events in life are celebrated with food and there is no reason why vegans should miss out on these important occasions because of their diet. There will, of course, be times when the menu doesn't offer much suitable food, but remember that the food is not the purpose of the event and enjoy the things that are most important. Also, whenever you receive an invitation to a dinner party, wedding or other event, it is a good idea to remind your host of your diet. Many people and caterers are getting accustomed to providing for those with special diets and so you will probably be easily provided for.

Hosting your own parties can be a little daunting at first but it is really no different than for anybody else, and may in fact be easier – you will not have to supply different food for meat-eaters and vegetarians, for one thing. It can also be more relaxing to be at a party where you have created the menu, and it is a great opportunity to show off all the delicious dishes that vegans eat.

Below: Often the simplest dishes are the most delicious. This Pea Soup with Garlic will be a great crowd pleaser.

Above: Artichokes with Beans and Almonds will make an ideal dish for a sophisticated dinner party.

Dinner parties

There are few things in life more pleasant than sharing good food with friends. When hosting your own dinner party, the main trick is to serve the food you love to eat and let your guests share your passion.

Ensure that you are aware of any allergies your guests may have before planning your menu. Many vegans find themselves catering for dedicated meat-eaters, which can be an enjoyable experience because you get a chance

Above: Curried Leek and Squash Gratin is perfect for serving a group of hungry friends at an informal gathering.

to show them the array of colours, flavours and tastes of well-produced vegan cuisine. If you are aiming for a classy dinner party then spend accordingly on your meal. Look to include a few exotic ingredients in the dishes, and present your food with plenty of style.

The trick to a successful dinner party is to have as much as possible prepared ahead so you actually get to spend time with your guests rather than being stuck in the kitchen. Perhaps serve soup or a cold appetizer, then something that just needs taking out of the oven and heating up gently while you eat your first course.

The presentation will be much more impressive if you make individual portions of items such as pies or tarts. Other dishes, such as rice or stir-fries, can be presented in a large hollowed out tomato, half a green (bell) pepper, a large flat mushroom or a potato skin. You can easily make filo baskets by draping the pastry over an oiled ramekin and then baking it before filling with your food.

Informal gatherings are good for a big pan of food from which people can help themselves. Pots full of casseroles, stews and curries are ideal for this situation and often you can simply have a side serving of rice, couscous or

bread to go along with the main dish. You can also top pots of stew or curry with pastry or potato scallops or mashed sweet potato sprinkled with seeds, if you like.

For dessert, try pre-prepared scoops of vegan ice cream covered in melted chocolate and served with hot whisky or orange liqueur. If you feel confident you can even create a flaming dessert – very impressive in a romantically lit room. Other options for a dinner party dessert include creating a sorbet using fresh fruit, such as pears or clementines, and then packing the sorbet in the hollowed-out fruit.

Large parties

Occasionally you may need to feed a lot of people at a large gathering such as a birthday party or a wedding. The easiest way to feed a lot of people is to make a serve-yourself buffet rather than have a sit-down affair. Aim for plenty of bitesize finger food that is easy to eat while standing up. There's absolutely no reason why you should compromise on your personal principles just because there are lots of meat-eaters to feed.

Below: Spice up your side dishes and serve a selection of vegetables for a crowd of friends.

Above: When catering for large parties, it may be easier to prepare a vegan buffet with lots of choice.

Just make sure there is enough choice so no-one goes hungry. The range of buffet food that can be eaten on a vegan diet will astound many of your guests, and the meat-eaters probably won't notice the missing sausage roll.

For very special occasions you could get vegan caviar and vegan champagne – or make a delicious vegan cake.

Below: Vanilla, Date and Saffron Pears will make an excellent dessert for a dinner party.

Here are a few suggestions and ideas for delicious vegan buffet food that non-vegans will enjoy too:
• Cherry tomatoes stuffed with smoked tofu pâté
• Mini Scotch eggs with ackee or a cauliflower floret encased in soya sausage meat
• Puff pastry soya sausage and herb rolls
• Mini savoury tarts with mushrooms and walnuts
• Mini artichoke and wild mushroom pizzas with melted vegan cheese
• Vegan caviar on mini oatcakes
• Falafels
• Pakora, onion bhajis and samosas
• Spring rolls
• Vegetable dumplings
• Avocado and red (bell) pepper sushi
• Mini vegetable kebabs
• Tofu satay sticks
• Stuffing balls
• Blinis with tofu cream cheese
• Stuffed button (white) mushrooms
• Stuffed baby potatoes
• Baked marinated tofu triangles
• Celery sticks stuffed with tofu cheese
• Vegetable tempura
• Edamame
• Savoury rice balls

Alcohol

The vegan problems with alcohol are the manufacturing processes, which often use isinglass (from a fish swim bladder), gelatin, milk protein, eggs or chitin from shellfish to speed up the clearing and fining process of beers and wines. Most spirits, however, are vegan.

Manufacturers are not obliged to label ingedients so it is difficult to tell a vegan wine or beer from a non-vegan one. Look for Eastern European wines, traditionally fined with betonite (a clay), German beers that are subject to a purity law that forbids contaminants, or beers and wines from more modern breweries and wineries that filter their products rather than add chemicals. Traditional bottled ales are usually a safe vegan bet too – particularly if there is a little natural sediment in the bottle.

Eating out

A vegan diet is not the end to dining in restaurants and cafés that many people assume it to be. A bit more knowledge and planning may be required but there are plenty of ways to enjoy a meal out in a variety of establishments.

The restaurant trade has recently become more aware that they need to provide cuisine for people who follow different diets. A vegetarian option has been widely available for many years but, thanks to a better understanding of various food allergies and intolerances, restaurants are now accustomed to accommodating people on various other special diets.

The popularity of restaurants serving various world cuisines also provides good opportunities for seeking out a vegan-friendly meal. There are a few idiosyncrasies to watch out for in particular restaurants.

Chinese, Japanese and Thai

These restaurants frequently offer a range of vegetarian dishes on their menus. Chinese restaurants are a common feature in many towns and cities and you can be sure of getting a suitable meal. Tofu is a common

Below: Vegetable stir-fries are a good Chinese or Thai option for vegans, but watch out for egg noodles.

ingredient on the Chinese menu and staff will be able to add it to a number of vegetable dishes.

Japanese restaurants can be tricky due to the frequent use of dashi stock which contains dried fish. Try and find a dish that uses dashi made from seaweed only. Many varieties of vegetable sushi – which means vinegared rice not fish – are suitable for a vegan diet.

Choose: Vegetable sushi; tofu and vegetable stir-fries; Singapore glass/rice noodles; vegetable pancakes and dumplings; crispy seaweed.

Watch out for: Fish products in stocks and sauces – dashi, Thai fish sauce, oyster sauce; dried fish/shrimp powder on your crispy seaweed; prawn crackers; eggs in rice dishes, noodles and fortune cookies.

Mexican

Apart from their legendary relationship with beef, Mexican restaurants are generally a good choice for vegans. Be careful, however, that lard has not been used in the preparation of the dish, otherwise there are many bean-based meals and vegetable salsas that can be enjoyed in these establishments.

Choose: Vegetable fajitas, burritos and enchiladas – often featuring (bell) peppers and/or beans; vegetable chilli; refried beans; tortilla chips with salsa and guacamole.

Watch out for: Cheese sprinkled on dishes; chicken or beef stocks used for making soups and rice; yogurt.

Italian

Although finding meat-free options in an Italian restaurant is easy, it can be a little harder to omit the eggs and cheese. Italian food is more likely to use olive oil than butter, so look for things like bruschetta, which will usually be drizzled with oil. Pizza bases will usually be made with oil, too, so you can just omit the cheese topping. Pasta will often be made with egg, but check with the kitchen, and they may have egg-free

Above: A vegetarian pizza of grilled vegetables without the cheese topping is a great Italian choice for vegans.

varieties. Vegetable risottos can be a good choice but make sure the stock used is vegetable.

Choose: Pasta with mushrooms and pine nuts; salads with Mediterranean vegetables – olives, artichokes, asparagus, mushrooms, sun-dried tomatoes, etc; potatoes with garlic; bruschetta with tomatoes or mushrooms; vegetarian pizza without the cheese topping; vegetable risottos; polenta.

Watch out for: Parmesan in the pesto sauces and sprinkled over other dishes; cream; milk in the pizza base; egg in the pasta; anchovies in sauces and on pizzas; mozzarella cheese in the salad.

French

The cuisine of France is not famed for its vegetarian options, let alone its vegan-friendly dishes. In an authentic French restaurant you may have a difficult time choosing a meal.

Many vegetable dishes, such as soups, will be made with meat stock. Also, be cautious of salads as they may contain lardons, or eggs in the dressing.

However, the cuisine favours fresh produce, so vegan-friendly plates of vegetables, fungi and salads should take your mind off the lack of options.

Choose: Vegetable side dishes; cooked or raw salads; fruit; ratatouille and similar vegetable and tomato stews; vegetable soups, particularly onion and bean varieties.

Watch out for: Be cautious of anything that is not clearly a whole vegetable, fruit or fungi. Soups may be made with meat stock – even onion soup, which also has cheese-topped bread in it. Lardons, eggs or cheese may be in salad dressings.

Spanish

Although the Spanish have a special place in their cultural cuisine for ham, they also have a great tradition of natural health and an affinity with the environment. Many Spanish dishes lend themselves to vegan versions, and the Mediterranean habit of using oil instead of butter is also very helpful for vegans.

Choose: Vegetable paella; salads; bean and vegetable stews; vegetarian tapas – grilled vegetables, potato croquettes, spicy potatoes, olives, garlic mushrooms, etc.

Watch out for: Fish and meat stocks in stews, soups and paella; cheese, bacon and ham added to salads and vegetable side dishes; eggs.

Below: There are usually plenty of vegetable curries to choose from in Indian restaurants.

Indian

Many authentic Indian restaurants have a good understanding of the needs of vegetarian and vegan customers and are often willing to accommodate them. They may even have a vegetarian, or vegan, section on their menus. Watch out for the clarified butter, known as ghee, that is sometimes used for cooking – oil can often be used as a substitute. Yogurt may also be in the dough that is used to make naan breads.

Choose: Vegetable curries and dhals; rice dishes, such as biryani; breads, such as naans and chapatis; vegetable pakora and samosas; poppadums.

Watch out for: Ghee, which is used in many dishes; yogurt and milk products. Naan bread may contain dairy produce.

Middle Eastern

It is hard to go hungry as a vegan in restaurants that serve Middle Eastern cuisine, such as Lebanese, Iranian, Turkish and Egyptian establishments. There is a wealth of delights featuring chickpeas, couscous, sweet potatoes, olives, salads, wheat and fruit.

Choose: Vegetable tagine dishes with chickpeas, potatoes, apricots and olives; salads and dips, such as tabbouleh, hummus and baba ghanoush; stuffed vine leaves; pitta breads with vegetable kebabs and falafel; desserts such as Turkish delight, halva or stuffed dates.

Above: Falafel, the popular Turkish snack, is one of the many tasty vegan options from Middle Eastern cuisine.

Watch out for: Yogurt dressings on stuffed breads; meat stocks in tagines; gelatine in some Turkish delight.

RESTAURANT TIPS

Follow these few basic guidelines when dining out:

• Make sure that the establishment understands your needs. Some people do not know what a vegan is, so it is often better to simply describe the things that you do not eat. Phone ahead if you can.

• Beware of hidden ingredients. Particular cuisines have certain items to watch out for, such as ghee in Indian food and fish sauces in Asian cooking.

• Ask the staff to recommend a dish. In good restaurants the waiting staff should be trained to know what is suitable from the menu. If they are not sure, speak to the manager or chef.

• Pick and mix from the menu. Look for dishes that would be suitable for you with a little tweaking of the ingredients, and ask the kitchen to adapt the meal.

Pregnancy and children

Many health professionals recognize a balanced and varied vegan diet to be not only nutritionally adequate for people of all ages but positively beneficial. As with any diet it takes a little health-conscious effort to provide protection at key life stages, such as pregnancy and during infancy, childhood and adolescence. The body is working at its hardest at these times and its nutritional needs should be given special priority. A diverse and well-balanced vegan diet can easily satisfy the body's nutritional needs to promote normal growth at these times.

Pre-conception

In addition to following a healthy vegan diet, with plenty of fruits and vegetables, you should ensure adequate intake of folic acid and vitamin B12, iron and essential fats. You should try to avoid coffee and alcohol.

Pregnancy

For all women, vegan and non-vegan alike, the recommended intake of vitamins and minerals is higher than

Below: A nutritionally balanced diet can alleviate pregnancy symptoms such as cravings, aversions, stress and fatigue.

TIPS FOR MORNING SICKNESS

Vegan diets are often higher in carbohydrates than average. To ward off morning sickness try to increase the ratio of protein-rich foods such as buckwheat, hemp seeds and quinoa in your diet and nutrient-dense essential fats.
- Eat five small meals a day and always include protein-rich foods.
- Avoid eating fried foods and sugary snacks.
- Stay upright after eating.
- Eat oatcakes on waking or during the night.
- Try herbal teas, such as ginger, peppermint or chamomile.
- Try sipping a fresh fruit smoothie with added hemp protein or a pregnancy-safe green drink to avoid dramatic blood sugar fluctuations between meals.

normal during pregnancy. Increase your intake of folic acid, vitamin A (beta carotene), B1 (thiamine), niacin, riboflavin, B12, D2, calcium, iron, zinc and essential fats – particularly DHA (docosahexaenoic acid), which is needed to build babies' eyes and brains.

During pregnancy the mother's store of vitamin B12 is not readily available to the developing baby. The baby builds up its supply of vitamin B12 from the mother's daily intake. The mother must thus ensure she has enough in her diet for both of them. If vitamin B12 intake is low during pregnancy, the developing baby will struggle to have adequate stores of the vitamin, and this may lead to a deficiency in the child at some point after birth.

Adequate zinc intake should also be ensured otherwise human milk may not be a rich enough source of zinc. Breast-feeding infants would then have to draw on their own body reserves, laid down during the last three months in the womb.

Above: A herbal tea, such as ginger or peppermint, can help to ward off morning sickness.

The increase in calorie requirements during pregnancy is relatively small. There is little, if any, increase in calorie need during the first six months of pregnancy, but an extra 200 calories per day should be consumed during the third trimester. However, you need to ensure that each calorie counts and the calories you consume are dense in nutrients as your need for nutrients is greater during pregnancy.

Extra water is required by the body for making additional blood for the mother, the baby and for the amniotic fluid. Aim to drink at least six 200ml/7fl oz glasses per day of filtered water. Pregnancy-safe herbal teas, soya milk or vegetable juice could count toward this. Avoid coffee and tea, as caffeine has been associated with various problems during pregnancy, and avoid alcohol.

The basic advice for pregnant women on a vegan diet is to follow the nutritional guidelines established for all adults, ensuring an increased quantity of a mixture of vegan wholefoods. Many women (not just vegans) take a

Right: Persevere with breastfeeding; it can often take two to three weeks to start flowing properly, but those first few drops are the most important. Formula milk can mean your baby misses out on many of the nutrients found in perfectly natural mother's milk, such as essential fats and immune-system boosters.

daily multivitamin and mineral supplement during pregnancy as extra insurance to compensate for times when either healthy eating just will not fit into the day or food aversions develop. With a nutritionally balanced diet, typical pregnancy symptoms, such as food cravings, sickness, stress, fatigue and constipation, may be avoided.

Breastfeeding

The diet to follow when breast-feeding your baby is similar to the diet that is recommended for pregnancy, although the intakes of calories, protein, calcium, magnesium, zinc, copper, selenium and vitamin B12 should be slightly higher. Eating an increased quantity of vegan wholefoods is an ideal way to give yourself a nutritional boost while breastfeeding. In particular, ensure a regular intake of vitamin B12, D2 and essential fats at this time.

Birth to six months

During the first six months of your baby's life, all its basic nutritional needs will be met by regular feeds of breast milk. Breast milk provides a young baby with a natural and nutritionally balanced diet. Your baby will gradually move away from milk as the main source of nutrition, toward his or her first taste of solid foods.

If you find you have to resort to using bottled milk, it is possible to purchase a vegan formula. Ask any vegan organization, health-food store or pharmacy for details of vegan formulas currently available. Soya-based infant formulas can be used from birth onward. Infant formulas are often lacking DHA needed for brain building, so consult a health-care professional about essential nutrients and algae-based fatty acids. As is the case with dairy milk, standard soya milks, which are consumed by adults, should never be used as a straight replacement for breast milk or infant formula. They are lacking in the correct amount of nutrients that are required by a baby, which natural human breast milk contains.

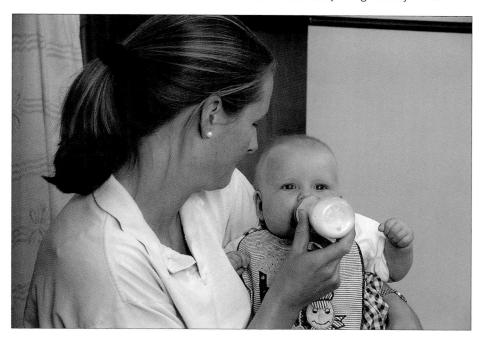

Left: A selection of soya-based vegan formulas are available if you choose to use bottled milk rather than breast milk.

Above: Introduce finger foods from eight months – try soft foods, such as fruits, that can be eaten easily.

First foods

The classic 'first food' should be organic baby rice, cooked millet or quinoa, or mashed banana. This can be followed by various vegetable purées such as cauliflower, broccoli, peas, carrot, and then fruit. If your baby's first taste of solid food is sweet banana, he or she is less likely to get excited about puréed broccoli. Persevere a number of times with a food that your child seems to be rejecting, as taste buds are constantly maturing.

Begin feeds with breast or bottle milk and gradually increase the amount of solid food afterward. Solids should never be added to a bottle of milk. Do not add salt, sugar or spice to food. Move from solid food at one feed per day to solids at two feeds and so on, following and responding to the baby's appetite and pace.

Remember that after four or five months of age, your baby may not receive enough vitamin B12 or D2 from breast milk if your body's stores are depleted. Fortified soya milks intended for infants must contain vitamin B12 and D2 by law.

Seven months

By this stage, your baby will be becoming more active and will be ready to try slightly more lumpy foods with more variety of taste. In addition to breast or bottled milk, you can introduce blended oats, millet, rice, quinoa or buckwheat breakfast cereal to the baby's diet, and a variety of vegetables, such as avocado, cooked and mashed broccoli, carrots, sweet potatoes and parsnips.

Eight to ten months

Gradually adjust your baby's feeds to fit in with the family's meals. Provide foods which contain soft lumps, such as mashed peas and potato, so your baby can use the spoon. Your baby will be ready for fresh fruits, such as pears, peaches, apricots, figs, plums and melons. You can also try finger foods.

By now your baby may also be ready to take a drink from a cup. Other than breast or bottled milk, you can try cooled boiled water or diluted fresh fruit juices, such as apple or pear and vegetable juices.

Ten to twelve months

Foods should be chopped, finely grated or blended. Your baby will be more inclined to hold a spoon, and may be moving toward eating on her own. A greater variety of vegetables should be offered at this point. Only introduce nut butters on the advice of your healthcare professional if you have a family history of nut allergies. As your baby starts to become more mobile, aim to boost greater energy needs from fat, such as coconut, hemp oil and avocado rather than sugary foods and fruit juice.

Twelve months plus

From twelve months of age your infant can share the same meals as the rest of the family, with additional snacks. Keep in mind the following key points, which will help to ensure that your child's diet has the optimum balance of nutrients that are necessary for their growth and development:

Use energy-dense foods These will help you keep up with your child's growing demands.
• Fruit smoothies, concentrated fruit spreads and dried figs
• Fortified plant-milks or infant formula
• Thick porridge with a little additional vegetable oil
• Nut butters, tahini and hummus (providing there is no genetic history of allergies to these foods)
• Coconut milk
• Avocados

Use soya and rapeseed (canola) oils These will encourage your child's brain and visual development.
• Use more rapeseed oil or hemp oil
• Add a little flax oil to sunflower oil

Boost vitamins and minerals
• Use black treacle (molasses) to increase iron intake
• Use tofu prepared with calcium sulphate, which contains more calcium than cow's milk
• Ensure access to sunshine and intake of foods fortified with vitamin D2
• Ensure adequate vitamin B12 intake
• Include foods that are rich in vitamin C in a meal to enhance iron absorption

Below: Energy-dense foods rich in vitamins and minerals are vital for your active and growing toddler.

Older children and teenagers

Vegetarianism among children is common, but you may encounter some people and health professionals that still feel veganism is a drastic step for a child or growing teenager. Arm yourself with the facts and key sources of nutrients, and your child's radiant health should speak for itself. You need to prove that your knowledge of nutrition is based on sound scientific fact, and that the meals you give to your growing children are both interesting and healthy.

The diet recommendations for older children and teenagers are the same as for all vegans, though children may need more frequent meals or snacks due to their high energy needs. A wide variety of wholefoods should be eaten daily, including fruits, vegetables, plenty of leafy greens, as well as wholegrain products, cereals, nuts, seeds, beans, peas and lentils. Ensure they have a reliable source of calcium and supporting vitamins and minerals (especially during growth spurts) and encourage regular weight-bearing exercise to help to build healthy bones.

Below: Teenagers following a vegan diet should ensure they get enough of the vitamins and minerals needed for growth.

Introducing a vegan diet

You may be in a position where you are adopting a vegan diet for children who have been raised to some extent on animal-based foods, or perhaps you have children and have decided to make the life-style change to veganism as a family.

Below: Making the transition to a vegan diet can be a huge change, both physically and mentally, for a family.

Above: Children may need more frequent meals or snacks as they use up a large amount of energy every day.

In this situation you should take time to plan how and when you are going to replace animal-derived products in your children's diets, rather than making a hurried overnight decision. It is important to think about what nutrients you are cutting out by eliminating all animal-derived products, and in what vegan form you can replace them in your diet.

It can also help to make the transition a gradual one, taking things one step at a time. This will ensure you understand the basic nutrition involved and are armed with plenty of menu ideas. Take the time to learn what specific nutrients are important at your child's stage of development and how you can make sure they get sufficient through their new diet. Start children with familar foods, such as peanut butter sandwiches, and gradually introduce new vegan foods.

Making the change a gradual one will also give your family time to get accustomed to the new diet, both physically and mentally. Talk about veganism with your children; they are bound to have lots of questions.

the
vegan
kitchen

For newcomers to vegan cooking it is useful to be reminded that you could actually be opening the door to more ingredients, not fewer. The seemingly endless variety of different fruits, vegetables, nuts, seeds, peas, beans, berries, fungi, herbs and spices will ensure that there is always a delicious meal that can be made for any occasion.

Replacing dairy products and eggs

One of the common questions for those starting a vegan diet is, 'How do I cope without milk and eggs?' Even for vegetarians changing to veganism, this is often a concern. It is, however, surprisingly easy to replace dairy products and eggs, and there is an ever-growing variety of foods on the market to enable you to do so.

You can make quiches using tofu, whisk ice cream using soya milk, set jellies using agar-agar and sprinkle a variety of special cheeses on your food. The options available will ensure that you will barely notice the absence of dairy and eggs.

What is soya?

The most popular and prolific dairy replacer is soya. Soya is a bean related to clover, peas and alfalfa. It contains an excellent balance of amino acids, and is considered the equivalent in protein quality to meat, milk and eggs, which is one reason it has become so popular. Soya has made an enormous impact on the processed food market in the West in recent years and is now used in a variety of products. Many foods have been developed from soya,

Below: Soya beans have been grown for over 5,000 years and are widely used in Asian foods.

but the most popular are miso, soya milk, soy sauce, tempeh and tofu. Soya beans and their derivatives are also used for a huge variety of non-food products such as paints, soaps, plastics, adhesives, candles and fabrics.

For centuries, the soya bean has been the basis of Asian cuisine, and is thought to have been cultivated in China for over 5,000 years. More soya beans are grown in the USA than anywhere else in the world, though over 90 per cent of them are used to facilitate the production of meat and dairy rather than to directly feed people. Other producers include Brazil, Argentina and China.

Soya beans are unique among beans as they contain compounds called isoflavones. These molecules have structures similar to the oestrogens produced in the body, hence the name plant- or phytoestrogen. There are many classes of active non-nutrients with oestrogenic activity, but interest has focused on the beneficial effects of a group of compounds belonging to the isoflavones. The two primary isoflavones in soya beans are daidzein and genistein. Research suggests soya may offer health benefits relating to heart disease, osteoporosis, menopause symptom relief and, possibly, cancer.

Above: There is a wide range of soya products available, which are perfect vegan substitutes for dairy products.

Soya beans are high in protein and are classed as a complete protein – meaning that they contain all the essential amino acids the human body needs. The beans also contain iron, calcium, zinc, B vitamins, vitamin E and fibre. Steamed tofu made with calcium sulphate contains over five times as much calcium as whole pasteurized cow's milk. Soya oil also contains the beneficial polyunsaturated fat. It is free from cholesterol and contains both linoleic and linolenic essential fatty acids.

Milk

Soya milk This is commonly used as a replacement for dairy milk. Various types of soya milk are available, including sweetened, unsweetened, concentrated, ready-to-drink and powdered. Flavoured varieties of soya milk include banana, carob, chocolate and strawberry. Each soya milk product has a slightly different taste and most people have their own preferred brand. Soya milk can be used in exactly the same way as cow's milk – in tea, coffee, custard, rice pudding, creamed soup, white sauce or poured over breakfast cereal.

Other milks Rice, oat, pea, quinoa, barley, hemp and nut milks are also available. Look for them in health-food stores and large supermarkets.

To make your own nut milk, add a handful of blanched almonds or cashew nuts to 475ml/16fl oz/2 cups cold water. Process the mixture in a blender or food processor until smooth and creamy.

Creams and desserts

Soya cream This is usually purchased as a pouring cream, although whipped creams, sour creams and creamed cheeses are also available.

Soya dessert A ready-to-use product that is similar in appearance and taste to custard. It is available in a variety of flavours, such as vanilla, chocolate, strawberry or carob.

Soya ice cream There are many soya-based ice creams which look and taste exactly like their dairy-based counterparts. They are available in a wide range of flavours.

Other ice creams Rice milk, chestnuts, coconut, cashew nuts or even bananas can all be used to make ice creams.

Yogurt

Soya yogurt Plain, flavoured and 'live' soya yogurts are available from health-food stores and most supermarkets. Soya yogurts are made from soya milk, and are used in the same way as dairy yogurts.

Tofu

Made from the curds of soya milk, tofu (also known as beancurd) has little flavour of its own but is highly versatile and absorbs other flavours well. Firm tofu is sold in a block, and can be seasoned and cubed for use in stews and stir-fries. A softer set tofu, called 'silken' tofu, is a good substitute for milk or cream in soups, puddings and desserts. For a simple dessert, blend silken tofu with sugar or maple syrup, a little vegetable oil and a flavouring, such as cocoa powder or vanilla extract.

Cheese

There is a variety of cheese alternatives available to vegans, which can be made from soya milk, seeds or nuts.

You can make a cheesy topping by blending soya milk with vegetable oil in equal quantities and emulsifying with a little vinegar. Add some mashed potato to thicken and a little ketchup and some yeast extract to give it a cheesy flavour.

Soya cheese Hard and soft vegan cheeses are now available, which are made from soya milk. Flavours include Cheddar, Cheshire, Gouda, Stilton, Edam, mozzarella and feta. A powdered Parmesan cheese is also sold for use on pasta dishes.

Below: This Tofu Berry Cheesecake, made with tofu and soya yogurt, is deliciously creamy.

Above: Tofu, a great dairy substitute for vegans, is nutritious, highly versatile and absorbs flavours well.

Other cheeses A variety of other alternatives are available, made from rice, brazil nuts, hemp seeds or cashew nuts.

Nutritional yeast flakes These 'cheesy' tasting flakes are grown for the health-food market (unlike brewer's yeast powder, which has a bitter taste). Use them to flavour sauces or sprinkle on top of hot savoury dishes.

Eggs

When eggs are not eaten on their own, they are used primarily to bind a dish or to lighten it by whipping air into the egg before mixing with other ingredients. Eggs are widely used in cooking, but there are many ways to replace them.

Binders Mashed potato or thick stocks can be used to bind vegetarian burger mixes, nut roasts and other savoury dishes. Bananas, soya milk or soya desserts can bind sweet dishes or cakes.

Raising agents Baking powder, or a mix of cider vinegar and bicarbonate of soda (which is ideal for chocolate cakes) are successful raising agents.

Whole eggs replacers Seasoned firm tofu is commonly used to replace whole eggs. Use it to make quiches, flans and eggless 'scrambled eggs'.

Fruit

An essential part of any diet is fresh fruit, packed full of vitamins and minerals. Make sure you eat enough fruit by adding it to savoury salads and main course dishes, rather than just grabbing it as a snack or dessert. Remember that some fruits contain more natural sugars than others.

Apples

Cultivated for more than 3,000 years, apples are a popular and versatile fruit. They can be enjoyed raw as a snack, grated into salad with nuts or added to a fruit salad. They can also be stewed and served as a sauce with nut roast, or baked and served as a classic dessert. Although fairly low in vitamin C, apples are rich in soluble fibre and pectin, both of which may help to lower cholesterol levels in the blood.

Apricots

The best apricots are sunshine-gold in colour and full of juice. They are delicious baked or used raw in salads. Extremely rich in beta carotene, minerals and vitamin A, apricots are a valuable source of fibre.

Cherries

These make a simple, tasty and refreshing dessert. They also provide a delicious and unusual start to a meal in the form of a chilled soup, which is light and easy to digest. Pitted cherries can be used in salads and are delicious with almonds in a soya yogurt dressing to accompany bean burgers or tempeh. They provide valuable amounts of the antioxidant vitamin C, which helps the body's resistance to infection.

Nectarines

Like a peach without the fuzzy skin, this sweet juicy fruit is named after the drink of the gods – nectar – and is delicious baked or raw. Both nectarines and peaches are extremely fragile and bruise easily, so buy them slightly underripe. When eaten raw, nectarines are especially rich in vitamin C. They aid digestion, reduce high blood pressure and cleanse the body.

Below: Peaches are a versatile fruit. Make sure you handle them gently as they bruise easily.

Above: Snack on fresh cherries to keep vitamin C levels topped up and help your body's immune system.

Peaches

These may be white- or yellow-fleshed. Make sure you select unblemished fruit as peaches bruise easily. They can be skinned in the same way as tomatoes, and at their peak they are best served plain as a tasty dessert or snack. They are also delicious served with fresh raspberry purée, in a sundae with nuts and tofu, in the form of a peach brûlée or poached in brandy. They are great in salads or they can be blended with tomato juice and tarragon to make a light and refreshing soup. Peaches are a valuable source of vitamin A in the form of carotene.

Pears

These do not keep very well, so it is best to buy them slightly underripe and store them at room temperature for a day or two. When they are ready for eating they will give slightly to pressure at the stalk end and have a delicate flavour with natural sweetness and melting flesh. Pears can be used in a salad with a tasty soya yogurt and herb dressing. They are also excellent when poached as a dessert. Despite their high water content, pears contain useful amounts of vitamin C, soluble fibre and potassium. In natural medicine, they are used as a diuretic and laxative.

Plums

These can be classed as either dessert or cooking varieties. Some cooking varieties have extremely dry flesh with little flavour and are best served stewed with cinnamon. Dessert plums, such as greengages or Victoria, are sweet and juicy, and they can also be used for cooking. Plums are an excellent fruit for making refreshing chilled soups and are also the main ingredient of plum sauce – a thick, dark sauce that is often used in Chinese cooking and goes particularly well with roasted tofu, as well as with foods made from wheat gluten, such as seitan and mock duck. Plums are relatively low in calories and rich in vitamins and minerals, and are therefore an ideal healthy snack for anybody, but in particular for those who are trying to lose weight.

Rhubarb

The trimmed stem of the rhubarb plant should be cooked before eating, and the leaves must never be eaten, whether raw or cooked, as they are poisonous. Any tough outer skin should be peeled off if the stems are large and coarse. Rhubarb can be gently stewed with a little sugar until soft and tender and is best flavoured with ginger, orange or cashew nuts. Rhubarb contains valuable calcium but also contains large amounts of oxalic acid, which prevents the body from absorbing minerals, such as calcium and iron. It is therefore not advisable to eat rhubarb more than twice a week.

Below: Pears can form the basis of many tasty desserts.

Above: Plums make a sweet and healthy snack eaten as they are, but can also be used in a variety of dessert recipes.

Oranges

These are valued for their high vitamin C content and also for the oils that they contain. Best eaten as soon as they are peeled, oranges start to lose vitamin C from the moment they are cut. The rind is used for its flavour and the flesh may be added to salads or used in a sweet and sour sauce with ginger. Orange juice is used in both sweet and savoury recipes, as a marinade or braising agent, or served as a refreshing drink. Oranges go well with dark (bittersweet) chocolate, almonds or cashew nuts. When orange segments are added to a fruit salad, the acidic juice helps to prevent other fruits from discolouring.

Above: Lemons are an essential ingredient in most kitchens and their juice and rind can be used in many dishes.

Grapefruits

These sharp and refreshing citrus fruits are often served as an appetizer or as a light, healthy breakfast. Grapefruit can also be used in salads with avocado, or served hot sprinkled with ground cinnamon and browned under a grill (broiler). Pink grapefruit are sweeter and juicier than yellow ones. Like other citrus fruits, grapefruit has high levels of vitamin C and is low in calories.

Lemons

These are indispensable for their juice and rind, which are used to accentuate the flavour of other foods and give a subtle tang. Lemon juice is good to use instead of vinegar in salad dressings. It helps to preserve the colour of other fruits or vegetables. Lemon wedges make an attractive garnish and are an essential accompaniment for many foods. Preserved lemons add tartness to vegetable stews and casseroles.

Limes

These sour green citrus fruits have a distinctive flavour and can often be used instead of lemon. Lime juice is essential in recipes such as guacamole, where it prevents the avocado from discolouring. A squeeze of lime juice in sparkling water on ice makes a refreshing summer drink.

Berries

Strawberries, raspberries, blackberries, blueberries and other berries are luscious, delicate fruits that need gentle handling. Look for bright and firm berries that show no signs of bruising, wetness or mildew.

Fat, juicy berries are all wonderful served with tofu, rice pudding, soya yoghurt or dairy-free ice cream. They can also be pushed through a sieve (strainer) or whizzed in a blender to make a delicious coulis or sauce. Strawberries make an attractive base for a summer fruit salad, salsa or a salad with mint and cucumber. All berries can be made into mousses, fools or smoothies, or used to decorate fruit cocktails or puddings.

Cranberries are hard, shiny berries with an acidic, slightly spicy taste. They are most commonly used for making cranberry sauce, or bought as juice in a refreshing drink that is rich in vitamin C.

All berries are abundant in nutrients. Blueberries contain vitamin C, fibre and B vitamins along with flavenoids that can aid the body's defences against infection. Raspberries contain high levels of folate, zinc and potassium, making them a really healthy choice.

Blackcurrants and redcurrants contain a useful amount of calcium and are one of the best possible sources of vitamin C. The stems and flower ends should be removed during preparation, unless the berries are going to be sieved (strained). Generally, currants are best used cooked otherwise they are extremely tart.

There are a host of dried 'superberries' now appearing on the store shelves, such as goji berries, açaí berries and noni berries, all boasting unusually high amounts of antioxidants and immune-boosting properties.

Grapes

There are many varieties of grape, most of which are grown for wine production. Grapes for eating are less acidic and have a thinner skin than those used for wine-making. Grapes contain iron, potassium and fibre. They are powerful detoxifiers and can improve the condition of the skin, and treat gout, liver and kidney disorders.

Below: Watermelon is one of many varieties of melon and makes a deliciously refreshing treat on a hot day.

Above: Raspberries are a delicate, soft fruit which can bruise easily and need delicate handling.

Melons

The high water content makes melon one of the most refreshing fruits. There are many different varieties of melon, including honeydew, cantaloupe and watermelon. To test if ripe, smell it and press the ends – it should have a strong fragrance and yield a little.

Melons are commonly eaten as a light appetizer, often flavoured with ginger or green peppercorns. They also make a tasty addition to a savoury salad, or can be eaten as a dessert piled with summer fruits, such as redcurrants, strawberries or raspberries. All varieties of melon are low in calories.

Figs

These delicate, thin-skinned fruits may be purple, brown or greenish-gold. Delicious raw, figs can also be poached or baked. Choose unbruised ripe fruits. Figs are a well-known laxative and an excellent source of calcium.

Dates

Like figs, dates are one of the oldest cultivated fruits. Fresh dates are sweet and soft and are a natural sweetener. Dates should be plump and glossy. Medjool dates from Egypt and California have a wrinkly skin, but most other varieties are smooth. They can be stored in the refrigerator for up to a week. Dates are high in vitamin C and a good source of potassium and soluble fibre.

Above: Passion fruit has a fragrant pulp inside that can be scooped out with a spoon.

Pineapples

Widely available fresh, canned or as juice, pineapple is refreshing in sweet or savoury salads. It goes well with rice and is a good ingredient for making sweet and sour sauce.

Pineapple contains a natural enzyme called bromelin, which helps with digestion so the fresh fruit is ideal for healthy salads (the enzyme is destroyed by heating, so canned fruit does not have the same effect). Pineapple contains magnesium, zinc and fibre as well as valuable antioxidants, which may neutralize cell damage by free radicals.

Mangoes

This tropical fruit has smooth, aromatic flesh. It has a large flat stone (pit) in the middle, which must be removed before eating. When buying a mango, choose one that is tender all over and yields slightly in the palm of your hand.

An extremely versatile fruit, mango goes well with savoury ingredients and can also be used in salsas, pickles or chutneys. It is good cooked in a curry and served with courgette (zucchini) ribbons and lemon slices. It is also a tasty addition to many desserts, such as fruit salads. An easy way to serve them is to remove the stone, then score a criss-cross pattern inside the two halves. Turn the mango halves inside out. Mangoes are very high in vitamin A.

Papayas

Similar to a sweet, peach-coloured melon but with a more intense flavour. Remove the seeds from the middle and peel off the skin. They are delicious when marinated and skewered as part of a kebab. They are reputed to have properties that protect your digestive system from bugs and parasites.

Bananas

A concentrated bundle of energy, bananas are also full of valuable nutrients. They are rich in dietary fibre, vitamins and minerals, especially potassium. Ripe bananas soothe the stomach and are believed to strengthen the stomach lining against acid and ulcers. Their high starch content makes them a good source of sustained energy, and they are an effective laxative. Bananas are rich in the amino acid tryptophan, which is known to lift the spirits and aid sleep.

Passion fruits

These are small and oval with a dark purple, leathery skin. Buy them when the skin is wrinkled as this denotes ripeness.

To eat, cut the passion fruit in half and scoop out the fragrant, full-flavoured pulp with a teaspoon. The black crunchy seeds should be eaten along with the pulp. It is outstanding with coconut ice cream, delectable in fruit salads or any other dessert, and it is a good source of carotene and iron.

Below: Papaya can be eaten on its own by simply removing the seeds and skin, or is also good barbecued on a kebab.

Lychees

These small exotic fruits are the size of a plum with a hard, red, knobbly skin. The ultimate pocket snack, the skin can be cracked and pulled away to reveal a ball of flesh that is translucent white and juicy with an aromatic, rosy scent. The stone in the middle must be removed.

Lychees make a wonderful addition to fruit salads, or can be blended in a smoothie. They are high in vitamin C.

Kiwi fruits

Also called a Chinese gooseberry, a kiwi fruit looks like a hairy brown egg with green flesh inside. They make a bright addition to salads, though they must be added just before serving as they quickly ferment. They are packed with vitamin C and can be eaten for breakfast in place of a boiled egg, using a teaspoon, served with some toast with nut butter.

Pomegranates

These are large, thick-skinned berries full of jewel-like seeds surrounded by a shiny pink pulp. The seeds are arranged in irregular compartments divided by tough skin. To eat, cut the pomegranate in half and scrape out the seeds. The seeds make an attractive topping for desserts or salads and are used in Middle Eastern dishes, Indian pakora and various rice dishes. Pomegranates can also be crushed to make a nutritious juice bursting with antioxidants.

Above: Kiwi fruits are excellent served in salads, or simply scoop out the flesh from the skin using a teaspoon.

Vegetables

It is important that we all eat enough vegetables. Nutritionists recommend a minimum of five portions of fresh vegetables per day. There are so many delicious vegetables available that they need never get boring for a vegan. Try to experiment with new recipes that feature more unusual varieties, or discover different ways of serving old favourites like cauliflower and cabbage.

Beetroot (Beets)

You can tell by the colour that this is going to be full of antioxidants. Beetroot is often included in juices as it is reputed to be an excellent intestinal cleanser and good for detoxing the liver and gall bladder. It is often served pickled in salads and it is the principal ingredient of borscht, a Russian soup.

Carrots

These bright orange root vegetables contain beta carotene that converts to vitamin A and is vital for good vision. Carrots are also rich in dietary fibre, antioxidants and minerals. They have a fragrant, sweet taste and baby carrots are available, which are more tender than the larger ones but have less taste.

The popularity of carrots all over the world means that there are plenty of dishes to make with them. They are good added to stews and soups, sautéed in orange juice, grated in a salad or in carrot cake.

Above: Carrots can be cooked in many dishes, or eaten raw as a healthy snack.

Celeriac

This root is closely related to celery, which explains its flavour – a cross between aniseed, celery and parsley. Similar in size to a small swede, it has ivory flesh and must be peeled before use. Grate and eat it raw in salads or steam and bake it in gratins. Celeriac can also be used in soups. Like celery, it is a diuretic. It also contains vitamin C, calcium, iron potassium and fibre.

Swedes (Rutabagas)

The globe-shaped swede has pale orange flesh with a delicate sweet flavour. Trim off the thick peel, then treat it the same way as other root vegetables. Swedes contain vitamins A and C.

Parsnips

This vegetable has a sweet creamy flavour and is delicious roasted or steamed. Parsnips are best purchased after the first frost of the year as the cold converts their starches into sugar, making them sweeter. Scrub before use and only peel if tough. Parsnips are effective detoxifiers and are believed to fight some cancers. They contain vitamins C and E, iron, folic acid and potassium.

Turnips

This humble root vegetable has many health-giving qualities, and small turnips with their green tops intact are especially nutritious. Small turnips can be eaten raw. You can steam, bake, or use them in casseroles and soups. Rich in beta carotene and vitamin C, turnips may halt the onset of certain cancers and maintain bowel regularity.

Above: Bright red beetroot is excellent for making soups, such as borscht, and is ideal for use in salads.

Potatoes

There are thousands of potato varieties, and many lend themselves to particular cooking methods. Discard any potatoes with green patches as these indicate the presence of toxic alkaloids called solanines. Vitamins and minerals are stored in, or just below, the skin, so it is best to use potatoes unpeeled. They are high in complex carbohydrates, and include both protein and fibre. They provide plenty of sustained energy, plus vitamins B and C, iron and potassium.

Sweet potatoes

These make a great change from potatoes and although they have a high sugar content, they are high in antioxidants and a useful part of the diet.

Broccoli

A versatile and nutritious superfood in the world of vegetables that should be eaten regularly by everybody, not just vegans. Broccoli is a versatile vegetable, whether stir-fried, roasted or steamed. It can be used as a base for baked dishes or served cold with chopped, roasted almonds and is delicious with ground nuts as a soup. Broccoli contains large amounts of vitamin A and C, folic acid and iron and a little calcium.

Above: Chinese leaves are a crisp variety of cabbage and are a good choice for stir-frying.

Cabbage

This everyday vegetable comes in a wide variety of forms, which are all extremely versatile and can be used either as side dishes or in salads. Coleslaw, the traditional white cabbage salad, which is made with grated carrot, onion and occasionally fennel, is delicious made with red cabbage as well. Red or white cabbage is extremely good cooked with pineapple, (bell) peppers and onion, or it can also be pickled and served as a condiment. Crisp varieties of cabbage, such as Chinese leaves (Chinese cabbage) and pak choi (bok choy) are popular choices for stir-frying and are common in Chinese dishes. Savoy cabbage can be wrapped around savoury fillings, such as mashed tofu or soya mince, and then baked in a rich tomato sauce. Cabbage contains carotene, iron, calcium and varying amounts of vitamin C, though it does not provide very much energy.

Cauliflower

This popular vegetable has a delicious flavour and crunchy texture. It is full of valuable nutrients, including potassium, fibre, vitamins C, K and E, folate and carotene. Be careful not to overcook it as it can turn mushy. It is best to cut cauliflower into fairly small, even florets so that they each take the same time to cook. Indian spices complement cauliflower extremely well, as do nutmeg or tomato. It is good mashed, served in place of rice as a low carbohydrate alternative. Raw cauliflower florets are great as crudités for dips or snacking.

Spinach

This is a delicious, dark green leafy plant that can be eaten raw when young, but it is better cooked when a little older and slightly tougher. The leaves take very little time to cook and they taste good stir-fried with garlic and tofu, in tarts and with creamy sauces to go over some pasta. Spinach is often added to lentil or potato curries. It is rich in vitamin A, iron and calcium. However, it also contains oxalic acid, which stops the body absorbing some of these minerals.

Kale

These tough dark green leaves are packed with nutrients including lots of iron and calcium, so it is worth trying to sneak it into your usual recipes. Try it shredded into stir-fries, stews, curries or pies, or as a base for Indian pakora.

Squashes

Winter squashes, such as acorn squash, butternut squash and pumpkins, have tough inedible skins, dense, fibrous flesh and large seeds. Summer squashes, such as cucumbers, courgettes (zucchini) and

Above: Young spinach leaves can be eaten raw in a salad or cooked and added to stir-fries and spicy curries.

marrows, are picked when still young and have thin, edible skins and tender, edible seeds. Look for firm, bright, unblemished vegetables that are heavy for their size. Winter squashes can be kept for several weeks if stored whole in a cool, dry place. Summer squashes do not keep as well and should be stored in the refrigerator for only a few days. Summer squashes are diuretics and their potassium content means they are beneficial for those with high blood pressure. Pumpkins are also a diuretic, as well as a laxative, and like other winter squash, contain high levels of Vitamin E, beta carotene and potassium. Summer squashes contain smaller amounts of beta carotene. All squash are low in calories.

Below: Cucumber is a summer squash that is easy to slice and add to salads.

Above: Choose local asparagus when it is in season rather than the variety that has been flown in from distant countries.

Above: Celery is often eaten raw but is also delicious cooked in stews and soups or braised with garlic.

Fennel

Similar in texture to celery, the base of this plant has a delicate aniseed-like flavour. Almost all of the plant is edible. The bulbous stalks are used as a vegetable, either raw or cooked, and can replace celery in Waldorf salads and similar dishes. It is also a very good partner for potato. The graceful green leaves of the plant are perfect used as a garnish, and the seeds can be added, ground or whole, to various sweet or savoury dishes such as nut roasts, curries and patés as a spice.

Asparagus

Due to the very short season and short shelf-life, asparagus is an all-too-brief luxury. They are now available pretty much all year but they have to travel halfway around the world to a shelf near you, so it is best to grab what you can when they are in season. Store them upright in a bowl of water.

Gently warm the spears in a little oil, puréed garlic, and season with a little sea salt and black pepper. Asparagus in jars are usually mushy and comparatively tasteless. Asparagus contain asparagine (said to stimulate the kidneys) and also phosphorus, potassium, folic acid, beta carotene, vitamin C and vitamin K.

Celery

This crunchy vegetable adds a distinctive flavour to soups and casseroles. It can be braised with grated ginger, sunflower seeds, carrot and onion in a simple and tasty vegetable dish to serve with pies and bean dishes. For buffets, raw celery stalks can be filled with vegetable pâté, puréed avocado or nut butters. Celery is delicious combined with apple, carrot or pear in a healthy juice. Stalks can also be eaten alone as a low-carbohydrate snack.

Celery is 95 per cent water, so it is extremely low in calories and a helpful way of getting fibre without the calories. It also contains a small amount of various valuable vitamins and minerals.

Aubergines (Eggplants)

This vegetable readily absorbs robust flavours and has a firm, velvety texture. Aubergines are a popular ingredient in Mediterranean recipes, such as moussaka from Greece and baked Italian dishes. They are popular in Moroccan tagine dishes and

Right: Tomatoes are a rich source of nutrients and are essential for a wide variety of vegan meals.

Indian curries and spiced snacks. Baby aubergines are tasty when roasted with a little olive oil and cumin seeds. Roasted aubergine flesh can be made into a dip seasoned with lemon juice and parsley.

They used to contain bitter juices that were removed by standing in salt, but this is not always necessary now.

Tomatoes

An indispensable flavouring and salad ingredient, tomatoes are a common fruit in most kitchens and can be used in a wide variety of ways. Small cherry tomatoes are perfect in salads, or can be roasted with balsamic vinegar, hollowed out and stuffed with mashed tofu with garlic and basil, or dunked into dips. Beefsteak tomatoes are ideal for stuffing or slicing into salads. Plum tomatoes have an intense, sweet flavour that makes them excellent for making soups and sauces.

Passata, or strained tomatoes, is readily available bottled, sometimes with herbs or spices added, and is a useful store-cupboard or pantry item for making a quick sauce to go with potatoes, rice or pasta. Dried tomatoes, particularly the sun-blushed variety, combine well with garlic and fresh herbs for an unusual salad. Tomato purée (paste) is useful for enriching and thickening sauces.

A valuable source of the vitamins E, C and carotene, tomatoes also contain the antioxidant lycopene, which may help protect the body against some cancers.

Chillies

These range from mild to very fiery, but they all need careful handling. Cut the chillies and remove the seeds under running water using the point of a sharp knife. Do not touch your face afterward (especially eyes) as the juices are a severe irritant. Wash your hands well afterward.You could use gloves if you are particularly sensitive or if handling potent varieties such as scotch bonnet peppers.

Avocados

This delicately flavoured fruit-vegetable is best when the flesh has ripened to the consistency of soft butter and is light yellow-green in colour. Halve it and serve with a teaspoon of vinaigrette or tomato mayonnaise dressing. It can be used to make soup, added to a leafy green salad, or served with tofu in a yogurt dressing. It is also good on pizza, or in a vegan 'tricolore' salad, combined with tofu and ripe tomatoes. It is the main ingredient in the traditional Mexican dip, guacamole.

Avocados are rich in protein, vitamins A and B, with virtually no carbohydrate content. They contain vitamin E rich oil. Although fairly high in calories, they are healthy and should be eaten regularly.

Below: Use avocados regularly as they are full of nutrients and add a delicious creaminess to dips and sauces.

Above: Red chillies, like Serrano chillies, have ripened for longer than green varieties, but are not necessarily hotter.

Bell peppers

Brightly coloured and fresh in flavour, peppers are useful served raw in salads, as crudités, or as a garnish. They can be cooked in casseroles, on kebabs or stir-fried. They can be stuffed or roasted with a little olive oil and make delicious lightly battered fritters, such as Japanese tempura. Raw peppers are high in vitamin C and beta carotene.

Peas

Petits pois (baby peas) are the smallest and sweetest of shelled peas and are good frozen. They are cropped in peak condition and frozen within hours of picking, which means they retain more nutrients, especially vitamin C, than store-bought fresh peas. Peas are a colourful and tasty addition to many dishes. They provide a good source of protein as well as vitamins and minerals.

Green beans

Often overlooked, green beans can be used in a variety of ways. French, runner and dwarf beans can be eaten pod and all. Simply top and tail them, then they can be steamed, fried in a little rapeseed (canola) oil with chopped onion and flaked (sliced) almonds, added to stir-fried dishes, served hot as an accompaniment to a variety of dishes with a teaspoon of vinaigrette dressing, or served in a vegan Niçoise salad. They are also an excellent ingredient for chutneys and pickles.

Green beans provide useful amounts of carotene and B vitamins. Remember to ensure that those with strings along the edge are trimmed before cooking.

Mangetouts (Snow peas)

These are a variety of pea with edible pods, which are eaten before the peas are formed. Ideally, they should be briefly steamed to enhance their sweet flavour and crunchy texture. They are good cooked in stir-fries or served raw for dipping.

Broad (Fava) beans

When young and fresh, the pods can be eaten whole; simply top and tail, and then slice. Usually, however, you will need to shell the beans as their skins can become tough. Broad beans can be eaten raw or lightly cooked.

Corn

Corn cobs are best eaten soon after picking. Remove the green outer leaves and cook whole or slice the kernels off with a sharp knife. Baby corn cobs can be eaten raw and are good in stir-fries. Look out for fresh, plump kernels and eat soon after purchase. Corn is a good carbohydrate food and is rich in vitamins A, B and C, and fibre. It contains useful amounts of iron, magnesium, phosphorus and potassium. Baby corn is high in folate, which is essential for maintaining the immune system.

Below: Frozen peas are shelled and frozen within hours of picking, which means they retain a lot of nutrients.

Onions

These ancient vegetables have numerous culinary uses as a flavouring, whether used raw or cooked. Onions can also be served as a vegetable in their own right, either roasted, baked or boiled. Red onions have a milder flavour and are more colourful, shallots are good roasted whole and spring onions (scallions) are popular in salads and stir-fries.

Although they contain few nutrients, their main value lies in the natural antibiotic properties of the compounds they contain, such as allicin. These have valuable cleansing properties, may help fight infections, lower cholesterol levels and help protect against cancer.

Leeks

Providing useful amounts of iron as well as the antioxidants carotene and vitamins E and C, leeks are a good vegetable to use in casseroles and soups. To prepare them, cut off the roots, remove any tough outer leaves and trim off the very green tops. Wash them well as dirt can get trapped between the layers. They can be steamed and served hot or cold, dressed with fresh parsley and a little vinaigrette dressing.They are the classic partner for potatoes in soup.

Garlic

For centures this wonder food has been praised for its medicinal powers. The flavour of garlic is milder when whole or sliced; crushing or chopping releases the oils, making the flavour stronger. Most garlic is semi-dried to prolong its shelf-life, yet the cloves should still be moist and juicy. Stored in a cool, dry place, garlic will keep for up to about eight weeks.

Although the antiviral, antibacterial and antifungal qualities of garlic are most potent when eaten raw, cooking does not inhibit its anti-cancer, blood-thinning and decongestant capabilities. It has also been found to lower cholesterol, reduce high blood pressure, boost the immune system, act as an anti-inflammatory, lift mood and have a calming effect.

Mushrooms

These are rich in the essential B vitamins niacin, pantothenic acid and biotin. Flat mushrooms are excellent for grilling (broiling), stuffing or making into pâté. Dried shiitake mushrooms are often used in Chinese cooking but must be soaked before use. Oyster mushrooms are quite firm and when cut into strips they make a great vegan replacement in traditional meat recipes such as stroganoff and bourguignon. Fresh wild mushrooms and gourmet varieties are becoming more widely available in supermarkets.

Above: Garlic is thought to have a multitude of medicinal properties, including anti-cancer capabilities.

Salad leaves

There are many varieties of salad leaves available, including lettuces, radicchio, rocket (arugula), sorrel and watercress. Buy leaves as fresh as possible and tear them by hand. Although all types of salad leaves are about 90 per cent water, they contain useful amounts of vitamins and minerals, particularly folate, iron and the antioxidants, vitamin C and beta carotene.

Sea vegetables

A valuable mineral-rich food to include in your diet, there are many varieties of sea vegetables available, mainly from Japan, Ireland, Scotland, France and Canada. Some sea vegetables, such as wakame, hijiki and kombu (or kelp) can be used in soups, stews and stir-fries, while others, such as agar-agar and carrageen, are used as a setting agent in jellies, mousses and cheesecakes.

Sea vegetables are usually sold dried and will keep for months. They are rich in the antioxidant beta carotene, contain some of the B complex vitamins and significant amounts of calcium, magnesium, potassium, phosphorus and iron, as well as useful amounts of selenium, zinc and iodine. This rich mineral content benefits the nervous system, helping to reduce stress. It also boosts the immune system, aiding the metabolism, while the iodine content helps thyroid function.

Above: Spring onions, red onions, shallots and white onions.

Lentils

Lens-shaped lentils, which come in many types, are the seeds of the lentil plant. They are classed as pulses (legumes) and are one of the oldest foods in the human diet, with evidence they were eaten 9,000 years ago. One of the first domesticated crops, the lentil originated in Asia and north Africa and continues to be cultivated in those regions, as well as in France and Italy. Lentils are hard even when fresh, so they are always sold dried. Unlike most pulses, they do not need soaking. They are a valuable staple in the vegan kitchen and can be used in a wide range of dishes.

Red lentils

These orange-coloured split lentils, sometimes known as Egyptian lentils, are one of the most familiar varieties and are widely available in supermarkets. They cook in just 20 minutes, eventually disintegrating into a thick purée, which makes them ideal for adding to soups and casseroles as they will help to thicken the dish. They are delicious when stewed with spices to make an Indian dhal. In the Middle East, red or yellow lentils are cooked and mixed with spices and vegetables to form balls, which are then fried or grilled (broiled) for a snack.

Below: Red split lentils are widely available and are perfect for thickening vegetable soups and stews.

Above: Puy lentils from France are highly prized and, because they retain their shape, they are ideal for salads.

Yellow lentils

Less well-known than other varieties, yellow lentils taste very similar to the red lentils and are used in much the same way. They are usually sold split in two and are widely used in Indian cuisine, especially for making spicy dhals and vegetable curries.

Below: Brown lentils are a suitable variety for use in salads because they keep their shape after cooking.

Green and brown lentils

Sometimes referred to as continental lentils, you often get a mixture of both green and brown lentils together. They look like little pills and these lentils retain their shape when cooked rather than going mushy like the red and yellow varieties, though they can go mushy if cooked for too long. They take longer to cook than the split lentils – approximately 40–45 minutes – and are ideal for adding to warm salads, casseroles and stuffings. Alternatively, either of these lentils can be cooked and blended with herbs or spices to make a tempting and nutritious pâté.

Puy lentils

These tiny, dark, blue-green marbled lentils grow in central France and are the only lentils identified by their area of cultivation – the Le Puy region. They are considered to be far superior in flavour and texture to the other varieties of lentils. They have a delicate peppery taste and they retain their bead-like shape during cooking, which takes around 25–30 minutes. Puy lentils are a delicious addition to simple dishes, such as warm salads, and are also extremely good braised in wine with fresh herbs.

Dried peas and beans

Along with lentils, the many varieties of peas and beans are referred to as pulses (legumes) and have long been a staple food in the Middle East, South America, India and the Mediterranean, but there is hardly a country that does not have its own favourite bean-based dish, from Boston baked beans in the USA to refried beans in Mexico. In China they are fermented for black bean and yellow bean sauces.

There is a vast range of peas and beans that are all packed with protein, vitamins, minerals and fibre, and are extremely low in fat. For the vegan cook, their ability to absorb the flavours of other foods means that these pulses can be used as the base for an almost infinite number of vegan dishes. Most pulses require soaking overnight in cold water before use, so it is wise to plan ahead when you want to make a dish using these pulses. Dried kidney beans and soya beans contain toxins, so you need to follow the cooking instructions carefully. After soaking, they need to be boiled vigorously before use.

Below: Most dried peas and beans require soaking for a few hours or overnight before cooking.

Peas

Dried peas come from the field pea not the garden pea, which is eaten fresh. Unlike lentils, peas are soft when young and require drying. They are available whole or split; the latter have a sweeter flavour and cook more quickly. Like split lentils, split peas do not hold their shape when cooked, making them perfect for use in Indian dhals, purées, casseroles and soups. They take about 45 minutes to cook. Marrowfat peas are larger in size and are used to make the traditional British 'mushy' peas. Like other whole peas, they require soaking overnight before use. They are delicious with mint as a pea pâté or pea and mint soup.

Although peas can be kept for up to a year, they toughen with time. Buy from stores that have fast stock turnover and look for bright, unwrinkled pulses that are not dusty. Store in airtight containers in a cool, dark place. Rinse before use.

Peas have an impressive range of nutrients including iron, selenium, folate, manganese, zinc, phosphorus and some B vitamins. Extremely low in fat and richer in protein than most pulses, peas are reputed to be important in fighting heart disease by reducing harmful LDL cholesterol in the body. They are high in fibre, which slows down the rate at which sugar enters the bloodstream, providing a steady supply of energy.

Above: Dried beans can be used to make many dishes, from soups and stews to dips and salads.

Aduki beans

Also known as adzuki beans, these tiny, deep-red beans have a sweet, nutty flavour and are popular in dishes from the Far East. In Chinese cooking they form the base of red bean paste. They are known as the 'king of beans' in Japan, where they are reputed to be good for the liver and kidneys. They cook quickly and can be used in casseroles and bakes. They are also ground into flour for use in cakes, breads and pastries.

Black-eyed beans

Known as black-eyed peas or cow peas in the USA, black-eyed beans are an essential ingredient in North American Creole cooking – which is influenced by French, Spanish and African cuisines – and some spicy Indian curries. The small, creamy-coloured bean is characterized by the black spot on its side where it was once attached to the pod. They are good in soups and salads, and can also be added to savoury bakes and casseroles. They are suitable to be used in place of haricot (navy) or cannellini beans in various dishes.

Above: The distinctive-looking black-eyed bean is a useful ingredient for a range of dishes.

Black beans

These shiny, black, kidney-shaped beans are often used in Caribbean cooking. They have a sweetish flavour, and their distinctive colour adds a dramatic touch to soups, mixed bean salads or casseroles. They are popular in China, where they are used to make the world-famous black bean sauce, which is great for serving with tofu.

Borlotti beans

These oval-shaped beans have red-streaked, pinkish-brown speckled skin and a bitter-sweet, slightly nutty flavour. When they are cooked, the speckled markings disappear and they have a tender, moist texture, which goes really well in Italian-style bean and pasta soups, as well as in hearty vegetable stews and casseroles. In most recipes, they are interchangeable with red kidney beans.

Right: Distinctively shiny black beans can be mixed with red and yellow peppers and orange butternut squash to create this vibrantly stunning Black Bean Hotpot, which is also extremely nutritious.

Right: Broad beans are usually sold fresh and green, but they change from green to brown when dried.

Broad (Fava) beans

These large beans were first cultivated by the ancient Egyptians. Usually eaten in their fresh form, broad beans change in colour from green to brown when dried, making them difficult to recognize in their dried state. The outer skin can be very tough and chewy, and some people prefer to remove it after cooking. They can also be bought ready-skinned. Broad beans are good added to falafel and are also sometimes sold roasted and spiced as a snack.

Butter beans and lima beans

Similar in flavour and appearance, both butter beans and lima beans are characterized by their flattish, kidney shape and soft, floury texture. Cream-coloured butter beans are familiar in Britain and Greece, while lima beans are popular in the USA. In Greek cooking, butter beans are oven-baked with tomato, garlic and olive oil until tender and creamy. The pale-green lima bean is the main ingredient in succotash, an American dish that also includes corn kernels. Butter and lima

beans are also good with creamy herb sauces. Care should be taken not to overcook both butter beans and lima beans as they are prone to becoming quite pulpy and mushy in texture.

Cannellini beans

These small, white, kidney-shaped beans have a soft, creamy texture and a mild, slightly nutty flavour when cooked. They are a particularly popular ingredient in Italian cooking. They can be added to soups and are often used in place of haricot beans. When dressed with olive oil, lemon juice, crushed garlic and fresh chopped parsley, they make an excellent tasty and nutritious warm salad.

Chickpeas

Also known as garbanzo beans, robust and hearty chickpeas resemble shelled hazelnuts and have a delicious nutty flavour and creamy texture. They need soaking and lengthy cooking before they are tender.

Chickpeas are frequently used in Mediterranean cuisine, where they are the principal ingredient in hummus (along with the sesame seed paste, tahini). They are also a favourite in Middle Eastern cuisines in dishes such as falafel, where they are ground with herbs and spices and then fried before being served with tahini and pitta bread. In India, chickpeas are known as gram and they are ground into a flour to make fritters, pakora and flat breads. Gram flour, which is also known as besan, can be found in health-food stores as well as Asian grocery stores.

Flageolet beans

These young French beans are removed from the pod when they are tender and just maturing, before they are fully ripe, hence their fresh delicate flavour. They range from a creamy white to a pretty, mint-green colour, and they are the most expensive bean to buy and are best treated simply. Cook them until they are tender, then season and drizzle with a little olive oil and lemon juice.

Above: Versatile cannellini beans are delicious used in a salad with a mixture of other vegetables and herbs.

Haricot beans

Called navy or Boston beans in the USA, these beans are most commonly used for canned baked beans. These versatile, ivory-coloured beans are small and oval in shape and suit slow-cooked dishes, such as casseroles and stews.

Below: Chickpeas, with their nutty flavour, are the main ingredient of Greek hummus and Middle Eastern falafel.

Pinto beans

A smaller, paler version of the borlotti bean, the savoury-tasting pinto has an attractive speckled skin – it is aptly named as pinto, meaning 'painted' in Spanish. One of the many relatives of the kidney bean, pinto beans feature extensively in Mexican cooking, most familiarly in refried beans, when they are cooked until tender and fried with garlic, chilli and tomatoes. The beans are then mashed, resulting in a wonderful, spicy, rough purée that is usually served with warm tortillas. Soya yogurt and garlic-flavoured guacamole are good accompaniments.

Ful medames

A member of the broad bean family, these small Egyptian beans form the base of the national dish of the same name, in which they are flavoured with ground cumin and then baked with olive oil, garlic and lemon. They have a strong, nutty flavour and tough, light brown outer skin. Ful medames need to be soaked overnight in cold water, then simmered slowly for about 1 hour until soft and tender.

Below: Delicately-flavoured flageolet beans are best served simply seasoned and drizzled with olive oil and lemon juice.

HOW TO SPROUT

Beans, peas and lentils are easy to sprout. This technique is suitable for mung and aduki beans, chickpeas, whole lentils, mustard, fenugreek and alfalfa seeds.

1 First pick over the beans or seeds, removing any tiny stems or stones, and rinse them in a sieve (strainer) under cold running water. Then put about 2 tbsp in a large, wide-necked jar (they should fill about one quarter of the jar) and soak them in plenty of warm water overnight.

2 The next day, drain off the water, cover the jar with a piece of muslin (cheesecloth) and fasten with string or an elastic band. Lay the jar on its side in a warm, well-ventilated place, out of direct sunlight.

3 Every night and morning, uncover the jar, fill with warm water, swirl around, then cover again and drain off the water completely through the muslin to prevent mould. Seeds should start to sprout after 2–3 days; beans and lentils after 5–7 days. When the sprouts have grown to 1–2cm (½–¾in) long, they are ready to eat. Rinse again before using.

Above: Red kidney beans are popular in South America and are an essential ingredient in any chilli.

Red kidney beans

Mahogany-red kidney beans retain their colour and shape when cooked. They have a soft, 'mealy' texture and are common in South American cooking. An essential ingredient in Mexican chillies, they can also be used to make refried beans (though this dish is traditionally made from pinto beans). Cooked kidney beans can form many salads, but are especially good combined with red onion, flat leaf parsley and mint, then tossed in an olive oil dressing.

It is essential to follow the cooking instructions for kidney beans as they contain a substance that causes food poisoning if they are not boiled vigorously for 10–15 minutes after soaking and before simmering. Skim off any scum that rises to the surface of the boiling water.

Mung beans

Instantly recognizable in their sprouted form as beansprouts, mung or moong beans are small, olive-coloured beans that are native to India. They are soft and sweet when cooked, and are used in the spicy curry, mung dhal. They are also good added to soups, stews and casseroles. Soaking is not essential, but if they are soaked overnight this will halve the 40 minutes cooking.

Above: Although it is not necessary to soak mung beans, it will reduce the cooking time considerably.

Soya beans

The vegan diet owes a lot to these extremely versatile beans. They are used to produce the vegan superfood, tofu, as well as being the foundation of many other soya products such as milk and yogurt. These small, oval beans vary in colour from creamy-yellow through brown to black. In China, they are known as 'meat of the earth' and were once considered sacred. For those on a vegan diet, soya beans contain all the nutritional properties of animal products but without the disadvantages. They are the most nutritious of all beans. Rich in high-quality protein, this bean contains all eight essential amino acids that cannot be synthesized by the body but are vital for cell and tissue renewal. They need to be soaked for at least 12 hours before cooking, as they are very dense.

They combine well with robust ingredients such as garlic, herbs and spices, and they make a healthy addition to soups, casseroles, bakes and salads. Soya beans are also used to make tempeh, textured vegetable protein (TVP), flour and soy sauce. In Japanese restaurants the fresh soya beans are known as edamame and are lightly steamed in their pods and served with soy sauce for dipping.

Soya bean products

Soya beans are a versatile food source with the highest nutritional value of all beans. They should form an important part of any vegan diet as they supply protein, B vitamins and unsaturated fats. Soya protein can help reduce blood cholesterol and it also provides phytoestrogens, which have health-promoting properties and may improve osteoporosis and help prevent some cancers.

Tofu

This is made from soaked, mashed and strained soya beans. It is white, milky and set in custard-like squares. Its texture can be soft (silken tofu) or firm. Fresh tofu should be kept covered with water in the refrigerator. Vacuum-packed, long-life tofu can be stored unopened at room temperature. Plain tofu absorbs the flavours of other ingredients well during cooking. Smoked and marinated tofu are also available.

Firm tofu This lightly pressed product is stored in cakes or blocks, either submerged in water or vacuum-packed, and can be cubed or sliced. It can be stir-fried, used in stews and soups, crumbled into salads or barbecued.

Silken tofu This product is the softest, most delicate form of tofu. A creamy version comes in tubs and can be used for dips, dressings or sweet dishes, such as fruit fools and non-dairy ice cream. A slightly firmer type of silken tofu comes in cubes, which break down very easily, so must be handled carefully.

Above: Tofu can be used to make delicious desserts, like this date and tofu ice, packed with protein.

Fried tofu At first glance, this doesn't look much like tofu. Slice the nut-brown block, however, and the white interior is exposed. The outer colour is the result of deep-frying in vegetable oil, a process that not only adds flavour, but also makes the beancurd more robust.

Tempeh

This is made by fermenting cooked whole soya beans in banana leaves, which gives the product a nutty, savoury flavour and causes it to solidify so that it can be cut into blocks. The beans remain visible under a velvety coating. It is firm and chewy in texture, and its strong flavour means it needs to be soaked or marinated with ingredients that have equally strong flavours.

Left: A selection of silken tofu, seared tofu and firm tofu.

Miso

This Japanese paste is made from fermented soya beans. It is very salty and should be used sparingly, for example in stews or spread on vegetables before grilling (broiling). It can also be dissolved in water and used as a base for soup.

Soy sauce

There are many types of soy sauce, which is made from fermented soya beans, but they are all salty and earthy-tasting. It does not contain the isoflavones that are associated with other soya products, such as tofu.

Right: Dark and light soy sauce.

IDEAS FOR USING TOFU
• Mash the tofu and make it into burgers with onion, herbs, spices and garlic.
• Use as a salad dressing: blend with chopped fresh coriander (cilantro) leaves and lemon juice.
• Thread cubes on to skewers with mushrooms, tomatoes and (bell) peppers; marinate in soy sauce and mustard before grilling.
• Whip with fresh herbs and Tabasco sauce as a dip for carrot sticks and other crudités.
• Blend with fresh fruit, such as strawberries or raspberries, to make a fruit fool.
• Stir-fry with Chinese mushrooms, bamboo shoots, pak choi (bok choy) and cashew nuts.
• Poach in a clear broth with seaweed and vegetable strips for a simple, light meal.

Above: Numerous varieties of miso are available, categorized by strength of flavour and colour.

Above: The soya beans remain visible and intact in tempeh, giving it a firm, chewy texture and strong, nutty flavour.

Textured vegetable protein (TVP)

This is manufactured from soya beans into different shapes and forms. It has a firm, sponge-like texture and can be flavoured to resemble meat or, alternatively, can be left as a natural soya product. TVP needs to be rehydrated with water or stock for a few minutes before being incorporated into recipes. It is available as chunks or resembling minced (ground) meat. It is fortified with vitamin B12 and is therefore a nutritious alternative to meat, or it can be combined with meat to extend a modest quantity and so reduce the overall saturated fat content. TVP can be treated in the same way as the cuts of meat it resembles, but it does not take up flavours as readily as other soya products.

Soya flour

High in protein and low in carbohydrate, this can be stirred into sauces, soups and gravies to add bulk and nutrients. It is made from roasted soya beans that have been ground into a powder. It is not suitable as a thickening agent and has a distinct flavour so should be combined with strong-flavoured ingredients, otherwise it can overwhelm a dish. It does not contain the high levels of isoflavones that are associated with other soya products. Soya flour should be stored in the refrigerator and used up fairly quickly. It is therefore best to buy it in small quanitities.

Soy protein

This is often mixed with wheat protein or pea protein to make nutritious meat- and dairy-free alternatives to almost anything you can think of. Tuna pâté, scampi (extra large shrimp), bacon, sausages, roast turkey, salad dressings, cheese, ice cream and fudge are just a few of the diverse products available.

PHYTOESTROGENS

Naturally occurring plant derivatives called phytoestrogens, such as isoflavones, are found in soya beans, as well as chickpeas and other legumes. Flax seeds are another source. They mimic oestrogen in the body and are particularly useful for menopausal women. A lot of research is taking place into their effect on health, and they have been associated with the following benefits:
• Improved symptoms for people suffering with osteoporosis, which is possibly due to the slowing of bone demineralization.
• A reduced risk of cardio-vascular disease due to a lowering effect on cholesterol.
• A lower risk of some cancers, such as breast and prostate cancer.
• The improvement of menstrual symptoms.
• The reduction of hot flushes in menopausal women.

Below: White and black soya beans are a natural source of health-promoting phytoestrogens, such as isoflavones.

Above: Textured vegetable protein (TVP) is available either minced or cubed.

Nuts

Rich in B complex vitamins, vitamin E, potassium, magnesium, calcium, phosphorus and iron, nuts offer the vegan an abundance of nutrients, although they contain a hefty number of calories. Most nuts are rich in monounsaturated and polyunsaturated fats, with the exception of brazil nuts and coconuts, which are high in saturated fat, but do not contain cholesterol. Numerous studies highlight the substantial health benefits of walnuts. According to one study, the essential fatty acids found in walnuts can decrease cholesterol levels and may reduce the risk of heart disease by 50 per cent. Almonds and hazelnuts have similar properties. Of all foods, brazil nuts are the richest in the vital mineral selenium, which is a mood enhancer. Nuts are also one of the richest vegetable sources of the antioxidant vitamin E.

Always buy nuts in small quantities from a store with a high turnover of stock, because if kept for too long, they can turn rancid. Nuts in their shells should feel heavy for their size. Store nuts in airtight containers in a cool, dark place or in the refrigerator and they should keep fresh for at least 3 months.

Below: For the best flavour, buy shelled almonds in their skins and blanch them yourself to remove the skin.

Almonds

There are two types of almond: sweet and bitter. The best sweet varieties are the flat and slender Jordan almonds from Spain. Heart-shaped Valencia almonds from Portugal and Spain, and the flatter Californian almonds are also widely available. For the best flavour, buy shelled almonds in their skins and blanch them yourself: cover with boiling water, leave for a few minutes, then drain and the skins will peel off easily.

Almonds are available ready-blanched, flaked (sliced) and ground. The latter adds a richness to cakes, tarts, pastry and sauces. Bitter almonds are much smaller and are used in almond oil and extract. They should not be eaten raw as they contain traces of the lethal prussic acid.

Brazil nuts

These are, in fact, seeds, and are grown mainly in the Amazon regions of Brazil and other neighbouring countries. Between 12 and 20 brazil nuts grow, packed snugly together, in a large brown husk, hence their three-cornered wedge shape. Brazil nuts have a sweet, milky taste and are used mainly as dessert nuts. They have a high fat content, so go rancid very quickly. They are a recommended source of the mineral selenium.

Cashew nuts

These are the seeds of the 'cashew apple' – an evergreen tree with bright-orange fruit. Cashew nuts have a sweet flavour and crumbly texture. They make delicious nut butters, or can be sprinkled into stir-fries or over salads. They are never sold in the shell and undergo an extensive and complex heating process that removes the seed from its outer casing.

Chestnuts

Most chestnuts are imported from France and Spain and they are excellent after roasting, which complements their soft, floury texture.

Above: Chestnuts have a soft floury texture and are excellent when roasted and eaten whole.

Raw chestnuts are not recommended as they are not only unpleasant to eat but also contain tannic acid, which inhibits the absorption of iron. Unlike other nuts, they contain very little fat. Out of season, they can be bought dried, canned or puréed. Add them whole to stews, soups, pies or stuffings. The sweetened purée is good in desserts.

Coconuts

This versatile nut grows all over the tropics. The white dense meat, or flesh, is made into desiccated (dry unsweetened shredded) coconut,

Below: Because of its high toxicity, the shell of the cashew nut is carefully removed and the nut is cleaned.

blocks of creamed coconut and a thick and creamy milk. A popular ingredient in Asian, African and South American cuisines, coconut lends a sweet, creamy flavour to desserts, curries, soups and casseroles. Use coconut in moderation, as it is particularly high in saturated fat.

When buying a coconut, make sure that there is no sign of mould or a rancid smell. Give it a shake – it should be full of liquid. Keep coconut milk in the refrigerator or freezer once opened.

Hazelnuts

Grown in the USA, Britain, Turkey, Italy and Spain, hazelnuts are usually sold dried, and can be bought whole, shelled and ground. They can be eaten raw, and the shelled nuts are especially good toasted. They can be grated or chopped for use in cakes and desserts, but they are also tasty in savoury dishes and can be added to salads, stir-fries and pasta.

Macadamia nuts

This round nut, about the size of a large hazelnut, is native to Australia, but is now grown in California and South America. Macadamia nuts are commonly sold shelled (the shell is extremely hard to crack). They have a crisp texture, a rich, buttery flavour and a very high fat content.

Below: Coconut Sorbet is just one of the many desserts you can make with this sweet and creamy, versatile nut.

Peanuts

Not strictly a nut but a member of the pulse family, peanuts bury themselves just below the earth after flowering – hence their alternative name, groundnuts. They are a staple food in many countries, and are widely used in South-east Asia, notably for satay sauce, and in African cuisines, where they are used as an ingredient in stews. In the West, peanuts are a popular snack food; the shelled nuts are frequently sold roasted and salted, and they are used to make peanut butter. Peanuts are particularly high in saturated fat and should be eaten in moderation.

Below: Hazelnuts can be eaten raw or grated or chopped into a variety of sweet and savoury dishes.

Above: Peanuts, the seeds of the peanut plant, can be made into tasty and nutritious Peanut and Tofu Cutlets.

Pecan nuts

A glossy, reddish-brown, oval-shaped shell encloses the pecan kernel, which looks like an elongated walnut but has a sweeter, milder flavour. This native American nut is a favourite in sweet pies, especially the classic pecan pie, but is also good eaten on its own, or added to salads. However, pecan nuts should be eaten only as an occasional treat, because they have one of the highest fat content of any nut, with a calorie content to match.

Below: Pecan nuts look similar to walnuts, but are longer in shape, and have a sweeter, milder flavour.

Pine nuts

Deceptively named, these are actually the tiny, cream-coloured seeds of the Mediterranean stone pine tree. They have a rich, aromatic flavour, which lends itself to toasting. Buy in small quantities as their high oil content quickly turns them rancid. Pine nuts are a key ingredient in Italian pesto sauce, where they are pounded with garlic, olive oil and basil, and in the Middle Eastern sauce, tarator, in which toasted pine nuts are combined with bread, garlic, and olive oil to make a creamy paste that has a similar consistency to the chickpea-based hummus. They are an excellent source of zinc.

Pistachio nuts

Incredibly 'moreish' when served as a simple snack, pistachio nuts have pale-green flesh and thin, reddish-purple skin. Sold shelled or in a split shell, these mild nuts are often used chopped as a colourful garnish, sprinkled over both sweet and savoury foods. Pistachio nuts have a wonderful flavour, they are good in all manner of desserts and can be made into a delicious ice cream. They are widely used in Turkish and Arabic sweets, notably nougat and Turkish delight. Check before buying pistachio nuts for cooking, as they can often be sold salted.

Above: Add hazelnuts and walnuts to a mixture of seeds, oats and dried fruits for a tasty and healthy Granola.

ROASTING AND SKINNING NUTS

The flavour of most nuts, particularly hazelnuts and peanuts, is improved by roasting. It also enables the thin outer skin to be removed more easily.

1 Place the nuts in a single layer on a baking sheet. Bake at 180°C/350°F/Gas 4 for 10–20 minutes or until the skins begin to split and the nuts are golden.

2 Tip the nuts on to a dish towel, rub to loosen and remove the skins.

Left: Pine nuts can be expensive due to the labour-intensive process of extracting them from the pine cone. Right: Walnuts are delicious in a range of cakes and desserts.

Walnuts

This versatile nut has been around for hundreds of years. When picked young, walnuts are referred to as 'wet' and have fresh, milky-white kernels, which can be eaten raw, but are often pickled.

Dried walnuts have a bitter-sweet flavour and can be bought shelled, chopped or ground. They can be used to make excellent cakes and cookies as well as rich cake fillings, but are equally good added to savoury dishes, such as stir-fries and salads – a Waldorf salad combines whole kernels with celery and apples in a vegan mayonnaise dressing. Walnuts are a good source of the essential fat omega-3.

Seeds

They may look very small and unassuming, but seeds are nutritional powerhouses for the vegan, packed with vitamins and minerals, as well as beneficial oils and protein. They can be used in a huge array of sweet and savoury dishes, and will add an instant, healthy boost, pleasant crunch and nutty flavour when added to rice and pasta dishes, salads, stir-fries, soups and soya yogurt. You can of course just eat them as they are.

Seeds contain valuable amounts of the antioxidant vitamin E, which enhances the immune system and protects cells from oxidation. Vitamin E also improves blood circulation, and promotes healing and normal blood clotting as well as reducing infections associated with ageing.

Seeds, particularly hemp seeds, may help to reduce blood cholesterol levels in the body because they contain plentiful amounts of linoleic acid and linolenic, which are more commonly known as omega-6 and -3 fatty acids.

For their size, seeds contain a huge amount of iron. Sesame seeds are particularly rich – just 25g/1oz provides nearly half the daily requirement of iron, and 50g/2oz pumpkin seeds provide almost three-quarters of the iron we need each day. Sunflower seeds are often prescribed by natural medicine practitioners for their restorative qualities.

Above: Sesame seeds are an excellent way of getting all the essential iron that your body needs.

Seeds are best bought in small quantities from shops that have a high turnover of stock. It is recommended to purchase whole seeds, rather than ground, and store them in a cool, dark place as they can be prone to turning rancid. After opening the packet, decant the seeds into an airtight container.

Sesame seeds

These tiny, white or black seeds are a feature of Middle Eastern and Asian cooking. In the Middle East they are ground into tahini, a thick paste that is a key component of hummus. Sesame seeds are also ground to make halvah, a sweet confection found in Greece, Israel and Turkey. Gomassio, or gomashio, is the name of a crushed sesame seed condiment used in Japan. It can easily be made at home: firstly, toast the seeds, then crush them with a little sea salt in a mortar using a pestle. Try a ratio of one part salt to five parts sesame seeds. The flavour of sesame seeds is improved by roasting them in a dry frying pan; it gives them a distinctive nuttiness. The toasted seeds make a good addition to salads and noodle dishes. Unroasted seeds can be used as a topping for breads, buns, cakes and cookies, and they can be added to pastry dough.

Try to buy seeds that have been mechanically rolled – the tell-tale sign is a matt appearance. Seeds that have been subjected to other processing methods, such as salt-brining or a chemical bath, are usually glossy. Salt brining can affect the flavour of the seeds, as can chemical processing, which also damages their nutritional value. Sesame seeds are a good source of calcium and complementary essential amino acids.

Sunflower seeds

These are the seeds of the sunflower, which is a symbol of summer and an important crop throughout the world. The impressive, golden-yellow flowers are grown for their seeds and for making sunflower oil; the leaves are used to treat malaria and the stalks are made into fertilizer. Rich in vitamin E, the pale-green, tear-drop-shaped seeds have a semi-crunchy texture and an oily taste that is much improved by roasting them in a dry frying pan. You could try sprinkling sunflower seeds over salads, rice pilaffs and couscous, or use them in bread dough, muffins, casseroles and baked dishes. Sunflower seeds are rich in the polyunsaturated essential fat omega-6.

ROASTING SEEDS

The flavour of seeds can be much improved by 'roasting' them in a dry frying pan. Black poppy seeds won't turn golden brown when roasted, so watch them carefully to make sure that they don't scorch.

1 Spread out a spoonful or two of seeds in a thin layer in a large, non-stick frying pan and heat gently.

2 Cook over a medium heat for 2–3 minutes, tossing the seeds frequently, until they are golden brown.

Above: The addition of pumpkin, sesame and sunflower seeds gives this Three Seed Loaf superb flavour and texture.

Hemp seeds

The cultivation of hemp has a long and heroic history. As recently as World War II governments were still encouraging and subsidizing the farming of this versatile, easy-to-grow crop. Due to various political reasons, along with pressure from the paper, tobacco and oil industries, hemp was demonized and subsequently fell out of fashion. Today, however, hemp is making a comeback as a valuable crop and a nutritious food. It is available as hemp milk, hemp nut butter, hemp oil, hemp protein powder, hemp pasta, hemp soy sauce and even hemp beer.

Hemp seeds are delicious lightly roasted, or buy the shelled variety (the husks are quite tough), which are like a cross between sesame seeds and cashew nuts. Hemp can be sprinkled on salad and used raw in a variety of sweet and savoury dishes. Hemp seeds are packed with essential amino acids and essential fats. They have a perfect ratio of omega-3, -6 and -9 essential fats, thus hemp oil is a good economic alternative to expensive balanced blended oils claiming to do the same thing.

Pumpkin seeds

These small, flat green seeds are richer in iron than any other seed, as well as being an excellent source of zinc. Subtly sweet and nutty, pumpkin seeds make a tasty and nutritious snack eaten on their own. You could also add them to muesli, granola or other breakfast cereals, as well as to nut and seed roasts. They are delicious lightly toasted, tossed in a little toasted sesame oil or soy sauce, and stirred into a mixed leaf or rice salad. Pumpkin seeds are widely used in South American cooking, where they are generally roasted and ground to make into sauces.

Below: Linseeds and hemp seeds are fantastic sources of the essential fatty acids.

Poppy seeds

These are the seeds of the opium poppy but without any of the habit-forming alkaloids. Poppy seeds can be blue (usually described as black) or white. The black variety looks good sprinkled over cakes and breads, adding a pleasant crunch. Black poppy seeds can be used to make delicious seed cakes and teabreads, and they are used in German and Eastern European pastries, strudels and tarts. In India, the ground white seeds are used to thicken sauces, adding a nutty flavour. Poppy seeds can be made into a tahini-like spread that is full of protein and delicious spread on wholemeal (whole-wheat) toast.

Flax seeds/linseeds

Linseed oil has long been used as a drying oil to embellish wooden furniture and cricket bats and for making putty. However, the brown or golden seed, also known as flaxseed, is a rich source of polyunsaturated fat, including the essential fatty acid, omega-3 linoleic acid. Linseeds can be added to muesli, granola and other breakfast cereals, mixed into bread dough or sprinkled over salads. Flax grown in nothern climates is reputed to be high in lignans which may assist with hormonal imbalances, protect the heart and even possess some anti-cancer properties.

Grains

There is a wide selection of delicious and healthy grains available to vegans, from wheat in all its various forms to lesser known grains such as the highly nutritious quinoa. Many of these grains have been cultivated for thousands of years, and together they are the staple foods, in one form or another, for the majority of the world's population.

Rice

This grain has been cultivated for thousands of years and is a staple food for about half the world's population. It comes in many varieties and is usually classed by the grain size. Long-grain rice comes in brown and white varieties, and includes basmati rice, which has a delicately perfumed taste and is essential in many spicy Indian dishes.

Short-grain rice has more starch than long-grain types so sticks together more after cooking, which is why it is a popular choice in the Far East as it is easier to eat with chopsticks. The Italian arborio rice is a short-grain type and is used to make creamy risottos.

Brown varieties of rice are one of the ultimate grains, in terms of taste, nutrition and healing potential. They are

Below: Wild rice has a deliciously nutty taste and is great for using in cold rice salads.

easily digested, and simultaneously comforting and satisfying to eat, particularly when served with crisp stir-fried vegetables.

White rice has a much shorter cooking time than brown rice, but it is less nutritious, since many minerals and vitamins are lost when the bran and germ of the grain is removed.

Wild rice

Also known as Indian rice, this looks like a plump, black basmati rice but it is really an aquatic freshwater grass native to the USA. It has a delicious nutty flavour and nice texture, and it offers 12–15 per cent protein, complementary nutrients and a decorative addition to rice dishes. It also is excellent for using in cold dishes, such as salads.

Wheat

The use of wheat as a staple food around the world is second only to rice. It is the planet's most prolific commercially

Below: White rice is a convenient choice for speedy meals due to its quick cooking time.

Left: Wheat is used to make white and brown breads.

grown grain, largely thanks to the gluten it contains. It is used worldwide in bread, breakfast cereals, pasta, noodles, pizza bases, and even French fries, sausages and sauces – it is not easy to avoid it.

Modern wheat has been bred to grow faster and more fruitfully, which has resulted in much more gluten contained in the grain. Try ancient varieties, such as spelt wheat used by the Romans, if you have problems with ordinary wheat. Wheatgrass juice is considered to be one of the healthiest ways to enjoy wheat. Wheat bran is a waste product – use wholemeal (whole-wheat) products and eat plenty of fruit and vegetables.

Barley

This ancient grain is used in various dishes from cereals to soups, such as Scotch broth. Pearl barley comes in a variety of sizes and is used in winter-warming vegetable stews and to make barley water, a refreshing summer drink. Barley malt is used in the production of beer and whisky.

Rye

This grain does not contain much gluten, so when it is milled into flour it creates dense breads, such as pumpernickel bread from Germany. It is used around the world to make crispbreads, gin, beer and whisky. It is good added to a muesli (granola) mix for breakfast.

Bulgur wheat

This pale, sand-coloured grain, made from dried and crushed cooked wheat berries, is nutty in flavour and comes in varying degrees of coarseness. When cooked, by soaking in double its volume of boiling water for 15–20 minutes, bulgur wheat is similar in appearance to couscous but is heavier, and has more flavour. Bulgur is usually served cold – combined with flat leaf parsley, mint, tomatoes, cucumber, onion and a lemon and oil dressing, it forms the basis of the Middle Eastern salad, tabbouleh.

Buckwheat

This is a native of Russia and, despite its name and use as a grain, it is a plant, not a grass, with no connection to wheat. The seeds are made into flour, which is used to make the Russian pancakes, blinis, and soba noodles in Japan. The larger grains are crushed kernels and are cooked in a similar way to rice. High in protein, it contains all eight amino acids.

Millet

Another under-used but essential grain, millet contains all the essential amino acids. It is the only alkaline grain, making it easily digestible. It is also a rich source of silicon, which helps to build collagen for keeping skin, eyes, nails and arteries healthy, vibrant and flexible. Widely eaten in much of Africa, the small round grain is cream in colour, with a pleasant taste.

Below: Home-made muesli is an ideal way to get a daily dose of the nutrients offered by various grains and seeds.

Above: Pleasant-tasting millet contains all the essential amino acids and is easily digestible.

Oats

This grain is extraordinarily high in soluble fibre and is a fundamental food for heart health. A bowl of porridge or oat-rich muesli is a great foundation for the day, giving excellent stores of energy. Oat-based muesli is readily available, but it is also easy to make at home. Simply add chopped hazelnuts, linseeds, sunflower and pumpkin seeds to an oat base, then sweeten the mixture by stirring in chopped dried fruit. Store the muesli in an airtight container in a dry cupboard, and the muesli will last as long as the nuts – about three months.

Organic versions of muesli not only retain their micro-nutrients but also tend to contain less refined sugar and salt than non-organic varieties, supporting healthier energy levels and moderating moods throughout the day. For a special treat, make a classic Bircher muesli by soaking equal quantities of oats and dairy-free milk overnight. Stir in an equal quantity of soya yogurt and honey the next morning, with a freshly grated apple and one other chopped fresh fruit. Oats are also widely used in baking and are delicious in flapjacks, added to the topping for a fruit crumble, or sprinkled on home-made breads.

Quinoa

A native of Bolivia, this tiny round grain was little known outside South America until recently but quinoa (pronounced 'keen-wah') is becoming increasingly popular. This is partly because it tastes delicious, but also because it is a good source of protein, fibre and B vitamins. Like brown rice, it tastes faintly nutty. It can be used as a replacement for rice, or for making stuffings, pilaffs and cereals.

Amaranth

This is a small grain, similar to quinoa in terms of its bountiful level of nutrients. Not quite as fluffy as quinoa, it is great for using in pâté and burger mixes.

Wheat berries

These are whole wheat grains with the husks removed. They are packed with concentrated goodness and have a sweet, nutty flavour and chewy texture. They are delicious added to salads and can be used to add texture to breads and stews, or be combined with rice or other grains. Soak them overnight, then cook in boiling water until tender. When germinated, the berries sprout into wheatgrass, a powerful cleanser and detoxifier.

Couscous

Although it looks like a grain, couscous is a form of pasta made by steaming and drying cracked durum wheat. When cooked, it is light and fluffy in texture. It is a mainstay of Middle Eastern cooking and its bland flavour provides a good foil for spicy dishes. It also tastes great flavoured with ginger or galangal and rose water and served as a traditional accompaniment to a Moroccan tagine.

Below: Bulgar wheat forms the basis of the Middle Eastern Salad, tabbouleh.

Pasta

Legend attributes the 14th-century explorer Marco Polo with introducing Italy to pasta from China, although medieval references to pasta have been found and traced back to Sicily. A combination of wheat flour and water produces the basic dough, which can then be formed into an infinite number of shape variations. Fresh pasta and some dried lasagne is often made with hen's eggs, and therefore unsuitable for vegan dishes.

The health benefits of pasta vary depending on the type used. Whole-wheat pasta is high in complex carbohydrates, which are broken down more slowly, providing energy over a longer period, and is more nutritious, containing a richer concentration of vitamins, minerals and fibre. Buckwheat pasta is particularly nutritious and rich in fibre; it contains all eight essential amino acids, thus a complete protein.

Dried pasta will keep almost indefinitely, but if you decant the pasta into a storage jar, it is a good idea to use up the remaining pasta before adding any from a new packet. If you make your own fresh pasta you will find it freezes well and should be cooked from frozen. Packs and bags of supermarket pasta have the advantage of being easy to store in the freezer.

Below: Various ingredients are added to coloured pasta, such as spinach, tomato and herbs.

Durum wheat pasta

This is the most readily available type of pasta and can be made without using egg. Durum wheat is perfect for pasta because it is a hard wheat. This type of pasta is nearly always used for straight long shapes, such as spaghetti and tagliatelle.

Buckwheat pasta

Pasta made from buckwheat flour has a nutty taste and is darker in colour than whole-wheat pasta. Pizzoccheri from Lombardy is the classic shape. These thin, flat noodles are traditionally sold in nests like tagliatelle (although pizzoccheri are about half the length), but they are also available cut into short strips. Buckwheat pasta is gluten-free and therefore suitable for people who are intolerant to gluten or wheat. It is also very nutritious; it is an excellent source of protein as it contains all eight amino acids, as well as useful amounts of calcium, zinc and B vitamins.

Other wheat-free pastas include those made from corn, rice, quinoa, spelt and even hemp. However, corn and rice pasta in particular have to be cooked carefully as they quickly turn to mush.

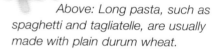

Above: Long pasta, such as spaghetti and tagliatelle, are usually made with plain durum wheat.

Coloured and flavoured pasta

A variety of ingredients can be added to pasta dough to give it both flavour and colour. The most common additions are tomato and spinach, but beetroot, saffron, fresh herbs such as basil, and even chocolate are used. Mixed bags of pasta are also available – the traditional combination of plain and spinach-flavoured pasta is called paglia e fieno, which means 'straw and hay'. There are many other mixtures, some with as many as seven different flavours and colours. Watch out for black pasta as this can be coloured with squid's ink.

Whole-wheat pasta

This pasta is made using wholemeal (whole-wheat) flour and contains more fibre than plain durum wheat pasta. It has a slightly more robust texture and nutty flavour and takes longer to cook. Whole-wheat spaghetti (bigoli), a traditional Italian variety from the Venice area, can be found in good Italian delicatessens, health-food stores and large supermarkets. An increasing range of whole-wheat shapes is now available.

Below: The range of shapes, colours and flavours of pasta will ensure that there is always a place for this staple food in the vegan kitchen.

Types of pasta

Long pasta Spaghetti is probably the best known form of dried long pasta, but there are many other varieties, from fine vermicelli to pappardelle – broad ribbon noodles. Tagliatelle, the most common form of ribbon noodles, is usually sold coiled into nests.

Short pasta There are hundreds of different short dried pasta shapes. Conchiglie (shells) are one of the most useful shapes because they are concave and trap virtually any sauce. Fusilli (spirals) are good with thick tomato-based sauces and farfalle (butterflies) can be served with creamy sauces, but are very versatile and work equally well with tomato- or olive oil-based sauces. Macaroni used to be the most common short shape, and being hollow, it is good for most sauces and baked dishes. However, penne (quills) have become more popular, perhaps because the hollow tubes with diagonally cut ends are perfect with virtually any sauce.

Flat pasta Lasagne is designed to be baked between layers of sauce, or cooked in boiling water, then layered, or rolled around a filling to make cannelloni. Spinach-flavoured lasagne sheets are also available.

Stuffed pasta The most common shapes of stuffed pasta are ravioli (squares), cappelletti (little hats), and tortellini (little pies), though other shapes are available from Italian delicatessens. Plain, spinach and tomato are the most usual doughs, and there is a wide range of vegan fillings, such as wild mushrooms. Check that they do not contain cheese.

Pasta for soup These tiny shapes are mostly made without egg from plain durum wheat pasta. There are hundreds of different ones, from tiny risi, which look like grains of rice, to alfabeti (alphabet shapes), which are popular with children. Larger shapes such as farfalline (little bows) and tubetti (little tubes) are used in thicker soups, such as minestrone.

Quick ideas for pasta

• To make a simple, but richly-flavoured tomato sauce, place some plum or cherry tomatoes in a baking dish and drizzle with a little olive oil. Roast them in a hot oven for 15 minutes, then add one or two peeled garlic cloves and continue roasting for about 15 minutes more. Transfer the tomatoes and garlic to a food processor and blend with basil leaves. Season with salt and ground black pepper and stir into cooked pasta. Serve imediately.

• Toss cooked pasta in a little chilli oil, then sprinkle over rocket (arugula) leaves and pine nuts. Serve immediately, sprinkled with roasted ground almonds.

• Stir a spoonful of black olive tapenade into cooked pasta, then sprinkle a few lightly toasted walnuts on top before serving.

• Roast a head of garlic, then squeeze out the soft cloves and mix well with olive oil. Toss with cooked pasta and sprinkle over fresh, chopped flat leaf parsley before serving.

• Olives, mushrooms, aubergines (eggplants) and artichokes bottled in olive oil make quick, delicious and nutritious additions to cooked pasta.

Below: Pasta is an excellent base for creating many substantial and wholesome vegan meals.

Noodles

The fast food of the East, noodles can be made from wheat flour, rice, buckwheat flour or mung bean flour. Like pasta, many varieties of noodles contain egg but they are often called egg noodles to warn you. Plain noodles are made from strong flour and water, they can be flat or round and come in various thicknesses. Both fresh and dried noodles are readily available in health-food stores and Asian stores as well as supermarkets. Noodles are low in fat and high in carbohydrates, so can provide a quick energy boost.

Whole-wheat noodles are richer in nutrients than normal wheat varieties. Buckwheat noodles not only contain all eight essential amino acids, they are particularly high in fibre. Cellophane noodles are made from mung bean starch, which is reputed to be one of the most powerful detoxifiers.

Packets of fresh noodles are found in the chiller cabinets of Asian stores. They usually carry a use-by date and must be stored in the refrigerator. Dried noodles will keep for many months if stored in an airtight container in a cool, dry place.

Below: Noodles can be used in an array of dishes, from soups and stir-fries to fresh-tasting cold salads.

Udon noodles
These thick Japanese noodles can be round or flat and are available fresh, dried or pre-cooked. They can be made from wheat or corn flour. Whole-wheat udon noodles have a more robust flavour.

Somen noodles
Usually sold in bundles held together by a paper band, these thin, white noodles are available from Asian stores and larger supermarkets. Beware of the yellowish version, called tamago somen, which are made with egg yolk.

Rice noodles
These fine, delicate noodles are made from rice and are opaque-white in colour. They come in various widths, from the very thin strands known as rice vermicelli, popular in Thailand and southern China, to the thicker rice sticks, which are used more in Vietnam and Malaysia. A huge range of rice noodles is available dried in Asian grocers and fresh ones are occasionally found in the chiller cabinets. Since all rice noodles are pre-cooked, they need only to be soaked in hot water for a few minutes to soften them before use in stir-fries and salads.

Buckwheat noodles
Soba are the best-known type of buckwheat noodles. They are a darker colour than wheat noodles – almost brownish grey. In Japan, they are traditionally served in soups or stir-fries.

Above: There is a wide variety of egg-free noodles suitable for those following a vegan diet.

Cellophane vermicelli and noodles
Made from mung bean starch, these translucent noodles, also known as bean thread vermicelli or glass noodles, come in a variety of thicknesses and are only available dried. Although very fine, the strands are firm and tough. Cellophane noodles are simply soaked in boiling water for 10–15 minutes. They retain their fantastic texture when cooked, never becoming soggy. Cellophane noodles are used as an ingredient in spring rolls.

Quick ideas for noodles
• To make a simple broth, dissolve mugi miso in hot water, add cooked soba noodles; sprinkle with chilli flakes and sliced spring onions (scallions).
• Cook udon noodles in vegetable stock. Add dark soy sauce, shredded spinach and grated ginger. Sprinkle with sesame seeds and fresh coriander (cilantro).
• Stir-fry sliced shiitake and oyster mushrooms in garlic and ginger, then toss with noodles. Sprinkle with fresh chives and a little roasted sesame oil.
• In a food processor, blend together some lemon grass, chilli, garlic, ginger, kaffir lime leaves and fresh coriander. Fry the paste in a little oil and combine with cooked noodles. Sprinkle with fresh basil and spring onions.

Oils and vinegars

A wide variety of oils, vinegars and condiments are suitable for a vegan diet. However, there are also a few to avoid. It is important to read the labels carefully, particularly on condiments, but if you are armed with the basics listed here, you should be able to make informed choices and avoid any hidden animal ingredients.

Oils

Produced from a number of sources, oils are an indispensable item in any kitchen. They can be made from cereals, such as corn; fruits, such as olives; nuts, such as walnuts, almonds and hazelnuts; and seeds, such as rapeseed (canola), safflower and sunflower.

Oils are undeniably high in calories and should always be used in moderation, but they also have a number of health benefits. Monounsaturated fats, found particularly in olive oil, help to keep cholesterol levels down. Olive oil contains vitamin E, a natural antioxidant that helps fight off free radicals. Polyunsaturated fats provide essential fatty acids known as omega-3 (alpha-linolenic) and omega-6 (linolenic acid). Omega-3, which is found in walnut, rapeseed, hemp and flax oils, has been found to reduce the likelihood of heart disease and blood clots; while omega-6, which is provided by safflower, sunflower and soya oils, reduces cholesterol levels. Cooking oils such as soya, sunflower and safflower keep

Left: Use extra virgin olive oil in salad dressings.

longer than nut or seed oils. To keep them at their peak, store in a cool, dark place. Keep opened nut and seed oils in the refrigerator.

Olive oil Indisputably the king of oils, it varies in flavour and colour, depending on how it is made and where it comes from. Climate, soil, harvesting and pressing all influence the end result. Olive oil is rich in monounsaturated fat, which has been found to reduce cholesterol, which subseqently reduces the risk of heart disease. It is also rich in omega-9 fats.

There are various different grades. Extra virgin olive oil is a premium oil with a superior flavour. It comes from the first cold pressing of the olives and has a low acidity. It is not recommended for frying, as heat impairs its flavour, but it is good in salad dressings, especially when combined with lighter oils. It is delicious as a sauce on its own, stirred into pasta with garlic and black pepper, or drizzled over steamed vegetables.

Also a pure first-pressed oil, virgin olive oil has a slightly higher level of acidity than extra virgin olive oil, and is used in much the same way.

Pure olive oil is refined and blended to remove impurities and has a lighter flavour than virgin or extra virgin olive oil. It is suitable for all types of cooking and can be used for shallow frying.

Corn oil One of the most economical and widely used vegetable oils, corn oil has a deep golden colour and a fairly strong flavour. It is suitable for cooking and frying, but not for dressings.

Rapeseed oil This bland-tasting, all-purpose oil, also known as canola, can be used for frying, cooking and in salad dressings. It contains a higher percentage of monounsaturated fat than any other oil, with the exception of olive oil.

Above: Walnut, sesame and hazelnut oils are some of the speciality oils that will add delicious depth of flavour to food.

Safflower oil This is a light, all-purpose oil, which comes from the seeds of the safflower. It can be used in place of sunflower and groundnut oils, but is a little thicker and has a slightly stronger flavour. It is suitable for deep frying, but is best used with other more strongly flavoured ingredients, and is ideal for cooking spicy foods. Safflower oil contains more polyunsaturated fat than any other type of oil and is low in saturated fat.

Sunflower oil Perhaps the best all-purpose oil, sunflower oil is very light and almost tasteless. It is extremely versatile, and can be used for frying and in cooking, or to make salad dressings, when it can be combined with a stronger flavoured oil such as olive oil or walnut oil. It is high in polyunsaturated fat and low in saturated fat.

Soya oil This neutral flavoured, all-purpose oil, which is extracted from soya beans, is probably the most widely used oil in the world. It is useful for frying because it has a high smoking point, and remains stable at high temperatures. It is also widely used in margarines. It is rich in polyunsaturated and monounsaturated fats and low in saturates. Try to find a brand that is not made from genetically modified soya beans.

Groundnut oil Also known as peanut oil, this relatively tasteless oil is useful for frying, cooking and dressing salads. Chinese peanut oil is darker and has a nuttier taste than groundnut oil. It is good in Asian salads and stir-fries.

Grapeseed oil A delicate, mild oil, which does not impose on other ingredients, this oil is pressed from grape seeds left over from wine-making. It is good in cooking and for frying, and can be used to make dressings, especially when mixed with a stronger flavoured oil.

Avocado oil Said to be the best to use for cooking due to its high smoke point.

Coconut oil Rich in saturated fat, it is good for cooking. Studies have shown that coconut oil is more easily turned into energy than saturated animal fats.

Speciality oils As well as the all-purpose oils that are used for everyday cooking, there are several richly flavoured oils that are used in small quantities, often as a flavouring ingredient in salad dressings and marinades, rather than for cooking. These include fragrant hazelnut oil, which adds a nutty taste to cakes and biscuits; delicate almond oil, which is used in confectionery; flavoursome pumkin seed oil, which is rich in omega-6; hemp seed oil, which has a perfect balance of omega-3, -6 and -9; sesame oil, which is common in Asian cuisine; and walnut oil, which is intensely flavoured and great in salad dressings and marinades.

Left: Rice vinegar (left) and brown malt vinegar have different uses.

Vinegars

One of our oldest condiments, vinegar is made by acetic fermentation, a process that occurs when liquid containing less that 18 per cent alcohol is exposed to the air. Most countries produce their own type of vinegar, usually based on their most popular alcoholic drink. Commonly used as a preservative in pickles and chutneys, it is also an ingredient in marinades and salad dressings.

Hippocrates prescribed vinegar as a cure for respiratory problems, and it may also be beneficial in cases of food poisoning. Cider vinegar, in particular, is said to have many therapeutic benefits.

Wine vinegar These can be made from red, white or rosé wine and are great for dressings, sauces or adding flavour to stews and soups. They may not be suitable for vegans, as they can be made from non-vegan fined wine.

Left: Caramel-coloured sherry vinegar can be used in the same ways as balsamic vinegar.

Balsamic vinegar This is a rich, dark, mellow vinegar, which has become hugely popular. From Modena in northern Italy, it is made from grape juice which is fermented in vast wooden barrels for a minimum of four years. Its concentrated flavour is delicious in dressings or sprinkled over roasted vegetables.

Sherry vinegar Often just as costly as balsamic vinegar, if left to mature in wooden barrels, it can be equally good. Sweet and mellow, it can be used in much the same way as balsamic vinegar.

Malt vinegar Made from soured beer, this is used in Britain and other northern European countries for pickling vegetables and sprinkling over potato chips. It has a robust, harsh flavour and is not suitable for salad dressings.

Cider vinegar Praised for its health-giving properties, cider vinegar is made in the same way as wine vinegar. It is a clear, pale-brown colour and has a slight apple flavour. Too strong and sharp for dressings, it is best kept for pickling fruits.

Rice vinegar Japanese rice vinegar is mellow and sweet and is most often used to flavour sushi rice; Chinese rice vinegar is much sharper.

Right: Balsamic vinegar is rich and dark.

Sauces, spreads and dressings

Any diet, including a vegan diet, can be enhanced with a whole range of sauces, spreads and dressings. Dressings bring out the flavours of salads and can be used to marinate vegetables and tofu. Sauces and salsas will spice up and transform even the most basic dish, and many vegans have a range of other spreads, pickles and chutneys in the kitchen, ready to bring taste and variety to their dishes.

Ready-made products

Sauces, dressings and spreads that are ready-made and store-bought can be a problem. The fat and sugar content are not always obvious. Hidden fats may be a polyunsaturated or hydrogenated oil that contains trans fatty acids, which are thought to have a worse effect than saturated fat on blood cholesterol.

There are lots of hidden ingredients which are unsuitable for vegans. Get to know the products you can use, but it is healthier and more satisfying to make many of these condiments yourself.

Pickles and chutneys

These accompaniments are essential additions to most spicy meals and can be used to accompany salads and for spreading in sandwiches. Chutneys are chopped fruits and vegetables simmered in vinegar, sugar and spices.

Right: A tasty vegan dressing is simple to make and can be whisked up in no time.

Pickles are fruits or vegetables that are preserved whole or in chunks. Bought pickles and chutneys have a high sugar content, so it is a good idea to make them yourself.

Pickles and chutneys with a high vinegar content do not depend on sugar to keep well. The sugar is included for a balanced sweet-sour flavour, so if you find a recipe with lots of sugar, you can try to adapt it. Cook the ingredients (usually onions, vegetables and fruit) in the vinegar and omit the sugar. Pot and cover them as usual (sterilizing the pots), then sweeten individual portions to taste, if necessary, before use, with sugar or sweetener.

For extra sweetness, use sweet dessert apples instead of cooking apples. They do not soften as easily, so it is a good idea to chop them before adding. You can also try using dried fruit for sweetening – apricots, raisins, sultanas (golden raisins) or dates are all good options, which can also be used to sweeten vinegar-based preserves.

Below: Pickles and chutneys are an essential component to many meals.

Dressings

Home-made salad dressings are superior to bought dressings and you also know exactly what is in them. You can make a simple soya yogurt dressing by stirring in mustard, seasoning and chopped chives or spring onions (scallions) to soya yogurt. Add torn basil, chopped mint or finely chopped green chilli, if you like.

TOFU DRESSING

This is a delicious alternative to mayonnaise and cream sauces or toppings.

Makes 300ml/½ pint/1¼ cups

225g/8oz packet tofu
15ml/1 tbsp chopped parsley
15ml/1 tsp chopped chives
5ml/1 tsp Dijon mustard
15ml/1 tbsp pumpkin seed oil
15ml/1 tbsp hemp oil
juice of one lime
salt and ground black pepper

1 Blend together the tofu, chopped parsley, chopped chives, Dijon mustard, oils and lime juice in a food processor.

2 Season to taste.

• Add grated lemon or lime rind.
• Add chopped spring onions.

OIL AND VINEGAR DRESSING

This basic dressing is great for salads, vegetables, grilled (broiled) or pan-fried foods. It is a tasty marinade for tofu or vegetables.

Makes 300ml/½ pint/1¼ cups

5ml/1 tsp Dijon mustard
2.5ml/½ tsp sugar
100ml/3½fl oz/scant ½ cup cider vinegar
200ml/7fl oz/scant 1 cup extra
virgin olive oil
salt and ground black pepper

1 Mix the mustard, sugar, salt and pepper in a bowl. Add the vinegar and whisk well.

2 Pour in the oil and whisk again until emulsified. Alternatively, put everything in a screw top jar and shake.

• Add a finely chopped garlic clove.
• Add chopped herbs, such as chives, parsley, tarragon, thyme or oregano.
• Add some chopped capers.
• Add dried chilli flakes.

Above: Nut butters are a great substitute for dairy butter and can be used in salads, stir-fries and as dips.

Salsas and relishes

Home-made salsas and fresh relishes are fantastic alternatives to bottled sauces. They are simple and quick to make and they will keep in a covered container in the refrigerator for 2–3 days. You can also freeze them in small pots, ready for thawing in the microwave in minutes.

Nut butter

If you have a sturdy food processor in your kitchen, nut butter is easy to make in a large quantity. Use it for spreading instead of butter, as a dip for vegetables, as a dressing or for adding to stir-fries.

Simply roast plain peanuts, cashew nuts or skinless almonds in the oven at 180°C/350°F/Gas 4 for about 40 minutes, or until they are browned, stirring occasionally. Process them in a food processor until finely ground, add a little salt and continue grinding until the nuts begin to clump, then trickle in a little olive oil with the motor running. Process until creamy. The hot nut butter should have a thick pouring consistency.

Spoon the nut butter into jars. Tap the jars so that air bubbles inside rise to the surface. Top the nut butter with a little olive oil, then cover the jar loosely and leave until cold before covering and storing in the refrigerator.

Cashew cream

This is a great alternative to dairy cream, which can be used in desserts, dips, savoury toppings and dressings.

Grind plain cashew nuts to a powder in a food processor. With the motor running, gradually trickle in a little unsweetened natural apple juice. Add the juice slowly, allowing time for the nuts to combine with the juice. The mixture will gradually become pale and creamy as it emulsifies. The consistency should be like whipped cream. The trick is to make sure that the nuts are thoroughly ground before adding any juice, then to add the juice very slowly – otherwise the mixture will separate and become grainy. Store in the refrigerator for up to 5 days.

SPICY TOMATO SALSA

This is a scorchingly hot salsa. Tone down the heat by using milder chillies.

Serves 4–6

3 haberaño chillies or Scotch bonnets
2 ripe tomatoes
4 standard green jalapeño chillies, halved, deseeded and finely sliced
30ml/2 tbsp chopped fresh parsley
30ml/2 tbsp olive oil
15ml/1 tbsp balsamic or sherry vinegar
salt

1 Skewer the haberaño chillies and tomatoes one at a time on a fork and hold in a gas flame until the skin blackens and blisters.

2 Remove the skins from the chillies and tomatoes, halve them, discard the seeds and chop finely.

3 Mix with the remaining ingredients.

SALSA VERDE

There are many versions of this classic green salsa.

Serves 4

2–4 green chillies, halved and deseeded
8 spring onions (scallions), trimmed
2 garlic cloves, halved
50g/2oz salted capers, excess salt rubbed off
fresh tarragon sprig
bunch of fresh parsley
grated rind and juice of 1 lime
juice of 1 lemon
90ml/6 tbsp olive oil
green Tabasco sauce, to taste
black pepper

1 Pulse the chillies, spring onions and garlic in a food processor until roughly chopped. Add the capers and herbs. Pulse until finely chopped.

2 Transfer to a bowl and add the remaining ingredients. Stir lightly.

Condiments and stocks

Store-cupboard basics such as condiments and stock (bouillon) cubes are essentials in most households. They are quick and convenient and can spice up the simplest of dishes.

Table-top sauces can enhance lots of meals, for vegans and non-vegans alike. Take the time to become aware of the mass-produced condiments that are suitable for vegans and those which are not. Many of the most common condiments are actually suitable for vegans but they might not be marketed as so. Read labels carefully for any hidden flavourings, and if in doubt, buy them from specialist vegan stores.

Ketchup
Traditionally made the world over with tomatoes, vinegar and sugar, tomato ketchup is almost an obligatory accompaniment for chips. Watch out for the recent trend of manufacturers adding dairy into ketchup.

Worcestershire sauce
This fermented condiment contains anchovies, so look out for vegetarian versions. It is great for adding extra flavour to stews and casseroles.

Below: Premium French mustards may contain honey and are therefore not suitable for vegans.

HOME-MADE VEGETABLE STOCK
Bought stock (bouillon) cubes, and powder and chilled stocks from the supermarket are often high in salt and may contain flavour enhancers as well as other artificial additives. The best option, therefore, especially for vegans, is to make your own stock so you can be sure of exactly what goes into it. It is really easy to make using a selection of vegetables, with fresh mixed herbs added for flavour and whole black peppercorns for seasoning.

Makes 1 litre/1¾ pints/4 cups

750g /1lb 10oz vegetables
  (such as onions, leeks, celery,
  carrots, fennel, swede (rutabaga),
  turnip, squash, broccoli and
  mushrooms), trimmed, peeled if
  necessary, and roughly chopped
bunch of fresh herbs (such as bay
  leaf, thyme, oregano, rosemary,
  tarragon or parsley stalks)
large strip of lemon zest
6 black peppercorns

1 Put all the ingredients in a large pan and pour over 1.5 litres/2½ pints/6¼ cups of cold water. Bring to the boil, then reduce the heat, partially cover the pan and simmer gently for about 40 minutes.

2 Remove from the heat, strain the stock through a sieve (strainer) or colander and discard the vegetables.

3 Leave to cool, then pour into a plastic container. Keep chilled in the refrigerator and use within 4 days, or store in the freezer for up to 6 months. Thaw in a microwave, or slowly in a pan, before using.

Brown sauce and BBQ sauce
These piquant, savoury, vinegar-based, thick brown sauces usually contain dates or tamarind and are fairly well spiced. A favourite with sausages.

Mustard
Made from mustard seeds, it comes in a variety of flavours and textures. It is usually vegan unless honey is added as in some premium French varieties.

Horseradish sauce
This sauce usually contains eggs and dairy products. Vegan versions are rare, but you can make it by mixing fresh or dried horseradish with vegan mayonnaise.

Soy sauce
This salty sauce is made from fermented soya beans and is great in stir-fries.

Japanese miso, yeast extract, Vegemite and Marmite
These all add a savoury flavour to rich sauces, marinades, pâtés, soups and casseroles. They are generally vegan but check the packaging of individual brands.

Tabasco
This hot pepper sauce is made from tabasco peppers, vinegar and salt.

Stock (bouillon) cubes
Vegetable stock is often used to add extra flavour to soups and stews. Stock cubes are a quick and easy way of adding flavour to dishes when time is short. Although most vegetable stock cubes are suitable for vegans, it is advisable, as with all store-cupboard condiments, to check the label carefully. If you have time, you can make your own.

Healthy cooking techniques

While following a vegan diet, you need to ensure that you get the maximum nutrient value from your food. However, certain vitamins and minerals are destroyed by heat and are water-soluble, so it is essential that such losses are reduced by thoughtful preparation and cooking.

Raw food

Fruit and vegetables are an excellent source of many vitamins and minerals, yet some of these nutrients are lost during even the most careful cooking. B group vitamins and vitamin C are water-soluble and also destroyed by prolonged heating, so eat plenty of raw produce, provided that it can be easily digested. Always wash thoroughly or peel, use a sharp knife to cut with and prepare shortly before eating. Here are some ideas:

• Raw vegetable crudités with dips.
• Plenty of main meal and side salads.
• Use sprouted seeds in salads.
• Enjoy fruit at any time as a quick snack or dessert.
• Add a variety of chopped fresh fruit to probiotic yogurt.
• Make a chilled soup, like gazpacho.

Below: Raw carrots, red peppers and small florets of broccoli make ideal crudités for dips.

Above: Fruit juices are a convenient way of increasing your vitamin intake.

Juicing

This is a quick and convenient way of enjoying raw fruit and vegetables, increasing your intake and benefiting from the many nutrients they contain.

Most fruit and vegetables can be juiced, although some are particularly well suited. A blender or food processor is suitable for juicing tender produce, such as berries, mangoes, melons and bananas, but for firmer-fleshed raw fruit and vegetables, such as apples, pears, carrots, celery and beetroot (beets), you will need a proper juicer.

Juices make nourishing drinks, ideal for breakfast or as a snack, but juices should not replace eating a variety of whole fruit and vegetables daily.

Juices are best drunk freshly made, because their vitamin content soon begins to diminish, but if made ahead, keep it in an airtight container in the refrigerator and drink within 24 hours.

You can also now buy many good quality fresh juices and fruit smoothies (not those made from concentrate) that are convenient when you are out and about or if you do not have the time or right equipment to make your own.

Boiling

Plunge vegetables into boiling water, use the minimum amount of liquid and cook them for the shortest time needed to make them tender. Vegetables cooked in soups and stews retain water-soluble vitamins in the cooking liquid.

Above: Cook vegetables in a steamer set over a pan of simmering water.

Stir-frying

This method is quick, uses the minimum liquid and fat, and preserves maximum nutrients. Peel, chop and slice all the ingredients into bitesize pieces before you start cooking so that they are ready for use and they cook quickly and evenly. Add them to the wok in the order of cooking time – crunchy vegetables such as carrots and baby corn first, then quick-cooking vegetables, such as mangetouts (snow peas) and (bell) peppers, and finally delicate leafy vegetables.

Place the wok or frying pan over the heat, then when hot, dribble drops of oil, necklace fashion, on to the inner surface just below the rim. This coats the sides, then puddles in the base. You will only need about a teaspoon of oil. When the oil is hot add the food. Keep it moving.

Steaming

This method of cooking is nutritionally excellent as the food does not come into direct contact with the water, so few soluble nutrients are lost and it retains maximum nutritional value. The flavour and texture of the food is retained and there is no need to use oil or fat.

The many types of steamer available include electrical tiered steamers, insert pans with stepped bases, or Chinese-style bamboo or expanding steamer baskets, which are placed above a pan of simmering water. You can improvise with a foil-covered wire sieve (strainer) set over a pan of simmering water.

breakfasts, juices and smoothies

There is no reason why a vegan diet should mean that breakfast is no longer the most important meal of the day. This chapter features plenty of delicious options for getting all the necessary nutrients to see you through to lunchtime. Choose from luxurious twists on the traditional bowl of muesli, hearty pancakes with various fruit accompaniments, boosting juices and smoothies, or indulge in the classic cooked breakfast with all the trimmings.

Quick breakfast ideas

The first meal of the day is also one that has plenty of choices for vegans. It is the perfect opportunity to fill up on nutrients, or to enjoy a long leisurely treat – perfect for a lazy Sunday morning. Below are a few ideas to whet your appetite, whether you are looking for a quick snack before work or something hot and altogether more substantial.

COLD BREAKFAST IDEAS

Early morning on a workday is not always the best time to fire up the stove and get out the pots and pans. Yet there are plenty of options for a quick, cold breakfast available to the vegan, and the best news is that many of them are healthy and nutritious.

Fresh fruit

For the ultimate quick and healthy breakfast, grab a piece of seasonal fresh fruit. If you have a selection, make yourself a refreshing fruit salad including berries, pomegranate seeds, kiwi fruit and apricots. Add a little soya yogurt, if you like, for a substantial and delicious start to the day.

Dried fruit

There is a wide variety of dried fruits to choose from and they are ideal for making a simple and nutritious breakfast. They are great if combined with fresh fruit in a bowl with a little soya yogurt. and are also ideal for adding sweetness to a bowl of cereal.

Below: Have a selection of fruit at the ready for a quick and healthy breakfast.

There is now a fantastic range of dried fruit to choose from, including common favourites like raisins, sultanas (golden raisins), apricots, prunes, figs and dates as well as cranberries, blueberries, cherries and strawberries. There are also smaller, chopped pieces of apple, mango, papaya, banana and pineapple. Apricots, in particular, are one of the richest fruit sources of iron.

Cereal

Many of the pre-packed cereals in the supermarket are suitable for vegans. So you should have no trouble finding a bowl of nutritious cereal for breakfast, from muesli and cornflakes to bran flakes and other proprietary brands. Ensure that the variety that you choose is vegan-friendly. It is also easy to make your own from a selection of grains, flakes and seeds, as shown later in this chapter. Add soya milk or rice milk and sliced fresh or dried fruit, if you like.

For something more substantial, go for a hot cereal such as instant porridge (oatmeal). It is one of the best ways to start the day, especially if you sprinkle it with shelled hemp seeds and throw on a handful of berries.

HOT BREAKFAST IDEAS

Sometimes only a hot and filling breakfast will do, and there are plenty of delicious options for those on a vegan diet. Try some of these ideas for a hearty start to the day or a leisurely weekend treat.

Bubble and Squeak

If you have any left-over cabbage, leeks or peas and mashed potato then this is a good way to use them up. Just fry a handful of finely chopped cabbage with some chopped onion until they start to soften and turn golden brown. Add an equal amount of mashed potato. Season with salt and pepper, mould into patties, or press into the pan to make one large cake, sprinkle with seeds and then fry until golden brown on both sides, or bake in a hot oven for 20–25 minutes.

BAKED TOMATOES

Roasting ripe tomatoes in the oven for breakfast is simplicity itself and helps to intensify their delicious fresh flavour.

Serves 2

6 large ripe tomatoes
30ml/2 tbsp olive oil, for drizzling
sea salt and ground black pepper
4 slices wholemeal (whole-wheat)
  bread, for toasting (optional)

1 Preheat the oven to 190°C/350°F/ Gas 4. Cut the tomatoes in half and season with salt and ground black pepper, then drizzle with olive oil.

2 Bake for about 15–20 minutes until tender and turning brown. Serve on toasted wholemeal bread, if you like.

POTATO SCONES

Tattie scones are a breakfast favourite. Serve them as part of a big breakfast extravaganza or spread with jam or yeast extract.

Serves 2

115g/4oz/1 cup wholemeal
 (whole-wheat) flour
60ml/4 tbsp mashed potato
115g/4oz/½ cup dairy-free
 margarine spread
10ml/2 tsp arrowroot or
 cornflour (cornstarch)
5ml/1 tsp baking powder

1 Put all ingredients in a mixing bowl and blend thoroughly.

2 Roll out on a lightly floured surface into a large round and lightly brush with oil.

3 Bake at 190°C/350°F/Gas 4 for 25 minutes. Cut into triangles.

GARLIC MUSHROOMS

Fry up some thickly sliced mushrooms with shallots, garlic and lemon juice for a deliciously tasty breakfast. Serve on chunky slices of wholemeal (whole-wheat) toast for a perfect start to the day.

Serves 4

90ml/6 tbsp avocado or coconut oil
3 shallots, finely chopped
2 garlic cloves, finely chopped
675g/1½lb field (portabello)
 or chestnut mushrooms,
 thickly sliced
75ml/5 tbsp lemon juice
45ml/3 tbsp chopped fresh parsley
4 slices wholemeal (whole-wheat)
 bread, for toasting
salt and ground black pepper

1 Heat the avocado or coconut oil in a frying pan and cook the finely chopped shallots and garlic for 5 minutes until golden.

2 Add the thickly sliced mushrooms and toss them well with the shallots and garlic to coat them in the oil. Fry for 1 minute.

3 Pour in the lemon juice and season with salt and ground black pepper. Cook until the mushrooms are tender. Add the parsley and serve on wholemeal toast.

PANCAKES

Quick and easy to make, pancakes make a tasty and satisfying breakfast for vegans and non-vegans alike. Serve them with a squeeze of lemon juice, sliced fresh fruit, jam, or drizzle them generously with maple or agave syrup.

Makes about 10

115g/4oz/1 cup wholemeal
 (whole-wheat) self-raising
 (self-rising) flour
10ml/2 tsp arrowroot
25g/1oz/2 tbsp soft light brown sugar
250ml/8fl oz/1 cup rice milk
 or sweetened soya milk
10ml/2 tsp coconut oil
pinch of salt

1 Mix together the flour, arrowroot, sugar and salt in a bowl.

2 Add a quarter of the rice or soya milk and mix well, then gradually add the rest to make a batter.

3 Heat the oil in a frying pan and add 30ml/2 tbsp of batter for each pancake. Cook 2–3 pancakes at a time, for 3 minutes on each side or until golden.

CINNAMON TOAST

Spruce up your toast with this tasty topping, perfect for a morning snack. Serve with chopped fresh fruit, if you like.

Serves 2

75g/3oz/6 tbsp soya margarine
 or dairy-free spread
10ml/2 tsp ground cinnamon
15ml/1 tbsp agave syrup
5ml/1 tsp tahini
4 slices wholemeal (whole-wheat) bread

1 Cream the soya margarine or dairy-free spread with the cinnamon, agave syrup and the tahini.

2 Toast the wholemeal bread on both sides and spread with the cinnamon mixture.

Luxury muesli

Ready-made muesli has added sugar, and many types have added milk or cream powder, making them unsuitable for vegans. This healthier version is delicious and satisfying, and provides slow-release carbohydrate with natural sugar from the dried fruit for a great start to the day.

Serves 4

50g/2oz/scant ½ cup sunflower seeds
25g/1oz/¼ cup pumpkin seeds
30ml/2 tbsp ground almonds
115g/4oz/generous 1 cup rolled oats
115g/4oz/generous 1 cup buckwheat flakes
115g/4oz/generous 1 cup barley flakes
115g/4oz/scant 1 cup raisins
115g/4oz/1 cup chopped hazelnuts, roasted
115g/4oz/½ cup ready-to-eat dried
   apricots, chopped
50g/2oz/4 cups dried apple slices, halved
25g/1oz/½ cup goji berries

Cook's tip
Add some shelled hemp seeds and hemp oil to boost omega-3 levels.

1 Put the sunflower and pumpkin seeds in a dry frying pan and cook over a medium heat for 3 minutes until golden, tossing the seeds regularly to prevent them burning.

2 Mix the toasted seeds with the remaining ingredients until throughly combined. Leave to cool, then store in an airtight container.

Variations
• For a crunchy roasted mix, use jumbo oat flakes instead of rolled oats and roast them with barley and rye flakes in a large roasting pan in the oven until lightly browned. Roast the seeds in the oven in a separate pan. Mix and leave to cool completely before adding the nuts.
• Experiment with other muesli ingredients such as freeze-dried berries, walnuts or puffed quinoa.
• Make muesli in a huge batch, making sure it is completely cool before storing in an airtight container. It will keep for three months in a cool, dark place.

Light granola

Store-bought granola, like most breakfast cereals, tends to have a fairly high sugar content. This version has dried fruit for sweetness, so it will not send blood glucose levels soaring.

Serves 4

115g/4oz/generous 1 cup rolled oats
115g/4oz/1 cup jumbo oats
15ml/1 tbsp poppy seeds
50g/2oz/scant ½ cup sunflower seeds
30ml/2 tbsp sesame seeds
50g/2oz/½ cup hazelnuts, roasted
25g/1oz/¼ cup walnuts, roughly chopped
600ml/1 pint/2½ cups orange juice
50g/2oz/scant ½ cup raisins
50g/2oz/½ cup dried cranberries

Cook's tip
For a super-healthy breakfast, spoon a generous portion of low-fat soya yogurt into a bowl, and top with a generous layer of fruit salad.

1 Preheat the oven to 160°C/325°F/ Gas 3. Mix together the oats, seeds and nuts in a large bowl.

2 Pour the orange juice into the oat mixture and stir well so that all the ingredients are equally moist. If you have plenty of oranges, use freshly squeezed juice. You can also use a mix of oranges, lemons and grapefruits.

3 Transfer the mixture on to one or two baking sheets, spreading it out evenly using a metal spatula.

4 Place the baking sheets in the oven for about 1½ hours. Stir the mixture occasionally so it cooks evenly.

5 When the mixture is crisp and well browned, remove from the oven and mix in the raisins and cranberries. Leave the granola to cool, then store in an airtight container.

Variation
If you prefer a sweeter cereal, add a spoonful of agave syrup and swap the pecans for walnuts.

Energy 813kcal/3411kJ; Protein 20.8g; Carbohydrate 100.9g, of which sugars 33.4g; Fat 39g, of which saturates 5.5g; Cholesterol 0mg; Calcium 145mg; Fibre 12.4g; Sodium 55mg.
Energy 638kcal/2674kJ; Protein 14.4g; Carbohydrate 72.3g, of which sugars 27.9g; Fat 34.3g, of which saturates 2.9g; Cholesterol 0mg; Calcium 132mg; Fibre 6.9g; Sodium 39mg.

Pecan crunch

Serve this tasty crunchy cereal simply with soya or rice milk or, for a real treat, with soya yogurt and a handful of seasonal fresh fruits such as raspberries or blueberries.

Serves 6

200g/7oz/1¾ cups jumbo oats
150g/5oz/1¼ cups pecan nuts,
   roughly chopped
90ml/6 tbsp agave syrup
75g/3oz/6 tbsp soya margarine or other
   dairy-free spread

1 Preheat the oven to 160°C/325°F/ Gas 3. Put all the ingredients together into a bowl and mix well.

2 Spread the mixture on to a large baking tray. Bake for 30–35 minutes, or until golden and crunchy. Leave to cool, then break up into clumps and serve.

Variation

For a gluten-free version, use a mixture of buckwheat, quinoa flakes and puffed rice in place of the rolled oats.

Cook's tip

This crunchy oat cereal will keep in an airtight container for up to two weeks. Store the container in a cool, dry place.

Energy 443kcal/1847kJ; Protein 6.5g; Carbohydrate 37.7g, of which sugars 13.1g; Fat 30.6g, of which saturates 4.6g; Cholesterol 1mg; Calcium 38mg; Fibre 3.4g; Sodium 152mg.

Granola breakfast bars

A gloriously dense fruity, nutty and oaty mixture, packed with goodness and delicious too, these bars are an ideal breakfast when you are short of time in the morning.

Makes 12

175g/6oz/¾ cup soya butter or dairy-free
   margarine, diced
150g/5oz/⅔ cup agave syrup
250g/9oz/generous 1 cup demerara
   (raw) sugar
350g/12oz/3 cups jumbo oats
5ml/1 tsp ground cinnamon
75g/3oz/¾ cup pecan nut halves
75g/3oz/generous ½ cup raisins
75g/3oz/¾ cup ready-to-eat dried
   papaya, chopped
75g/3oz/scant ½ cup ready-to-eat dried
   apricots, chopped
50g/2oz/scant ½ cup pumpkin seeds
50g/2oz/scant ½ cup sunflower seeds
50g/2oz/4 tbsp sesame seeds
50g/2oz/½ cup ground almonds

1 Preheat the oven to 190°C/375°F/ Gas 5. Line a 23cm/9in square cake tin (pan) with baking parchment.

2 Put the butter and agave syrup in a large heavy pan and heat gently until the butter has melted and the mixture is completely smooth.

3 Add the demerara sugar to the pan and heat very gently, stirring the mixture constantly, until the sugar has completely dissolved.

4 Bring the butter mixture to the boil and continue to boil for 1–2 minutes. Stir the mixture constantly to prevent it sticking until it has formed a smooth caramel sauce.

5 Add the remaining ingredients and mix together. Transfer the mixture to the tin and press down with a spoon. Bake for 15 minutes until the edges turn brown.

6 Place in the refrigerator and chill well. Turn out of the tin, peel off the parchment and cut into bars.

Energy 522kcal/2189kJ; Protein 8.4g; Carbohydrate 63.8g, of which sugars 40.9g; Fat 27.7g, of which saturates 8.9g; Cholesterol 31mg; Calcium 93mg; Fibre 4.3g; Sodium 108mg.

Classic cooked breakfast

There are few more famous – or more filling – breakfasts than the classic full English breakfast. Thankfully there is no need to give up this traditional favourite because there are vegan versions of everything from vegan bacon and sausages to black pudding and haggis. This version also features a delicious tofu and corn mixture, soya cheese on toast and smoked tempeh. Feel free to use ingredients based on your preferences or what is available.

Serves 2

1 medium plum tomato
30ml/2 tbsp olive oil
15ml/1 tbsp soy sauce
2 vegan sausages
2 frozen potato croquettes or potato waffles
6 medium mushrooms
2 slices smoked soya tempeh
15ml/1 tbsp soya cream cheese
15ml/1 tbsp tomato ketchup
2.5ml/½ tsp yeast extract
2.5ml/½ tsp mustard
2 slices wholemeal (whole-wheat) bread
20ml/4 tsp fresh tofu
30ml/2 tbsp frozen or canned corn
5ml/1 tsp soya margarine or dairy-free spread
200g/7oz can baked beans
salt and ground black pepper

1 Preheat the oven to 180°C/350°F/ Gas 4. Cut the tomato in half lengthways and season with salt and pepper.

2 Mix the olive oil with the soy sauce in a cup and lightly brush the mix on to the sausages. Place the sausages on a baking tray with the tomato halves and the potato croquettes or waffles and bake for 10 minutes in the oven.

3 Meanwhile, lightly brush the oil mixture over the mushrooms and the soya tempeh.

4 Mix the soya cream cheese with the tomato ketchup, mustard and yeast extract until well blended. Spread the mixture evenly over one of the slices of wholemeal bread.

5 When the sausages have been in the oven for 10 minutes, turn them over. Add the mushrooms, tempeh and slices of bread – one of which is topped with the cheese mix – and return everything to the oven. Cook for another 10–15 minutes until everything is golden brown and tender.

6 Blend together the tofu and the corn with the margarine or dairy-free spread. Season with salt and pepper. Place the mixture in a pan and simmer gently, stirring frequently, until heated through.

7 In a separate pan, simmer the baked beans for about 5 minutes until piping hot. Cut the toasted bread slices in half diagonally and divide everything between two plates. Serve immediately with freshly squeezed juice, herb tea, tomato ketchup, brown sauce, mustard and a Sunday newspaper.

Energy 526kcal/2205kJ; Protein 23.8g; Carbohydrate 53.9g, of which sugars 9.7g; Fat 27.8g, of which saturates 4.7g; Cholesterol 0mg; Calcium 409mg; Fibre 9.2g; Sodium 1744mg.

Porridge with apple-date purée

Fresh dates and sweet apples add a delicious flavour and natural sweetness to porridge, making additional sugar unnecessary. They also contribute fibre and fruity food value.

Serves 4

175g/6oz/generous 1 cup fresh dates
2 eating apples, peeled, cored and cubed
225g/8oz/generous 2 cups rolled oats
475ml/16fl oz/2 cups soya milk
50g/2oz/⅓ cup shelled, unsalted pistachio
   nuts, roughly chopped
pinch of salt

Cook's tip
When fresh dates are available, purée a big batch of them with fresh pineapple or mango as well as the apple. Place the purée in ice cube trays in the freezer. When frozen, push the cubes out into bags for storage.

1 First make the date purée. Halve the dates and remove the stones (pits) and stems. Cover the dates with boiling water and leave to soak for 30 minutes, until softened. Strain the dates, reserving 30ml/2 tbsp of soaking water.

2 Process the dates and apples to a smooth purée using a food processor or blender.

3 Place the oats in a pan with the milk, 300ml/½ pint/1¼ cups water and salt. Bring to the boil, then reduce the heat and simmer for 4–5 minutes until cooked and creamy, stirring frequently.

4 Serve the porridge in warm serving bowls, topped with a spoonful of the date purée and sprinkled with chopped pistachio nuts.

Apricot and ginger compote

Serve this delicious and refreshing fruit compote with lots of soya yogurt or tofu, either by spooning the yogurt into the bowl first or adding more at the table. Add whole almonds to the dish, if you like, to give it an extra calcium boost.

Serves 4

200g/7oz/scant 1 cup ready-to-eat
   dried apricots
4cm/1½in piece fresh root ginger,
   peeled and finely chopped
600ml/1 pint/2½ cups soya yogurt
   or tofu

1 Cover the dried apricots with boiling water, then leave them overnight to soak.

Health benefit
Fresh root ginger is a brilliant, feel-good ingredient. It is enlivening and stimulating, in savoury and sweet dishes.

2 Place the apricots and their soaking water in a heavy pan. Add the chopped ginger to the pan and bring the mixture to the boil.

3 Reduce the heat and simmer the apricots for about 10 minutes or until the apricots are soft and plump. The water should have reduced and become syrupy.

4 Strain the apricots over a bowl to catch the syrup. Pour the syrup into a serving jug (pitcher) so diners can help themselves at the table.

5 Serve the apricots while warm with the reserved syrup. Spoon over the soya yogurt or tofu.

Cook's tips
• To freeze fresh root ginger, peel the root and store it in a plastic bag in the freezer. It will grate while frozen. Or, grate or chop it before freezing.
• For a more substantial breakfast, round off with slices of stoneground wholemeal (whole-wheat) toast with plenty of melted nut butter.

Energy 411kcal/1730kJ; Protein 13.5g; Carbohydrate 61.1g, of which sugars 19.8g; Fat 13.8g, of which saturates 1.3g; Cholesterol 0mg; Calcium 73mg; Fibre 6.2g; Sodium 127mg.
Energy 187kcal/795kJ; Protein 9.5g; Carbohydrate 24.1g, of which sugars 24.1g; Fat 3g, of which saturates 0.9g; Cholesterol 3mg; Calcium 37mg; Fibre 3.2g; Sodium 7mg.

Pecan nut and caramel banana porridge pancakes

These pancakes are more like drop scones than the classic thin French crêpes. Bananas and pecan nuts, cooked in maple syrup, make a sweet and delicious topping.

Serves 5

75g/3oz/⅔ cup plain (all-purpose) flour
50g/2oz/½ cup wholemeal (whole-wheat) flour
50g/2oz/generous ½ cup rolled oats
5ml/1 tsp baking powder
10ml/2 tsp arrowroot
25g/1oz/2 tbsp soft light brown sugar
15ml/1 tbsp rapeseed (canola) oil, plus extra for frying
250ml/8fl oz/1 cup soya milk
pinch of salt

For the caramel bananas and pecan nuts
50g/2oz/¼ cup soya margarine
15ml/1 tbsp maple syrup
3 bananas, halved and quartered lengthways
25g/1oz/¼ cup pecan nuts

1 To make the pancakes, mix together the two flours, oats, baking powder, arrowroot, salt and sugar in a bowl.

2 Make a well in the centre of the flour mixture and add the oil and a quarter of the milk. Mix well, then gradually add the rest of the milk to make a thick batter. Leave to rest for 20 minutes in the refrigerator.

3 Heat a large, heavy, lightly oiled frying pan. Using about 30ml/2 tbsp of batter for each pancake, cook two to three pancakes in the pan at a time. Cook for about 3 minutes on each side or until golden. Keep warm while you cook the remaining pancakes.

4 To make the caramel bananas and pecan nuts, wipe out the frying pan and add the soya margarine. Heat gently until the butter melts, then add the maple syrup and stir well. Add the bananas and pecan nuts to the pan.

5 Cook, turning once, for about 4 minutes or until the bananas have just started to soften and the sauce has caramelized.

6 To serve, place two pancakes on each of five warm plates and top with the caramel bananas and pecan nuts. Serve immediately.

Cook's tips
• Pecan nuts are one of the richest sources of vitamin B6, which can help relieve the symptoms of PMS (premenstrual syndrome), as well as giving our immune system a boost. However, they are high in fat, so eat in moderation.
• Bananas are a good source of energy, making them an excellent food to start the day. They also contain potassium, which is essential for the functioning of all the cells in our bodies.
• Porridge oats contain useful amounts of soluble fibre, which has been found to lower cholesterol levels in the body.

Energy 417kcal/1744kJ; Protein 6.8g; Carbohydrate 48.8g, of which sugars 21.3g; Fat 22.8g, of which saturates 5.1g; Cholesterol 2mg; Calcium 42mg; Fibre 3.2g; Sodium 109mg.

Buckwheat pancakes with apple and cinnamon

Buckwheat is a great source of all eight essential amino acids. Spiced pan-fried apple slices create a scrumptious topping for these nutritious buckwheat pancakes.

Serves 4

3 cooking apples, peeled, cored and sliced
50ml/2fl oz/¼ cup agave syrup
50g/2oz/¼ cup soya margarine
30–45ml/2–3 tbsp brandy or lemon juice
5–10ml/1–2 tsp ground cinnamon
fresh mint sprigs, to garnish
soya cream cheese, to serve

For the pancakes
50g/2oz/½ cup buckwheat flour
50g/2oz/½ cup rice flour
15ml/1 tbsp coconut oil
300ml/½ pint/1¼ cups soya milk
10ml/2 tsp arrowroot
rapeseed (canola) oil, for frying
salt

1 Make the pancakes. Place the buckwheat flour, rice flour and a pinch of salt in a bowl and make a well in the centre of the flour. Add the coconut oil and a little of the milk, beating well with a wooden spoon.

2 Gradually beat in the remaining milk, drawing the flour in from the sides to make a smooth batter.

Variation
Use pears in place of the apples and mixed (apple pie) spice instead of the cinnamon. Fresh apricots work well in this recipe too.

3 Heat a little rapeseed oil in an 18cm/7in non-stick frying pan. Pour in enough batter to coat the base of the pan thinly. Cook until golden brown, then turn and cook on the other side.

4 Transfer the cooked pancake to a warmed plate and keep hot. Repeat with the remaining batter to make eight pancakes. Place the cooked pancakes on top of one another with baking parchment in between to prevent them from sticking together.

5 Toss the apple slices in the agave syrup in a mixing bowl until the pieces are evenly coated.

6 Melt the soya margarine in a large frying pan, add the apple slices to the pan and cook over a high heat, stirring frequently for about 5 minutes, or until the apple slices have softened slightly and the sugar has caramelized.

7 Remove the pan from the heat and sprinkle the cooked apple slices with the brandy or lemon juice and the ground cinnamon.

8 Place the warm pancakes on plates, allowing two per person. Top with the cooked apples and some soya cream cheese sprinkled with a little extra ground cinnamon, if you like. Serve immediately, garnished with a few fresh mint leaves.

Energy 305kcal/1272kJ; Protein 4.3g; Carbohydrate 40.3g, of which sugars 17.3g; Fat 14.5g, of which saturates 7.1g; Cholesterol 2mg; Calcium 21mg; Fibre 1.7g; Sodium 160mg.

Zingy salad

This refreshing, fruity salad makes a lovely light breakfast. It is ideal for enjoying on a warm summer's morning. Choose really ripe, fragrant papayas for the best flavour.

Serves 4

2 large ripe papayas
1 fresh lime
2 pieces preserved stem ginger, finely sliced

Variation
This refreshing fruit salad is also delicious made with other tropical fruit. Pick whatever looks good in the supermarket. Try using two mangoes in place of the papayas. Ensure you get ripe fruit and then peel and remove the stone (pit) before slicing.

1 Cut the papayas in half lengthways and scoop out all the seeds using a teaspoon.

2 Using a sharp knife, cut the papaya flesh into thin slices and arrange them on a serving platter.

3 Pour the lime juice over the papaya slices and sprinkle the finely sliced stem ginger over the top. Serve immediately.

Energy 55kcal/233kJ; Protein 0.8g; Carbohydrate 13.4g, of which sugars 13.4g; Fat 0.2g, of which saturates 0g; Cholesterol 0mg; Calcium 35mg; Fibre 3.3g; Sodium 8mg.

Orange blossom

Avocados are extremely good for the skin, mainly because of their high vitamin E content. Combined with parsley, asparagus and orange, this juice makes a great cleanser and skin tonic.

Serves 2

1 small avocado
small handful of fresh parsley
75g/3oz tender asparagus spears
2 large oranges
squeeze of lemon juice
ice cubes
mineral water
orange wedges, to decorate

4 Halve the oranges and squeeze out the juice. Pour into the mixture with a squeeze of lemon juice. Blend briefly until the mixture is very smooth.

5 Pour the juice into two glasses until two-thirds full, then add ice cubes and mineral water. Decorate with chunky orange wedges.

Cook's tip
The orange and lemon juice in this blend means that the avocados will not discolour, so you might want to refrigerate a glass for later on. If it has thickened slightly, stir in a little extra mineral water.

1 Halve the avocado using a sharp knife and discard the stone (pit). Scoop out the flesh and place it in a blender or food processor.

2 Remove any tough stalks from the parsley and add to the blender or food processor.

3 Roughly chop the asparagus and add to the avocado. Blend thoroughly until smooth, scraping the mixture down from the side of the bowl, if necessary.

Energy 123kcal/507kJ; Protein 2.3g; Carbohydrate 6.1g, of which sugars 5.4g; Fat 9.9g, of which saturates 2.1g; Cholesterol 0mg; Calcium 21mg; Fibre 2.4g; Sodium 9mg.

Veggie boost

This simple blend makes a great juice boost. It has pure clean flavours and a chilli kick that is guaranteed to revitalize flagging energy levels. Tomatoes and carrots are rich in the valuable antioxidant beta carotene, which is reputed to fight cancer, and they contain a good supply of vitamins A, C and E, all of which are essential for good health.

Serves 2

3 tomatoes
1 fresh red or green chilli
250g/9oz carrots
juice of 1 orange
crushed ice

Cook's tip
Non-organic carrots often contain a lot of chemicals in their skins. If you use these, scrub them well or wash and peel them before use.

1 Quarter the tomatoes and roughly chop the chilli. (If you prefer a milder juice, remove the seeds and white pith from the chilli before chopping.) Scrub the carrots and chop them roughly.

2 Push the carrots through a juicer, then follow with the tomatoes and chilli. Add the orange juice and stir well to mix. Fill two tumblers with crushed ice, pour the juice over and serve.

Energy 83kcal/351kJ; Protein 2.7g; Carbohydrate 16.9g, of which sugars 16.3g; Fat 1g, of which saturates 0.3g; Cholesterol 0mg; Calcium 52mg; Fibre 4.5g; Sodium 49mg.

Very berry

Fresh and frozen cranberries are often in short supply, but dried berries are available all year round and make a tasty dairy-free shake when combined with soya milk. Tiny crimson redcurrants make the perfect partner for the dried cranberries in this refreshingly tart, sparkling smoothie, and this low-fat blend is packed with natural sugars, essential nutrients and vitamins.

Serves 1

25g/1oz/¼ cup dried cranberries
150g/5oz/1¼ cups redcurrants, plus extra
   to decorate
10ml/2 tsp agave syrup
50ml/2fl oz/¼ cup soya milk
sparkling mineral water

1 Put the cranberries in a small bowl, pour over 90ml/6 tbsp boiling water and leave to stand for 10 minutes.

2 String the redcurrants by drawing the stems through the tines of a fork to pull off the delicate currants.

3 Put the redcurrants in a food processor or blender with the cranberries and soaking water. Blend well until smooth.

4 Add the agave syrup and milk to the processor or blender and whizz briefly to combine the ingredients.

5 Pour the berry mixture into a large glass, then top up with a little sparkling mineral water to lighten the drink and add a little fizz. Drape the extra redcurrants decoratively over the edge of the glass so they hang down and serve the smoothie immediately.

Cook's tip
Allowing time for the dried cranberries to rehydrate means they will become plump and juicy. This will make them much easier to blend and will also maximize their deliciously tangy flavour.

Energy 126kcal/539kJ; Protein 3.8g; Carbohydrate 27.1g, of which sugars 27.1g; Fat 0.9g, of which saturates 0.2g; Cholesterol 0mg; Calcium 115mg; Fibre 7g; Sodium 25mg.

Pear, rhubarb and cranberry cooler

For best results this delicious smoothie should be made with really ripe and extremely juicy pears, so if the ones you buy are hard, leave them in the fruit bowl for several days before making this fresh and fruity treat. Do not forget to cook the rhubarb well in advance so that it has plenty of time to cool down before you start blending.

1 Using a small, sharp knife, trim the rhubarb, discarding the leaves, and cut the main stems into 2cm/¾in pieces.

2 Place the rhubarb slices in a pan with 90ml/6 tbsp water. Cover with a tight-fitting lid and bring the water to the boil.

3 Reduce the heat and cook the rhubarb gently for about 5 minutes or until the slices are tender. Transfer to a bowl and leave to cool completely, putting several pieces aside to use as a garnish.

4 Peel, quarter and core the pears and transfer the flesh to a blender or food processor along with the cranberries, the rhubarb and its cooking juices and the sugar.

5 Blend the mixture until smooth, scraping down the side of the bowl, if necessary. Thin with mineral water, if you like, then serve, garnished with the rhubarb pieces.

Serves 3–4

400g/14oz early rhubarb
2 large ripe pears
130g/4½oz/generous 1 cup fresh or
  frozen cranberries
90g/3½oz/½ cup caster (superfine) sugar
mineral water (optional)

Cook's tip
If you are using frozen cranberries, do not bother to thaw them first. They will still blend, and their icy coolness will chill the smoothie to just the right temperature.

Energy 138kcal/590kJ; Protein 1.4g; Carbohydrate 34.9g, of which sugars 34.9g; Fat 0.2g, of which saturates 0g; Cholesterol 0mg; Calcium 115mg; Fibre 3.6g; Sodium 7mg.

Soya mango

Mango makes the richest, creamiest, most indulgent drinks. This delicious drink is made using soya milk, which is particularly good in milkshakes and smoothies. It has a lovely caramel flavour that blends very well with fruit purées, especially those based on fruits with a sweet, intense taste such as apricots, papayas or mangoes.

Serves 2

1 medium mango
300ml/½ pint/1¼ cups soya milk
finely grated rind and juice of 1 lime, plus
    15ml/1 tbsp extra juice
15–30ml/1–2 tbsp agave syrup

1 Peel the mango and cut the flesh off the stone (pit). Place the chopped flesh in a food processor or blender, and add the soya milk, lime rind and juice and a little agave syrup. Blend until smooth and frothy.

2 Taste the mixture and add a little more agave, if necessary. Whizz again until well mixed, then pour over crushed ice in tall glasses.

Variation
For those with a sweet tooth, choose soya milk sweetened with apple juice for this recipe. It is available in supermarkets.

Energy 113kcal/477kJ; Protein 4.9g; Carbohydrate 17.7g, of which sugars 17.5g; Fat 2.6g, of which saturates 0.6g; Cholesterol 0mg; Calcium 31mg; Fibre 2g; Sodium 70mg.

Muesli smoothie

Another great breakfast booster, this store-cupboard smoothie can be a vegan's lifesaver if you have run out of fresh fruit. It is also a perfect option for breakfast in bed without the crumbs. Any leftovers can be covered and stored overnight in the refrigerator.

Serves 2

1 piece preserved stem ginger,
   plus 30ml/2 tbsp syrup from the
   ginger jar
50g/2oz/¼ cup ready-to-eat dried
   apricots, halved or quartered
40g/1½oz/scant ½ cup natural
   muesli (granola)
200ml/7fl oz/scant 1 cup soya milk

Cook's tip
You can try sneaking in a little chlorella algae or green drink powder made from freeze-dried plant extracts; just add a little at a time so you do not overpower it and make it taste 'too healthy'. Add a spoonful of hemp oil for omega-3.

1 Chop the ginger and put it in a food processor or blender with the syrup, apricots, muesli and milk.

2 Process the mixture until smooth, adding more milk if necessary. Pour into glasses and serve immediately.

Energy 203kcal/862kJ; Protein 6.4g; Carbohydrate 40.1g, of which sugars 30.9g; Fat 3.2g, of which saturates 1.3g; Cholesterol 6mg; Calcium 163mg; Fibre 2.9g; Sodium 163mg.

Cranachan smoothie

Although a steaming bowl of porridge makes a great vegan breakfast on a cold winter's morning, this sumptuous smoothie makes an ideal, light alternative in the warmer months. Just a spoonful or so of oats gives substance to this tangy, invigorating drink.

Serves 1

25ml/1½ tbsp medium rolled oats
150g/5oz/scant 1 cup raspberries
5–10ml/1–2 tsp agave syrup
45ml/3 tbsp soya yogurt

1 Put the rolled oats into a heatproof bowl. Pour in about 120ml/4fl oz/ ½ cup boiling water and leave the oats to stand in a warm place for about 10 minutes.

2 Put the soaked rolled oats in a food processor or blender and add all but two or three of the raspberries. Reserve these few raspberries for decorating the finished drink.

3 Add the agave syrup, depending on taste, and about 30ml/2 tbsp of the soya yogurt to the food processor or blender.

4 Process the ingredients until smooth, scraping down the side of the bowl halfway through if necessary, to ensure an even, consistent purée.

5 Pour the processed smoothie into a large serving glass, swirl in the remaining soya yogurt and serve with the reserved raspberries by the side.

Cook's tips
• If you do not like raspberry pips (seeds) in your smoothies, press the fruit through a sieve (strainer) to make a smoother purée, then process with the rolled oats and soya yogurt as above.
• If you can, start to prepare this drink before it is needed. Allowing plenty of time for soaking the raw rolled oats will result in a much creamier smoothie.

Energy 185kcal/789kJ; Protein 7.5g; Carbohydrate 30.8g, of which sugars 12.6g; Fat 3.4g, of which saturates 0.4g; Cholesterol 1mg; Calcium 53mg; Fibre 5.5g; Sodium 26mg.

soups
and
appetizers

Whether you want a warming soup, a tempting appetizer or a party snack, this chapter is full of delicious ideas. Roasted Root Vegetable Soup or Red Bean Soup with Salsa are ideal for a vegan diet, providing a simple and satisfying way to get lots of essential nutrients. Hummus or Aubergine Dip make a great snack with pitta bread, or for a special occasion you can impress guests with tofu Dragon Balls or Spicy Pea Pakora.

Pea soup with garlic

This fresh-tasting soup is simple and quick to prepare. It has a wonderfully sweet flavour and smooth texture, and is great served with crusty bread and garnished with mint.

Serves 4

30ml/2 tbsp olive oil
1 garlic clove, crushed
900g/2lb/8 cups frozen peas
1.2 litres/2 pints/5 cups vegetable stock
25g/1oz/2 tbsp soya margarine
salt and ground black pepper

1 Heat the olive oil in a large pan and add the garlic. Fry gently for about 2–3 minutes, until softened, then add the peas. Cook for 1–2 minutes more, then pour in the stock.

Cook's tip
If you keep a bag of frozen peas in the freezer, you can rustle up this soup at very short notice.

2 Bring the soup to the boil, then reduce the heat to a simmer. Cover and cook for 5–6 minutes, until the peas are tender. Leave to cool slightly, then transfer the mixture to a food processor and process until smooth (you may have to do this in two batches).

3 Return the soup to the pan and heat through gently. Season with salt and pepper to taste and stir in the soya margaine.

Energy 283kcal/1167kJ; Protein 15.5g; Carbohydrate 25.5g, of which sugars 5.2g; Fat 14g, of which saturates 3.7g; Cholesterol 1mg; Calcium 48mg; Fibre 10.6g; Sodium 52mg.

Pumpkin soup with cinnamon

Colourful pumpkin is full of flavour, making it ideal for this delicious winter soup. Garnish with rice and serve with crusty bread for a substantial and warming meal.

Serves 4

1.1kg/2lb 7oz pumpkin
750ml/1¼ pints/3 cups vegetable stock
750ml/1¼ pints/3 cups soya milk
10–15ml/2–3 tsp agave syrup
75g/3oz/½ cup cooked rice
5ml/1 tsp ground cinnamon
30ml/2 tbsp pumpkin oil
salt and ground black pepper

Variation

This soup is also delicious if made with butternut squash in place of the pumpkin.

1 Cut the pumpkin into wedges. Remove the seeds, cut off the peel and chop the flesh into chunks.

2 Place the pumpkin in a pan and add the stock, milk and syrup, and season with salt and black pepper.

3 Bring the mixture gently to the boil, then reduce the heat and simmer for about 15–20 minutes, or until the pumpkin is tender.

4 Drain the pumpkin, reserving the cooking liquid, and purée it in a food processor or blender, then return it to the pan with the liquid and add the ground cinnamon.

5 Bring the soup back to the boil for a minute. Check the seasoning and pour into warmed bowls. Garnish with some cooked rice, a sprinkling of ground cinnamon and a drizzle of pumpkin oil. Serve immediately.

Energy 182kcal/759kJ; Protein 8.1g; Carbohydrate 15.8g, of which sugars 8.2g; Fat 9.5g, of which saturates 1.7g; Cholesterol 0mg; Calcium 111mg; Fibre 2.8g; Sodium 67mg.

Potato and dulse soup

Dulse seaweed, with its uniquely tangy taste, is an excellent ingredient for vegans. It is a good source of minerals and vitamins and has a high protein content.

Serves 6–8

50g/2oz/¼ cup soya margarine
2 large onions, peeled and finely chopped
30ml/2 tbsp dried dulse seaweed
675g/1½lb potatoes, diced
about 1.75 litres/3 pints/7½ cups hot
   vegetable stock
a little soya milk, if necessary
sea salt and ground black pepper
chopped fresh chives, to garnish

1 Melt the soya margarine in a large heavy pan and add the onions, turning them until well coated. Cover and leave to sweat over a very low heat for about 10 mintues.

2 Add the seaweed and potatoes to the pan, and mix well. Season with salt and pepper, cover and cook without colouring over a gentle heat for about 10 minutes. Add the stock, bring to the boil and simmer for 25 minutes, or until the vegetables are tender.

3 Remove from the heat and allow to cool slightly. Purée the soup in batches in a blender or food processor.

4 Reheat the soup over a low heat and adjust the seasoning. If the soup seems too thick, add a little stock or milk.

5 Serve the soup very hot, sprinkled with chopped chives.

Cook's tip
For the best results use floury potatoes in this dish, such as Golden Wonder.

Energy 125kcal/523kJ; Protein 2.1g; Carbohydrate 17.7g, of which sugars 4g; Fat 5.6g, of which saturates 2.3g; Cholesterol 1mg; Calcium 18mg; Fibre 1.6g; Sodium 166mg.

Spanish almond and onion soup

The combination of onions, sherry and saffron gives this pale yellow soup a beguiling and distinctive flavour. It will make the perfect appetizer to a special vegan meal for friends or family.

Serves 4

45ml/3 tbsp coconut oil
2 large yellow onions, thinly sliced
1 small garlic clove, finely chopped
pinch of saffron threads
50g/2oz blanched almonds,
   toasted and finely ground
750ml/1¼ pints/3 cups vegetable stock
45ml/3 tbsp sherry
2.5ml/½ tsp paprika
salt and ground black pepper

To garnish

30ml/2 tbsp flaked (sliced) almonds, toasted
chopped fresh parsley

1 Heat the coconut oil in a heavy pan over a low heat. Add the onions and garlic, stirring to ensure that they are thoroughly coated in the oil.

2 Cover the pan and cook very gently, stirring frequently, for about 20 minutes, or until the onions have softened and turned golden yellow.

3 Add the saffron threads to the pan and cook, uncovered, for 3–4 minutes, then add the finely ground almonds and cook, stirring the ingredients constantly, for a further 2–3 minutes.

4 Pour the vegetable stock and sherry into the pan and stir in 5ml/1 tsp salt and the paprika. Season with plenty of black pepper. Bring to the boil, then lower the heat and simmer gently for about 10 minutes.

5 Pour the soup into a food processor or blender and process until smooth, then return it to the rinsed pan. Reheat slowly, without allowing the soup to boil, stirring occasionally. Taste for seasoning, adding more salt and pepper if required.

6 Ladle the soup into warmed bowls. Garnish each serving with the toasted flaked almonds and a little chopped fresh parsley and serve immediately.

Variation

This soup is also delicious served chilled. Add a little more vegetable stock to the soup to make it slightly thinner. Leave it to cool completely after cooking before chilling in the refrigerator for at least 4 hours. Just before serving, taste the soup for seasoning, and garnish as specified above.

Energy 255kcal/1054kJ; Protein 5.8g; Carbohydrate 11.5g, of which sugars 8.1g; Fat 19.6g, of which saturates 6.1g; Cholesterol 21mg; Calcium 82mg; Fibre 3.2g; Sodium 68mg.

Roasted root vegetable soup

Roasting the vegetables gives this winter soup a wonderful depth of flavour. You can use other vegetables, if you wish, or adapt the quantities depending on what is in season.

Serves 6

50ml/2fl oz/¼ cup olive oil
1 small butternut squash, peeled, seeded
  and cubed
2 carrots, cut into thick rounds
1 large parsnip, cubed
1 small swede (rutabaga), cubed
2 leeks, thickly sliced
1 onion, quartered
3 bay leaves
4 thyme sprigs, plus extra to garnish
3 rosemary sprigs
1.2 litres/2 pints/5 cups vegetable stock
salt and ground black pepper
soya yogurt, to garnish

1 Preheat the oven to 200°C/400°F/ Gas 6. Pour the olive oil into a large mixing bowl.

2 Add the prepared vegetables to the bowl and toss thoroughly with a spoon until they are all coated in the oil.

3 Spread out the vegetables in a single layer on one large or two small baking sheets. Tuck the bay leaves and the thyme and rosemary sprigs among the vegetables.

4 Roast the vegetables for 50 minutes or until tender, turning them occasionally to make sure they brown evenly.

5 Remove from the oven, discard the herbs and transfer the vegetables to a large pan.

6 Pour the stock into the pan and bring slowly to the boil. Reduce the heat, season to taste, then simmer gently for about 10 minutes.

7 Transfer the soup to a food processor or blender, or use a hand blender if you prefer, and process for a few minutes until thick and smooth.

8 Return the soup to the pan and heat it through for a minute or two. Season with salt and pepper and add a swirl of soya yogurt. Garnish each bowl with a sprig of thyme.

Energy 113kcal/473kJ; Protein 2.5g; Carbohydrate 12.4g, of which sugars 5.1g; Fat 6.3g, of which saturates 1g; Cholesterol 0mg; Calcium 50mg; Fibre 3.5g; Sodium 11mg.

Red bean soup with salsa

This mildly spiced soup is perfect for lunch on a lovely summer's day. A delicious cooling salsa of avocado and lime is added as a garnish for a special finishing touch.

Serves 6

30ml/2 tbsp olive oil
2 onions, chopped
2 garlic cloves, chopped
10ml/2 tsp ground cumin
1.5ml/¼ tsp cayenne pepper
15ml/1 tbsp paprika
15ml/1 tbsp tomato purée (paste)
2.5ml/½ tsp dried oregano
400g/14oz can chopped tomatoes
2 x 400g/14oz cans red kidney beans,
  drained and rinsed
900ml/1½ pints/3¾ cups vegetable stock
salt and ground black pepper
Tabasco sauce, to serve

For the guacamole salsa
2 avocados
1 small red onion, finely chopped
1 green chilli, seeded and finely chopped
15ml/1 tbsp chopped fresh coriander (cilantro)
juice of 1 lime

1 Heat the oil in a large, heavy pan and add the onions and garlic. Cook for about 4–5 minutes, until softened. Add the cumin, cayenne and paprika, and cook for 1 minute, stirring continuously.

2 Stir the tomato purée into the pan and cook for a few seconds, then stir in the oregano. Add the chopped tomatoes and kidney beans, and then pour in the vegetable stock.

3 Bring the tomato and bean mixture to the boil and simmer for 15–20 minutes. Cool the soup slightly, then purée it in a food processor or blender until smooth. Return to the rinsed-out pan and add seasoning to taste.

Cook's tip
This is the perfect soup to make in a big batch and freeze in small portions ready to thaw.

4 To make the guacamole salsa, halve, stone (pit) and peel the avocados, then dice them finely. Place in a small bowl and gently, but thoroughly, mix with the finely chopped red onion and chilli, and the coriander and lime juice.

5 Reheat the soup and ladle into bowls. Spoon a little guacamole salsa into the middle of each and serve, offering Tabasco sauce for those who want to spice up their soup.

Energy 302kcal/1265kJ; Protein 11.7g; Carbohydrate 33.2g, of which sugars 11.8g; Fat 14.5g, of which saturates 2.8g; Cholesterol 0mg; Calcium 125mg; Fibre 11.8g; Sodium 537mg.

Lentil soup with lemon and garlic

This traditional soup is made with red lentils and vegetables, which are cooked and puréed, then sharpened with lots of lemon juice. Lentils are a good complex carbohydrate, making this a satisfying and sustaining soup for those on a vegan diet. Garlic and lemon juice, added for flavour, both help to aid the digestion as well as offering many health benefits.

Serves 4

45ml/3 tbsp olive oil
1 onion, chopped
2 celery sticks, chopped
1–2 carrots, sliced
4 garlic cloves, chopped
1 potato, peeled and diced
250g/9oz/generous 1 cup red lentils,
    picked over and rinsed
1 litre/1¾ pints/4 cups vegetable stock
2 bay leaves
1–2 lemons, halved
2.5ml/½ tsp ground cumin, or to taste
cayenne pepper or Tabasco sauce,
    to taste
ground black pepper
lemon slices and chopped fresh flat leaf
    parsley, to garnish

1 Heat the oil in a large pan. Add the onion and cook for 5 minutes. Stir in the celery, carrots, half the garlic and all the potato. Cook for a few minutes until beginning to soften.

2 Add the lentils and stock to the pan and bring to the boil. Reduce the heat, cover and simmer for 30 minutes.

3 Add the bay leaves, remaining garlic and half the lemons to the pan and cook the soup for a further 10 minutes, until the lentils and vegetables are tender. Remove the bay leaves. Squeeze the juice from the remaining lemons, then stir into the soup, to taste.

4 Pour the soup into a food processor or blender and process until smooth. (You may need to do this in batches.) Transfer the soup back to the pan, stir in the cumin, cayenne pepper or Tabasco sauce, and season to taste.

5 Ladle the soup into bowls and top each portion with lemon slices and a sprinkling of chopped fresh flat leaf parsley.

Energy 349kcal/1474kJ; Protein 16.7g; Carbohydrate 52.5g, of which sugars 7.2g; Fat 9.5g, of which saturates 1.4g; Cholesterol 0mg; Calcium 59mg; Fibre 5.4g; Sodium 53mg.

Peanut and coriander soup

Peanut soup is a firm favourite throughout Central and South America. As in many Latin American recipes, the peanuts are toasted and ground, and then used as a thickening agent, with unexpectedly delicious results. To achieve the traditional 'beefy' flavour in this vegan version we use yeast extract or Japanese miso.

Serves 6

60ml/4 tbsp peanut oil
1 onion, finely chopped
2 garlic cloves, crushed
1 red (bell) pepper, seeded and chopped
250g/9oz potatoes, peeled and diced
2 fresh red chillies, seeded and chopped
200g/7oz can chopped tomatoes
150g/5oz/1¼ cups unsalted peanuts
1.5 litres/2½ pints/6¼ cups vegetable stock
10ml/2 tsp yeast extract or miso
salt and ground black pepper
fresh coriander (cilantro) sprigs,
  to garnish

1 Heat the oil in a large heavy pan over a low heat. Stir in the onion and cook for 5 minutes, until beginning to soften. Add the garlic, pepper, potatoes, chillies and tomatoes. Stir well to coat the vegetables evenly in the oil, cover and cook for 5 minutes, until softened.

2 Meanwhile, toast the peanuts by gently cooking them in a large dry frying pan over a medium heat. Keep a close eye on them, moving the peanuts around the pan until they are evenly golden. Take care not to burn them.

3 Set 30ml/2 tbsp of the peanuts aside, to use later as a garnish. Transfer the remaining peanuts to a food processor or blender and process until they are finely ground. Add the vegetables and process again until smooth.

4 Return the mixture to the pan and stir in the stock and yeast extract or miso. Bring to the boil, then lower the heat and simmer for 10 minutes.

5 Pour the soup into heated bowls. Garnish each portion with a sprig of coriander and the remaining peanuts.

Energy 260kcal/1079kJ; Protein 8g; Carbohydrate 14.7g, of which sugars 6.2g; Fat 19.2g, of which saturates 3.6g; Cholesterol 0mg; Calcium 30mg; Fibre 3g; Sodium 20mg.

Leek and vegetable soup with sun-dried tomato bread

Thickening this dish with a little oatmeal provides extra protein and fibre to this tasty and nourishing soup. The tangy tomato bread makes the perfect accompaniment.

Serves 4

2 small parsnips, quartered lengthways
4 red onions, cut into thin wedges
4 carrots, thickly sliced
4 leeks, thickly sliced
1 small swede (rutabaga), cut into chunks
4 medium potatoes, cut into chunks
30ml/2 tbsp olive oil
few sprigs of fresh thyme, plus a few extra
   sprigs to garnish
1 bulb garlic, broken into cloves, unpeeled
1 litre/1¾ pints/4 cups vegetable stock
90ml/6 tbsp rolled oats
salt and ground black pepper

For the sun-dried tomato bread
1 ciabatta loaf (about 275g/10oz)
60ml/4 tbsp olive oil
1 garlic clove, crushed
4 sun-dried tomatoes, finely chopped
30ml/2 tbsp chopped fresh parsley

1 Preheat the oven to 200°C/400°F/ Gas 6. Cut the thick ends of the parsnip quarters into four, then place them in a large roasting pan. Add the onions, carrots, leeks, swede and potatoes, and spread them in an even layer.

2 Drizzle the olive oil over the vegetables. Add the thyme and unpeeled garlic cloves. Toss well and roast for 45 minutes, until all the vegetables are tender and well browned in places.

3 Meanwhile, to make the sun-dried tomato bread, cut diagonal slits along the loaf, taking care not to cut right through it. Mix the olive oil with the garlic, chopped sun-dried tomatoes and parsley.

4 Carefully spread the mixture into each slit in the loaf, then press the bread back together. Wrap the loaf in foil and bake in the hot oven for 15 minutes, opening the foil for the remaining 4–5 minutes so that the top of the loaf can crisp up slightly.

5 Discard the thyme from the roasted vegetables. Squeeze all the garlic cloves from their skins over the other vegetables in the pan.

6 Process about half the vegetables with the stock and oats in a food processor or blender until smooth.

7 Pour the pureé into a pan, bring to the boil and season to taste. Add the remaining vegetables and heat through.

8 Ladle the soup into bowls and garnish with fresh thyme sprigs. Serve the hot tomato bread with the soup.

Variation
Try using cooked pearl barley or wild rice in place of the oats.

Energy 684kcal/2878kJ; Protein 19.2g; Carbohydrate 104.6g, of which sugars 28.1g; Fat 23.9g, of which saturates 3.2g; Cholesterol 0mg; Calcium 288mg; Fibre 16.6g; Sodium 458mg.

Pearl barley and haricot bean soup with mushrooms

This hearty main meal vegetable soup is perfect on a freezing cold day. Serve in warmed bowls, with plenty of rye or pumpernickel bread on the side.

Serves 6

30ml/2 tbsp haricot (navy) beans,
   soaked overnight
2 litres/3½ pints/8 cups water or
   vegetable stock
45ml/3 tbsp green split peas
45ml/3 tbsp yellow split peas
90ml/6 tbsp pearl barley
1 onion, chopped
3 celery sticks, diced or sliced
5 garlic cloves, sliced
2 carrots, sliced
1 large baking potato, peeled and cut
   into chunks
10g/¼oz mixed dried mushrooms
ground black pepper
chopped fresh parsley, to garnish

1 Put the beans in a large pan, cover with water or vegetable stock and bring to the boil. Boil for 10 minutes, then skim any froth from the surface. Add the green and yellow split peas, pearl barley, onion, celery and garlic.

2 Bring the mixture to the boil, then reduce the heat, cover and simmer gently for about 1½ hours, or until the beans are tender.

Cook's tip
Dried beans should be soaked in a bowl of cold water overnight to reduce the cooking time.

3 Add the carrots, potato and dried mushrooms and cook for a further 30 minutes, or until the beans and vegetables are tender.

4 Season to taste, then ladle into bowls, garnish with parsley and serve with rye or pumpernickel bread.

Energy 162kcal/689kJ; Protein 6.8g; Carbohydrate 34.1g, of which sugars 4.3g; Fat 0.8g, of which saturates 0.1g; Cholesterol 0mg; Calcium 34mg; Fibre 2.9g; Sodium 30mg.

Japanese miso broth with tofu

This flavoursome broth is simple and highly nutritious. In Japan, it is traditionally eaten for breakfast, but it also makes a great appetizer or light lunch.

2 Heat the mixture over a low heat until boiling, then lower the heat and simmer for 10 minutes. Strain the broth, return it to the pan and reheat until simmering. Add the green sliced spring onions or leeks and the pak choi or Asian greens and tofu. Cook for 2 minutes.

3 In a small bowl, combine the miso with a little soup, then stir the mixture into the pan. Add soy sauce to taste.

4 Coarsely chop the coriander leaves and stir most of them into the soup with the white part of the spring onions or leeks. Cook for 1 minute.

5 Ladle the soup into warmed bowls. Sprinkle with the remaining chopped coriander and the shredded fresh red chilli, if using, and serve immediately.

Serves 4

1 bunch of spring onions (scallions) or
   5 baby leeks
15g/½oz fresh coriander (cilantro)
3 thin slices fresh root ginger
2 star anise
1 small dried red chilli
1.2 litres/2 pints/5 cups dashi or
   vegetable stock
225g/8oz pak choi (bok choy) or other Asian
   greens, thickly sliced
200g/7oz firm tofu, cut into 2.5cm/1in cubes
60ml/4 tbsp red miso
30–45ml/2–3 tbsp Japanese soy sauce
1 fresh red chilli, seeded and
   shredded (optional)

1 Cut the coarse green tops off the spring onions or baby leeks and slice the rest of the spring onions or leeks finely on the diagonal. Place the green tops in a large pan with the stalks from the coriander, the ginger, star anise, dried chilli and dashi or stock.

Cook's tip
Accompany with rice cakes, or for a more substantial snack, add noodles, simmered for the time suggested on the packet.

Energy 71kcal/297kJ; Protein 7.2g; Carbohydrate 4.2g, of which sugars 3.5g; Fat 2.9g, of which saturates 0.4g; Cholesterol 0mg; Calcium 372mg; Fibre 2.6g; Sodium 884mg.

Hummus

This classic Greek dip is flavoured with garlic and tahini – sesame seed paste. For a fuller flavour, add a little ground cumin or roasted red (bell) pepper. Serve with toasted pitta bread.

Serves 4–6

400g/14oz can chickpeas, drained
60ml/4 tbsp tahini
2–3 garlic cloves, crushed
60ml/4 tbsp rapeseed (canola) oil
juice of ½–1 lemon
salt and ground black pepper

Health benefit

Hummus makes a good filling for baked potatoes, lowering their overall GI value and adding protein, especially served with a mixed salad or followed by fresh fruit.

1 Set aside a few of the chickpeas to use as a garnish, then coarsely mash the rest in a mixing bowl using a potato masher. If you prefer a smoother purée, then process the chickpeas in a food processor or blender until they form a smooth paste.

2 Mix the tahini into the bowl of chickpeas, then stir in the crushed garlic cloves and rapeseed oil, and add lemon juice, to taste. Season with salt and black pepper and garnish the top with the reserved chickpeas. Serve the dip at room temperature.

Energy 140kcal/586kJ; Protein 6.9g; Carbohydrate 11.2g, of which sugars 0.4g; Fat 7.8g, of which saturates 1.1g; Cholesterol 0mg; Calcium 97mg; Fibre 3.6g; Sodium 149mg.

Aubergine dip

Known as baba ghanoush in the Middle East, this dip has a delicious taste and a soft, velvety texture. Eat with pitta bread, breadsticks or tortilla chips, or spread on slices of bread.

Serves 4–6

1 large aubergine (eggplant)
30ml/2 tbsp olive oil
1 small onion, finely chopped
2 garlic cloves, finely chopped
45ml/3 tbsp chopped fresh parsley
75ml/5 tbsp silken tofu
Tabasco sauce, to taste
juice of 1 lemon, to taste
salt and ground black pepper

Cook's tip
You can roast the aubergine in the oven at 200°C/400°F/Gas 6 for 20 minutes, if you prefer.

1 Preheat the grill (broiler). Place the whole aubergine on a baking sheet and place it under the hot grill for about 20–30 minutes, turning occasionally. Cook until the skin has turned black and become wrinkled, and the aubergine flesh feels soft and tender when pressed with a fork.

2 Cover the aubergine with a clean dish towel and then set it aside to cool for 5 minutes.

3 Heat the olive oil in a frying pan and cook the finely chopped onion and garlic for 5 minutes, or until softened but not browned.

4 Peel the skin from the aubergine. Mash the flesh into a pulpy purée.

5 Stir in the onion mixture, parsley and tofu. Add the Tabasco sauce, lemon juice and seasoning to taste.

6 Serve spread on toast or crusty bread or use as a dip with pitta bread or corn chips, if you prefer.

Energy 129kcal/535kJ; Protein 3.3g; Carbohydrate 1.9g, of which sugars 1.6g; Fat 12.2g, of which saturates 1.6g; Cholesterol 0mg; Calcium 85mg; Fibre 2.5g; Sodium 4mg.

Dolmades

For a tasty appetizer to start a vegan dinner party, try these vine leaves stuffed with spiced brown rice, nuts and fruit. The filling is infused with sumac, which has a sharp lemon flavour.

Serves 4–5

20 vacuum-packed vine leaves in brine
90g/3½oz/½ cup long grain brown rice
25ml/1½ tbsp olive oil
1 small onion, finely chopped
50g/2oz/½ cup pine nuts
45ml/3 tbsp raisins
30ml/2 tbsp chopped fresh mint
2.5ml/½ tsp ground cinnamon
2.5ml/½ tsp ground allspice
10ml/2 tsp ground sumac
10ml/2 tsp lemon juice
30ml/2 tbsp tomato purée (paste)
salt and ground black pepper
lemon slices and mint sprigs, to garnish

1 Rinse the vine leaves well under cold running water, then drain. Bring a pan of lightly salted water to the boil. Add the rice, lower the heat, cover and simmer for 10–12 minutes, or until almost cooked. Drain.

2 Heat 10ml/2 tsp of the olive oil in a non-stick frying pan, add the onion and cook until soft. Stir in the pine nuts and cook until lightly browned, then add the raisins, chopped mint, cinnamon, allspice and sumac, with salt and pepper to taste. Stir in the rice and mix well. Leave to cool.

Cook's tip
Vacuum-packed vine leaves are available from Middle Eastern food stores and good delicatessens.

3 Line a pan with any damaged vine leaves. Trim the stalks from the remaining leaves and lay them flat. Place a little filling on each. Fold the sides over and roll up each leaf neatly. Place the dolmades side by side in the leaf-lined pan, so that they fit tightly.

4 Mix 300ml/½ pint/1¼ cups water with the lemon juice and tomato purée in a small bowl. Whisk in the remaining olive oil until the mixture is well blended.

5 Pour the mixture over the dolmades in the pan and place a heatproof plate on top to keep them in place.

6 Cover the pan and simmer the dolmades for about 1 hour, or until all the liquid has been absorbed and the leaves are tender.

7 Transfer the dolmades to a platter, garnish with lemon slices and mint sprigs and serve hot or cold.

Energy 43kcal/181kJ; Protein 0.7g; Carbohydrate 6.7g, of which sugars 1.7g; Fat 1.1g, of which saturates 0.1g; Cholesterol 0mg; Calcium 12mg; Fibre 0.3g; Sodium 2mg.

Ruby vegetable crisps

These tasty beetroot crisps make an appealing and healthy alternative to potato crisps, particularly for children, who will love the bright colour of this snack. Serve them with a bowl of creamy, garlicky soya mayonnaise or soya cream cheese, and use the crisps to scoop it up.

Serves 4

1 small fresh beetroot (beet)
fine salt, for sprinkling
olive oil, for frying
coarse sea salt and black pepper

Variation
Beetroot crisps are particularly flavoursome, but other naturally sweet root vegetables, such as carrots and sweet potatoes, will also taste delicious when cooked in this way.

1 Peel the beetroot and, using a mandolin or a vegetable peeler, cut it into very thin slices.

2 Lay the slices on kitchen paper and sprinkle them with fine salt.

3 Heat 5cm/2in oil in a deep pan until a bread cube turns golden in 1 minute. Cook the slices in batches, until they float to the surface and turn golden at the edge. Drain on kitchen paper and sprinkle with salt and pepper when cool.

Energy 130kcal/537kJ; Protein 0.3g; Carbohydrate 1.4g, of which sugars 1.3g; Fat 13.8g, of which saturates 1.9g; Cholesterol 0mg; Calcium 4mg; Fibre 0.4g; Sodium 13mg.

Roasted coconut cashew nuts

Serve these wok-fried hot and sweet cashew nuts in paper cones at parties. Not only do they look enticing and taste terrific, but the cones help to keep guests' clothes and hands clean and can simply be crumpled up and thrown away afterward.

Serves 6–8

15ml/1 tbsp groundnut (peanut) oil
30ml/2 tbsp agave syrup
250g/9oz/2 cups cashew nuts
115g/4oz/1⅓ cups desiccated (dry
   unsweetened shredded) coconut
2 fresh red chillies, seeded and finely chopped
salt and ground black pepper

Variation
Reduce the heat of this snack by using paprika instead of chillies.

1 Heat the groundnut oil in a wok or large frying pan and then stir in the agave syrup. After a few seconds add the nuts and coconut and stir-fry until both are golden brown.

2 Add the chillies, with salt and black pepper to taste. Toss until all the ingredients are well mixed. Serve the nuts warm or cooled in paper cones or on saucers.

Energy 301kcal/1247kJ; Protein 7.2g; Carbohydrate 9.7g, of which sugars 5.5g; Fat 26.2g, of which saturates 11.1g; Cholesterol 0mg; Calcium 14mg; Fibre 3g; Sodium 95mg.

Beansprout and cucumber parcels

This is inspired by a typical Vietnamese snack. These delightful rice paper rolls filled with crunchy raw summer vegetables and fresh mint and coriander are light and refreshing, either as a snack or an appetizer to a meal. A great gluten-free option for friends who cannot have wheat.

Serves 4

12 round rice papers
1 medium lettuce, leaves separated and
    ribs removed
2–3 carrots, cut into julienne strips
1 small cucumber, peeled, halved lengthways
    and seeded, and cut into julienne strips
3 spring onions (scallions), trimmed and cut
    into julienne strips
225g/8oz mung beansprouts
1 small bunch fresh mint leaves,
    roughly chopped
1 small bunch fresh coriander (cilantro)
    leaves, roughly chopped
dipping sauce, to serve

1 Pour some lukewarm water into a shallow dish. Soak the rice papers, two or three at a time, for 5 minutes until pliable. Place the soaked papers on a clean dish towel and cover with a second dish towel to keep them moist.

2 Work with one paper at a time. Place a lettuce leaf toward the edge nearest to you, leaving about 2.5cm/1in to fold over. Place a mixture of the vegetables on top, followed by some mint and coriander leaves.

3 Fold the edge nearest to you over the filling, tuck in the sides, and roll tightly to the edge on the far side. Place the filled roll on a plate and cover with clear film (plastic wrap), so it does not dry out. Repeat with the remaining rice papers and vegetables.

4 Serve the rolls with a dipping sauce of your choice. If you are making these summer rolls ahead of time, keep them in the refrigerator under a damp dish towel, so that they remain moist.

Cook's tip
Rice papers are readily available in Chinese and Asian markets.

Energy 105kcal/441kJ; Protein 4g; Carbohydrate 20g, of which sugars 6.6g; Fat 1g, of which saturates 0.2g; Cholesterol 0mg; Calcium 74mg; Fibre 3.7g; Sodium 23mg.

Courgette fritters

A healthier twist on Japanese tempura, using Indian spices and gram flour – made from chickpeas – in the batter. The result is a wonderful snack that has a light, crispy coating, while the courgette baton inside becomes meltingly tender.

Serves 4

90g/3½oz/¾ cup gram flour
5ml/1 tsp baking powder
2.5ml/½ tsp ground turmeric
10ml/2 tsp ground coriander
5ml/1 tsp ground cumin
5ml/1 tsp chilli powder
250ml/8fl oz/1 cup bottled beer
600g/1lb 6oz courgettes (zucchini), cut
    into batons
sunflower oil, for deep-frying
sea salt
steamed basmati rice, soya yogurt and
    pickles, to serve

1 Sift the gram flour, baking powder, turmeric, coriander, cumin and chilli powder into a large bowl. Stir lightly to mix through.

2 Season the mixture with salt and then gradually add the beer, mixing gently as you pour it in, to make a thick batter – be careful not to overmix.

3 Fill a large wok or deep, heavy pan one-third full with sunflower oil and heat to 180°C/350°F or until a cube of bread, dropped into the oil, browns in about 45 seconds.

4 Working in batches, dip the courgette batons in the batter and then deep-fry for 1–2 minutes until crisp and golden. Lift out of the wok using a slotted spoon. Drain on kitchen paper and keep warm.

5 Serve immediately with steamed basmati rice, soya yogurt and pickles.

Energy 207kcal/857kJ; Protein 8.3g; Carbohydrate 10.8g, of which sugars 4.7g; Fat 14.8g, of which saturates 2.4g; Cholesterol 95mg; Calcium 104mg; Fibre 2.1g; Sodium 50mg.

Crispy onion fritters

These delicious Indian snacks are made with gram flour, otherwise known as chickpea flour or besan, which has a distinctive nutty flavour. Serve with chutney or a soya yogurt and mint dip.

3 Add the gram flour and baking powder to the onion mixture in the bowl, then use your hand to mix all the ingredients thoroughly.

4 Shape the mixture by hand into approximately 12–15 fritters, about the size of golf balls.

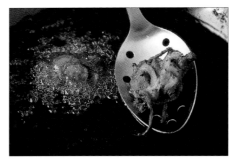

Serves 3–5

675g/1½lb onions, halved and thinly sliced
5ml/1 tsp sea salt
5ml/1 tsp ground coriander
5ml/1 tsp ground cumin
2.5ml/½ tsp ground turmeric
1–2 green chillies, seeded and
  finely chopped
45ml/3 tbsp chopped fresh coriander (cilantro)
90g/3½oz/¾ cup gram flour
2.5ml/½ tsp baking powder
rapeseed (canola) oil, for deep-frying

To serve
lemon wedges (optional)
fresh coriander (cilantro) sprigs
soya yogurt and herb dip (see Cook's tip)

1 Place the onions in a colander, add the salt and toss. Place on a plate and leave to stand for 45 minutes, tossing once or twice. Rinse the onions, then squeeze out any excess moisture.

2 Place the onions in a bowl. Add the ground coriander, cumin, turmeric, finely chopped chillies and chopped fresh coriander. Mix well.

Cook's tip
To make a herb dip, stir 30ml/ 2 tbsp each of chopped fresh coriander (cilantro) and mint into about 225g/8oz/1 cup soya yogurt.

5 Heat the rapeseed oil for deep-frying to 180–190°C/350–375°F, or until a cube of day-old bread browns in about 45 seconds. Fry the fritters in batches until golden brown all over. Remove with a slotted spoon, drain on kitchen paper and keep warm while the rest are frying.

6 Serve the fritters warm accompanied by lemon wedges and a herby dip.

Energy 245kcal/1016kJ; Protein 3.5g; Carbohydrate 26.4g, of which sugars 7.8g; Fat 14.1g, of which saturates 1.4g; Cholesterol 0mg; Calcium 64mg; Fibre 2.8g; Sodium 402mg.

Spicy pea pakora

These pakora make a delicious bitesize snack packed full of pulses, vegetables and spices.
For an extra healthy meal, try serving them in a wholemeal pitta bread with salad for lunch.

Serves 4–6

250g/9oz/generous 1 cup yellow split peas
   or red lentils, soaked overnight
3–5 garlic cloves, chopped
30ml/2 tbsp roughly chopped fresh
   root ginger
120ml/4fl oz/½ cup chopped fresh coriander
   (cilantro) leaves
2.5–5ml/½–1 tsp ground cumin
1.5–2.5ml/¼–½tsp ground turmeric
large pinch of cayenne pepper or ½–1 fresh
   green chilli, chopped
120ml/4fl oz/½ cup gram flour
5ml/1 tsp baking powder
30ml/2 tbsp couscous
2 large or 3 small onions, chopped
vegetable oil, for frying
salt and ground black pepper
lemon wedges, to serve

2 Add the cumin, turmeric, cayenne or fresh chilli, 2.5ml/½ tsp salt, 2.5ml/½ tsp pepper, the gram flour, baking powder and couscous to the mixture and combine. The mixture should form a thick batter. If it seems too thick, add a spoonful of soaking water and if it is too watery, add a little more flour or couscous. Mix in the onions.

3 Heat the oil in a wide, deep frying pan, to a depth of about 5cm/2in, until it is hot enough to brown a cube of bread in 45 seconds. Using two spoons, form the mixture into small balls, about the size of a walnut, and slip each one gently into the hot oil. Cook until golden brown on the underside, then turn and cook the second side until golden brown.

4 Remove from the hot oil with a slotted spoon and drain on kitchen paper. Transfer to a baking sheet and keep warm in the oven.

5 Serve the pakora hot or leave to cool and serve at room temperature with lemon wedges.

1 Drain the split peas or lentils, reserving a little of the soaking water. Put the chopped garlic and ginger in a food processor or blender and process until finely chopped. Add the drained peas or lentils, 15–30ml/1–2 tbsp of the reserved soaking water and the chopped coriander, and process the mixture to form a purée.

Variation
Finely chopped green beans or roughly mashed green peas can be added to the final pakora mix. They will add some extra colour and increase the nutritional value.

Energy 355kcal/1487kJ; Protein 13.5g; Carbohydrate 49.2g, of which sugars 5.3g; Fat 12.2g, of which saturates 1.2g; Cholesterol 0mg; Calcium 85mg; Fibre 4.7g; Sodium 25mg.

Pea and potato baked samosas

Most samosas are deep-fried but these healthier versions are baked in the oven. They are perfect for parties, since the pastries need no last-minute attention.

Makes 25

1 large potato, about 250g/9oz, diced
15ml/1 tbsp groundnut (peanut) oil
2 shallots, finely chopped
1 garlic clove, finely chopped
60ml/4 tbsp coconut milk
5ml/1 tsp hot curry paste
75g/3oz/¾ cup peas
juice of ½ lime
25 samosa wrappers or 10 x 5cm/4 x 2in
    strips of filo pastry
oil, for brushing
salt and ground black pepper

1 Preheat the oven to 220°C/425°F/ Gas 7. Bring a small pan of water to the boil, add the diced potato, cover and cook for 10–15 minutes, until tender. Drain and set aside.

2 Meanwhile, heat the groundnut oil in a wok or large frying pan. Add the shallots and cook over a medium heat, stirring occasionally, for 3–4 minutes.

3 Add the chopped garlic to the wok and cook for a further 2–3 minutes until the shallots are soft and golden.

4 Add the drained diced potato, the coconut milk, curry paste, peas and lime juice to the wok.

5 Mash the mixture coarsely with a wooden spoon. Season to taste with salt and pepper and cook over a low heat for 2–3 minutes. Remove the pan from the heat and set aside until the mixture has cooled a little.

6 Lay a samosa wrapper or filo strip flat on the work surface. Brush with a little oil, then place a generous teaspoonful of the mixture in the middle of one end. Turn one corner diagonally over the filling to meet the long edge.

7 Continue folding over the filling, keeping the triangular shape as you work down the strip. Brush with a little more oil if necessary and place on a baking sheet. Prepare all the other samosas in the same way.

8 Bake the samosas for 15 minutes, or until the pastry is golden and crisp. Leave them to cool for a few minutes before serving.

Energy 42kcal/178kJ; Protein 1.2g; Carbohydrate 8.5g, of which sugars 0.6g; Fat 0.6g, of which saturates 0.1g; Cholesterol 0mg; Calcium 14mg; Fibre 0.5g; Sodium 4mg.

Dragon balls

Tofu is wonderfully healthy and versatile. It is delicious in this Japanese dish, known as hiryozu, meaning flying dragon's head. They make excellent appetizers, or can be served as party snacks.

Serves 4

2 x 285g/10¼oz packets firm tofu
20g/¾oz carrot, peeled
40g/1½oz green beans
30ml/2 tbsp buckwheat flour
30ml/2 tbsp sake
10ml/2 tsp mirin
5ml/1 tsp sea salt
10ml/2 tsp light miso
10ml/2 tsp agave syrup
sunflower oil, for deep-frying

For the lime sauce
45ml/3 tbsp light miso
juice of ½ lime
5ml/1 tsp rice vinegar or mirin

To garnish
300g/11oz mooli (daikon), peeled
2 dried red chillies, halved and seeded
4 chives, finely chopped

1 Drain the tofu and wrap in a dish towel or kitchen paper. Set a chopping board on top and leave for 2 hours, or until it loses most of its liquid.

2 Cut the mooli for the garnish into about 4cm/1½in thick slices. Make three to four small holes in each slice with a skewer or chopstick and fill with chilli pieces. Leave for 15 minutes, then grate the mooli and chilli finely.

3 To make the tofu balls, chop the carrot finely. Trim and cut the beans into 5mm/¼in lengths. Cook both vegetables for 1 minute in boiling water.

4 In a food processor, blend the tofu, buckwheat flour, sake, mirin, salt, light miso and agave syrup until smooth. Transfer to a bowl and mix in the carrot and beans.

5 Fill a wok or pan with oil 4cm/1½in deep, and heat to 185°C/365°F.

6 Soak a piece of kitchen paper with a little vegetable oil, and lightly moisten your hands with it. Scoop about 40ml/2½ tbsp of the mixture in one hand and shape into a ball between your hands.

7 Carefully slide the ball into the oil and deep-fry until crisp and golden brown. Drain on kitchen paper. Repeat with the remaining mixture.

8 Arrange the tofu balls on a plate and sprinkle with chives. Put 30ml/2 tbsp grated mooli in each of four bowls. Mix the lime sauce ingredients in a bowl. Serve the tofu balls with the sauce to be mixed with mooli by each guest.

Energy 250kcal/1038kJ; Protein 12.4g; Carbohydrate 10.4g, of which sugars 3.1g; Fat 17.1g, of which saturates 2g; Cholesterol 0mg; Calcium 722mg; Fibre 0.5g; Sodium 649mg.

light lunches and salads

For speedy, light lunches and tempting, nutritionally balanced salads, this chapter is full of fresh ideas. A vegan diet is a joy to follow, with dishes such as Beetroot and Red Onion Salad, Vegetable Kebabs with a Harissa Dip, or Tabbouleh with Guacamole in a Tortilla Wrap. Quick to prepare and with plenty of vitamin-packed fruit and vegetables, these versatile dishes can be enjoyed at any time of day, all year round.

Herb and sundried tomato polenta with fried tomatoes

Golden polenta is a wheat-free vegan favourite but can taste a little bland on its own. Here it is flavoured with fresh summer herbs and then pan-fried and served with seasonal tomatoes.

Serves 4

750ml/1¼ pints/3 cups vegetable stock
5ml/1 tsp salt
175g/6oz/1 cup polenta
4 sun-dried tomatoes, chopped
25g/1oz/2 tbsp soya margarine
75ml/5 tbsp chopped mixed fresh parsley,
   thyme, chives and basil, plus extra,
   to garnish
olive oil, for greasing and brushing
4 large plum or beefsteak tomatoes
salt and ground black pepper

1 Prepare the polenta in advance. Place the stock or water in a heavy pan, with the salt, and bring to the boil. Lower the heat, slowly pour in the polenta and stir with a wooden spoon.

2 Stir the mixture constantly, using a figure-eight action, over a medium heat for 5 minutes, until the polenta begins to thicken and come away from the sides of the pan.

3 Add the sun-dried tomatoes to the polenta. Stir the mixture thoroughly so the tomatoes are well combined.

4 Remove from the heat and continue stirring for another minute or two. Stir in the soya margarine, freshly chopped parsley, thyme, chives and basil, and season with black pepper.

5 Transfer the mixture into a wide, greased tin (pan) or a glass or ceramic dish. Using a flexible spatula, spread the polenta mixture out evenly in the tin. Cover the surface closely with baking parchment, then put it in a cool place until it has set completely and is cold.

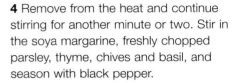

6 Turn out the polenta on to a board and stamp out eight rounds using a large biscuit or cookie cutter. You can also cut the polenta into eight squares with a knife, if you prefer. Brush with oil.

7 Heat a griddle pan and lightly brush it with oil. Cut the tomatoes in two, then brush them with oil and sprinkle with salt and pepper. Cook the tomato halves and polenta patties on the pan for 5 minutes, turning them once. Serve garnished with fresh herbs.

Energy 147kcal/612kJ; Protein 3.2g; Carbohydrate 23.4g, of which sugars 2.1g; Fat 4.2g, of which saturates 1.5g; Cholesterol 5mg; Calcium 6mg; Fibre 1.3g; Sodium 349mg.

Tabbouleh with guacamole in a tortilla wrap

Tabbouleh is a classic Middle Eastern dish that is perfect for a vegan diet. The combination of spring onions, lemon juice and plenty of fresh herbs creates a refreshing and healthy salad.

Serves 4–6

175g/6oz/1 cup bulgur wheat
30ml/2 tbsp chopped fresh mint
30ml/2 tbsp chopped fresh flat leaf parsley
1 bunch spring onions (scallions), sliced
½ cucumber, diced
50ml/2fl oz/¼ cup extra virgin olive oil
juice of 1 large lemon
salt and ground black pepper
4 wheat tortillas, to serve
flat leaf parsley, to garnish (optional)

For the guacamole
1 avocado, stoned (pitted), peeled and diced
juice of ½ lemon
½ red chilli, seeded and sliced (optional)
1 garlic clove, crushed
½ red (bell) pepper, seeded and finely diced

1 To make the tabbouleh, place the bulgur wheat in a large heatproof bowl and pour over enough boiling water to cover. Leave for 30 minutes until the grains are tender but still retain a little resistance to the bite. Drain thoroughly, then place back into the bowl.

2 Add the mint, parsley, spring onions and cucumber to the bulgur wheat and mix thoroughly. Blend together the olive oil and lemon juice and pour over the tabbouleh, season to taste and toss well to mix. Chill for 30 minutes to allow the flavours to mingle.

3 To make the guacamole, place the avocado in a bowl and add the lemon juice, chilli and garlic. Season to taste and mash with a fork to form a smooth purée. Stir in the red pepper.

4 Warm the tortillas in a dry frying pan for about 20 seconds on each side. Serve the tortillas either flat, folded or rolled up with the tabbouleh and guacamole. Garnish with parsley, if using.

Cook's tip
The soaking time for bulgur wheat can vary. For the best results, follow the instructions on the packet and taste the grain every now and again to check whether it is tender enough.

Variation
Use quinoa instead of bulgur wheat for a tasty and healthy alternative.

Energy 259kcal/1081kJ; Protein 5.1g; Carbohydrate 35g, of which sugars 1.9g; Fat 11.5g, of which saturates 1.9g; Cholesterol 0mg; Calcium 55mg; Fibre 1.7g; Sodium 52mg.

Peanut and tofu cutlets

These delicious patties make a filling and satisfying midweek meal served with lightly steamed green vegetables or a crisp salad, and a tangy salsa or ketchup.

Serves 4

90g/3½oz/½ cup brown rice
15ml/1 tbsp vegetable oil
1 onion, finely chopped
1 garlic clove, crushed
200g/7oz/1¾ cups peanuts
250g/9oz firm tofu, drained and crumbled
small bunch of fresh coriander (cilantro)
  or parsley, chopped (optional)
30ml/2 tbsp soy sauce
30ml/2 tbsp olive oil, for shallow frying

Variations

For a change you can try the following combinations:
• Walnuts with rosemary or sage
• Cashew nuts with coriander (cilantro) or parsley
• Hazelnuts with parsley, thyme or sage

1 Cook the rice according to the instructions on the packet until tender, then drain. Heat the vegetable oil in a large, heavy frying pan and cook the onion and garlic over a low heat, stirring occasionally, for about 5 minutes, until softened and golden.

2 Meanwhile, spread out the peanuts on a baking sheet and toast under a preheated grill (broiler) for a few minutes, until browned.

3 Place the toasted peanuts, onion, garlic, rice, tofu, coriander or parsley, if using, and soy sauce in a blender or food processor. Process until the mixture forms a thick paste. If it is too thick, add a little water.

4 Divide the paste into eight equal mounds and form each mound into a cutlet shape or square.

5 Heat the olive oil for shallow frying in a large, heavy frying pan. Add the cutlets, in two batches if necessary, and cook them for about 5–10 minutes on each side, until they turn golden and are heated through.

6 Remove the cooked cutlets from the pan with a metal spatula and drain on kitchen paper. Keep them warm in a low oven while you fry the remaining cutlets. Serve immediately with green vegetables or a crisp salad and salsa.

Energy 495kcal/2059kJ; Protein 20.2g; Carbohydrate 27.1g, of which sugars 5.3g; Fat 34.7g, of which saturates 5.9g; Cholesterol 0mg; Calcium 381mg; Fibre 4.4g; Sodium 543mg.

Falafel

These delicious chickpea fritters are popular in Turkey and throughout the Middle East. They are ideal for vegans and are delicious served stuffed into pitta bread, with salad and chilli sauce.

Serves 4

150g/5oz/¾ cup dried chickpeas
1 large onion, roughly chopped
2 garlic cloves, roughly chopped
60ml/4 tbsp roughly chopped parsley
5ml/1 tsp cumin seeds, crushed
5ml/1 tsp coriander seeds, crushed
2.5ml/½ tsp baking powder
salt and ground black pepper
olive oil
pitta bread, salad and soya yogurt, to serve

1 Put the chickpeas in a bowl with plenty of cold water. Leave to soak overnight.

2 Drain the chickpeas and cover with water in a pan. Bring to the boil. Boil rapidly for 10 minutes. Reduce the heat and simmer for 1 hour until soft. Drain.

3 Place in a food processor with the onion, garlic, parsley, cumin, coriander and baking powder. Add salt and pepper to taste. Process until the mixture forms a firm paste.

4 Preheat the oven to 180°C/350°F/ Gas 4. Divide the mixture into walnut-size pieces, roll into balls in your hands and then flatten them slightly. Roll the balls in a little olive oil, place on a baking sheet and bake in the oven for about 30 minutes.

5 Serve the falafel immediately, accompanied by some warmed pitta bread, a green salad and a helping of soya yogurt.

Cook's tip
Falafel are often served with a tahini sauce. Add some lemon juice and puréed garlic to light tahini.

Variation
Add a handful of chopped frozen broad (fava) beans into the mixture for additional protein.

Energy 303kcal/1282kJ; Protein 18.5g; Carbohydrate 44.7g, of which sugars 5.2g; Fat 6.9g, of which saturates 1.2g; Cholesterol 0mg; Calcium 88mg; Fibre 7.2g; Sodium 16mg.

Tofu and courgettes in tomato sauce

This Mediterranean-style dish can be eaten hot or cold, and improves given a day or two in the refrigerator. It is a delicious accompaniment to nut roast, or enjoy on its own with crusty bread.

Serves 4

30ml/2 tbsp olive oil
2 garlic cloves, finely chopped
4 large courgettes (zucchini), thinly sliced on
   the diagonal
250g/9oz firm tofu, drained and cubed
1 lemon
sea salt and ground black pepper

For the tomato sauce
10ml/2 tsp balsamic vinegar
5ml/1 tsp agave syrup
300ml/½ pint/1¼ cups passata (bottled
   strained tomatoes)
small bunch of fresh mint or parsley, chopped

1 First, make the tomato sauce. Place the vinegar, agave syrup and passata in a small pan. Heat the mixture gently, stirring occasionally, until just beginning to bubble. Add the fresh mint or parsley and heat through.

2 Meanwhile, heat the olive oil in a large non-stick wok or frying pan until very hot, then add the garlic and stir-fry for 30 seconds, until golden. Add the courgette slices and stir-fry over a high heat for about 5–6 minutes, or until golden around the edges. Remove from the pan.

3 Add the tofu to the pan and brown for a few minutes. Turn gently, then brown again. Grate the rind from half the lemon and reserve for the garnish. Squeeze the lemon juice over the tofu.

4 Season to taste with salt and black pepper, then leave to sizzle until all the lemon juice has evaporated. Gently stir the courgettes into the tofu until well combined, then remove the wok or pan from the heat.

5 Transfer the courgettes and tofu to a warm serving dish and pour the tomato sauce over the top. Sprinkle with the grated lemon rind. Taste and season with more salt and pepper, if necessary. Serve immediately with crusty bread or as a side dish to a nut roast, if you like.

Energy 141kcal/585kJ; Protein 8.8g; Carbohydrate 6.8g, of which sugars 6.3g; Fat 8.9g, of which saturates 1.3g; Cholesterol 0mg; Calcium 389mg; Fibre 2.4g; Sodium 181mg.

Vegetable kebabs with a harissa dip

These skewered vegetables are first coated in a spicy oil and lemon juice marinade before grilling. Serve with a fiery harissa and soya yogurt dip for a flavoursome, healthy meal.

Serves 4

2 aubergines (eggplants), cut into chunks
8 button (white) mushrooms
2 courgettes (zucchini), cut into chunks
2–3 red or green (bell) peppers, seeded and
 cut into chunks
12–16 cherry tomatoes
4 small red onions, quartered
60ml/4 tbsp olive oil
juice of ½ lemon
1 garlic clove, crushed
5ml/1 tsp ground coriander
5ml/1 tsp ground cinnamon
10ml/2 tsp dark soy sauce
10ml/2 tsp agave syrup
sea salt

For the harissa and yogurt dip
450g/1lb/2 cups soya yogurt or coconut cream
30–60ml/2–4 tbsp harissa
small bunch of fresh coriander (cilantro),
 finely chopped
small bunch of mint, finely chopped
salt and ground black pepper

1 Preheat the grill (broiler) on the hottest setting. Put all the vegetables in a large bowl. Mix together the olive oil, lemon juice, garlic, ground coriander, cinnamon, dark soy sauce, agave syrup and sea salt and pour the mixture over the vegetables.

2 Using your hands, turn the vegetables gently in the marinade until they are well coated. Thread them on to metal skewers, alternating the vegetables.

3 Cook the kebabs under the grill, turning them occasionally, until the vegetables are nicely browned all over.

4 Meanwhile make the dip. Put the yogurt in a bowl and beat in the harissa, making it as fiery in taste as you like. Add most of the chopped coriander and mint, reserving a little to garnish, and season well with salt and ground black pepper.

> **Cook's tip**
> Make sure you cut the vegetables into even chunks, so they will cook at the same time under the grill (broiler).

5 Serve the skewers immediately with the dip, garnished with the reserved herbs. While the vegetables are still hot, slide them off the skewers and dip them into the yogurt and harissa dip before eating. Serve with a green salad, brown rice or quinoa if you like, or inside a tortilla wrap.

Energy 305kcal/1267kJ; Protein 9.9g; Carbohydrate 24.8g, of which sugars 22.6g; Fat 19.1g, of which saturates 6.6g; Cholesterol 16mg; Calcium 230mg; Fibre 5.2g; Sodium 181mg.

White beans with green peppers

Jewish cuisine is peppered with dishes ideal for vegans due to kosher laws forbidding the eating of meat and dairy together. This dish mixes white beans in a spicy sauce with peppers.

Serves 4

750g/1⅔lb tomatoes, diced
1 onion, finely chopped
½–1 mild fresh chilli, finely chopped
1 green (bell) pepper, seeded and chopped
pinch of sugar
4 garlic cloves, chopped
400g/14oz can cannellini beans, drained
45–60ml/3–4 tbsp olive oil
grated rind and juice of 1 lemon
15ml/1 tbsp cider vinegar or wine vinegar
salt and ground black pepper
chopped fresh parsley, to garnish
pitta bread slices, to serve (optional)

1 Put the tomatoes, onion, chilli, green pepper, sugar, garlic, cannellini beans, salt and plenty of ground black pepper in a large bowl and toss together until well combined.

2 Add the olive oil, grated lemon rind, lemon juice and vinegar to the salad and toss lightly to combine. Chill before serving, garnished with plenty of chopped parsley.

Energy 391kcal/1654kJ; Protein 24g; Carbohydrate 53.8g, of which sugars 11.8g; Fat 10.4g, of which saturates 1.6g; Cholesterol 0mg; Calcium 120mg; Fibre 18.5g; Sodium 37mg.

Thai noodle salad

The coconut milk and sesame oil in the dressing gives this salad a delicious nutty flavour.
It makes an ideal summer treat for a picnic or a leisurely lunch in the garden.

Serves 4–6

350g/12oz egg-free noodles
1 large carrot, cut into thin strips
1 bunch of asparagus, trimmed
    and cut into 4cm/1½in lengths
1 red (bell) pepper, seeded and
    cut into fine strips
115g/4oz mangetouts (snow peas),
    trimmed and halved
115g/4oz baby corn cobs,
    halved lengthways
115g/4oz/½ cup beansprouts
115g/4oz can water chestnuts,
    drained and finely sliced

For the dressing

45ml/3 tbsp roughly torn fresh basil
75ml/5 tbsp roughly chopped fresh mint
250ml/8fl oz/1 cup coconut milk
30ml/2 tbsp dark sesame oil
15ml/1 tbsp grated fresh root ginger
2 garlic cloves, finely chopped
juice of 1 lime
2 spring onions (scallions),
    finely chopped
salt and cayenne pepper

To garnish

1 lime, cut into wedges
50g/2oz roasted peanuts,
    roughly chopped
fresh coriander (cilantro) leaves

1 To make the dressing, mix the basil, mint, coconut milk, sesame oil, ginger, garlic, lime juice and spring onions. Season with salt and cayenne pepper.

2 Cook the egg-free noodles in a pan of boiling water until just tender, following the instructions on the packet. Drain, rinse under cold running water and drain again, then set aside.

3 Cook the carrot, asparagus, pepper, mangetouts and baby corn cobs in a pan of boiling water until tender, but still crisp. Drain, plunge them immediately into cold water and drain again.

4 Toss the noodles, vegetables and dressing together to combine. Arrange in individual bowls and garnish with the lime wedges, peanuts and coriander.

Energy 365kcal/1521kJ; Protein 6g; Carbohydrate 55.1g, of which sugars 6.7g; Fat 12.8g, of which saturates 2.3g; Cholesterol 0mg; Calcium 61mg; Fibre 2.5g; Sodium 280mg.

Enokitake in fried tofu blankets

Tofu sheets are made by boiling soya milk and then lifting off the skin that forms on the top and drying it in sheets. They need to be immersed briefly in water before using to wrap around this tasty filling, which features delicately flavoured enokitake mushrooms.

Serves 4

30ml/2 tbsp groundnut (peanut) oil
50g/2oz fresh enokitake mushrooms,
    finely chopped
1 garlic clove, crushed
5ml/1 tsp grated fresh root ginger
4 spring onions (scallions), finely shredded
1 small carrot, cut into thin matchsticks
115g/4oz bamboo shoots,
    cut into thin matchsticks
15ml/1 tbsp light soy sauce
5ml/1 tsp chilli sauce
5ml/1 tsp agave syrup
15ml/1 tbsp cornflour (cornstarch)
8 tofu sheets (approximately
    18 x 23cm/7 x 9in each)
sunflower oil, for deep-frying
crisp salad leaves, to serve

1 Heat the groundnut oil in a wok over a high heat. Add the mushrooms, garlic, ginger, spring onions, carrot and bamboo shoots. Stir-fry for 2–3 minutes, then add the soy sauce, chilli sauce and agave syrup and toss to mix thoroughly.

2 Remove the vegetables from the heat and place in a sieve (strainer) to drain off the juices. Set aside to cool.

3 In a small bowl, mix the cornflour with 60ml/4 tbsp of cold water to form a smooth paste. Soak the tofu sheets in a bowl of warm water for 10–15 seconds and then lay them out on a clean work surface and pat dry with kitchen paper.

4 Brush the edges of one of the tofu sheets with the cornflour paste. Place 30–45ml/2–3 tbsp of the vegetable mixture at one end of the sheet. Fold the edges over toward the centre and roll up tightly to form a roll. Repeat with the remaining tofu sheets and filling.

5 Place the filled rolls on a baking sheet or tray lined with baking parchment, cover and chill for 3–4 hours.

6 To cook, fill a wok one-third full with sunflower oil and heat to 180°C/350°F or until a cube of bread, dropped into the oil, browns in 45 seconds.

7 Working in batches, deep-fry the rolls for 2–3 minutes, or until they are crisp and golden. Drain on kitchen paper and serve immediately with a crisp salad.

Cook's tip
Look for enokitake mushrooms in supermarkets or Asian food stores.

Energy 255kcal/1053kJ; Protein 3.8g; Carbohydrate 7.9g, of which sugars 3.4g; Fat 23.4g, of which saturates 2.8g; Cholesterol 0mg; Calcium 144mg; Fibre 1.2g; Sodium 228mg.

Sweet and sour vegetable noodles

This noodle dish has the colour of fire, but only the mildest suggestion of heat. Ginger and plum sauce give it a fruity flavour, while lime juice and tamarind paste add a delicious tang to the aromatic stir-fried vegetables and chopped coriander.

Serves 4

130g/4½oz dried rice noodles

30ml/2 tbsp groundnut (peanut) oil

2.5cm/1in piece fresh root ginger, sliced into thin batons

1 garlic clove, crushed

130g/4½oz drained canned bamboo shoots, sliced into thin batons

2 medium carrots, sliced into batons

130g/4½oz/½ cups beansprouts

1 small white cabbage, shredded

10ml/2 tsp tamarind paste

30ml/2 tbsp soy sauce

30ml/2 tbsp plum sauce

10ml/2 tsp sesame oil

15ml/1 tbsp agave syrup

juice of ½ lime

90g/3½oz mooli (daikon), sliced into thin batons

small bunch fresh coriander (cilantro), finely chopped

60ml/4 tbsp sesame seeds, toasted

1 Cook the noodles in a large pan of boiling water, following the instructions on the packet. Meanwhile, heat the oil in a wok or frying pan and stir-fry the ginger and garlic for 2–3 minutes, until golden. Drain the noodles and set aside.

2 Add the bamboo shoots to the wok, increase the heat to high and stir-fry for 5 minutes. Add the carrots, beansprouts and cabbage and stir-fry for a further 5 minutes, until they are beginning to char on the edges.

3 Stir in the tamarind paste, soy and plum sauces, sesame oil, agave syrup and lime juice. Add the mooli and coriander, toss to mix, then spoon into a warmed bowl, sprinkle with toasted sesame seeds and serve immediately.

Cook's tip

To prepare the cabbage: remove the outer leaves, cut into quarters, discard the core and slice thinly.

Energy 256kcal/1072kJ; Protein 7.1g; Carbohydrate 42.2g, of which sugars 14.1g; Fat 6.4g, of which saturates 1g; Cholesterol 0mg; Calcium 136mg; Fibre 4.2g; Sodium 858mg.

Sweet and sour vegetables with tofu

Crisp, colourful and nutritious, this is a hearty stir-fry that will satisfy even the hungriest appetite. Stir-fries make an easy and convenient meal for busy vegans, as the ingredients can be prepared ahead and then they can be cooked in barely any time at all.

Serves 4

30ml/2 tbsp vegetable oil
4 shallots, thinly sliced
3 garlic cloves, finely chopped
250g/9oz Chinese leaves
   (Chinese cabbage), shredded
8 baby corn, sliced on the diagonal
2 red (bell) peppers, seeded and thinly sliced
200g/7oz/1¾ cups mangetouts (snow peas),
   trimmed and sliced
250g/9oz firm tofu, rinsed, drained
   and cut in 1cm/½in cubes
60ml/4 tbsp vegetable stock
30ml/2 tbsp light soy sauce
15ml/1 tbsp agave syrup
30ml/2 tbsp rice vinegar
2.5ml/½ tsp dried chilli flakes
small bunch coriander (cilantro), chopped

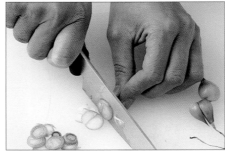

1 Heat the oil in a wok or frying pan and cook the shallots and garlic for 2–3 minutes over a medium heat, until golden. Do not let the garlic burn or it will taste bitter.

2 Add the shredded leaves, toss over the heat for 30 seconds, then add the corn and repeat the process.

3 Add the pepper, mangetouts and tofu, tossing each ingredient for 30 seconds before adding the next one.

4 Pour in the stock and soy sauce. Mix together the agave syrup and vinegar in a bowl. Add to the pan. Sprinkle over the chilli flakes and coriander, toss to mix well and serve immediately.

Energy 144kcal/604kJ; Protein 5.2g; Carbohydrate 23.7g, of which sugars 18.2g; Fat 3.7g, of which saturates 0.5g; Cholesterol 0mg; Calcium 73mg; Fibre 4.7g; Sodium 611mg.

Quinoa, cucumber and lime salad

Along with other staple crops such as amaranth, quinoa sustained the ancient American cultures of the Incas, Maya and Aztecs. Quinoa contains all the essential amino acids and can have up to 20 per cent protein. It is also ideal for those who are gluten-intolerant.

Serves 6

175g/6oz/1 cup quinoa
90ml/6 tbsp olive oil
juice of 2 limes
juice of 1 large orange
2 fresh green chillies
2 garlic cloves, crushed
½ cucumber, peeled
1 large tomato, seeded and cubed
4 spring onions (scallions), sliced
30ml/2 tbsp chopped fresh mint
15ml/1 tbsp chopped fresh flat
 leaf parsley
salt

Cook's tip
Sprinkle in some hemp seeds to add extra nutrition.

1 Put the quinoa in a sieve (strainer), rinse thoroughly under cold water, then transfer to a large pan. Pour in cold water to cover and bring to the boil. Lower the heat and simmer for about 10–12 minutes, until tender. Drain and leave to cool.

2 Make a dressing by whisking the oil with the citrus juices. Stir in the chillies and garlic and season with salt.

3 Cut the cucumber in half lengthways and, using a teaspoon, scoop out and discard the seeds. Cut into 5mm/¼in slices and add to the cooled quinoa with the tomato, spring onions and herbs. Toss well to combine.

4 Pour the dressing over the salad and toss again until all the ingredients are evenly coated. Check the seasoning, adjusting if necessary, and serve.

Energy 175kcal/727kJ; Protein 2.7g; Carbohydrate 16.1g, of which sugars 0.6g; Fat 11.5g, of which saturates 1.6g; Cholesterol 0mg; Calcium 31mg; Fibre 0.2g; Sodium 4mg.

Roasted cherry tomato, pasta and rocket salad

As well as being a meal in itself, this is a good side salad to accompany any main meal. Roasted tomatoes are very juicy, with an intense, smoky-sweet flavour.

Serves 4

450g/1lb ripe baby Italian plum tomatoes, halved lengthways
75ml/5 tbsp extra virgin olive oil
2 garlic cloves, cut into thin slivers
225g/8oz/2 cups dried wholemeal (whole-wheat) pasta shapes
30ml/2 tbsp balsamic vinegar
2 pieces sun-dried tomato in olive oil, drained and chopped
large pinch of sugar
1 handful rocket (arugula), about 65g/2½oz
salt and ground black pepper

Variation

If you are in a hurry and do not have time to roast the tomatoes, you can make the salad with halved cherry tomatoes instead.

1 Preheat the oven to 190°C/375°F/ Gas 5. Arrange the halved tomatoes cut side up in a roasting pan and drizzle 30ml/2 tbsp of the oil over them. Sprinkle with the slivers of garlic and salt and pepper to taste. Roast in the oven for 20 minutes, turning once.

2 Bring a pan of lightly salted water to the boil and cook the dried pasta shapes for 10–12 minutes, or according to the instructions on the packet.

3 Put the remaining oil in a large bowl with the vinegar, sun-dried tomatoes, sugar and a little salt and pepper to taste. Stir well to mix. Drain the pasta, add it to the bowl of dressing and toss to mix. Add the roasted tomatoes and mix gently.

4 Before serving, add the rocket leaves, toss lightly and taste for seasoning, adjusting if necessary. Serve either at room temperature or chilled.

Energy 344kcal/1444kJ; Protein 8.2g; Carbohydrate 46.2g, of which sugars 6.4g; Fat 15.3g, of which saturates 2.2g; Cholesterol 0mg; Calcium 51mg; Fibre 3.4g; Sodium 37mg.

Puy lentil and spinach salad with toasted cumin seeds

This wonderful, earthy salad is great for a picnic or at a vegan barbecue. It improves with standing and is at its best served at room temperature rather than chilled.

Serves 6

225g/8oz/1 cup Puy lentils
1 fresh bay leaf
1 celery stick
fresh thyme sprig
30ml/2 tbsp olive oil
1 onion or 3–4 shallots, finely chopped
10ml/2 tsp crushed toasted cumin seeds
400g/14oz young spinach
30–45ml/2–3 tbsp chopped fresh parsley,
    plus a few extra sprigs to garnish
salt and ground black pepper

For the dressing
75ml/5 tbsp extra virgin olive oil
5ml/1 tsp Dijon mustard
15–25ml/3–5 tsp red wine vinegar
1 small garlic clove, finely chopped
2.5ml/½ tsp finely grated lemon rind

1 Rinse the lentils and place them in a large pan. Add water to cover. Tie the bay leaf, celery and thyme into a bundle and add to the pan, then bring to the boil. Reduce the heat to a steady boil. Cook for 30–45 minutes, until just tender.

2 Meanwhile, make the dressing. Mix the oil, mustard, 15ml/1 tbsp vinegar, garlic and lemon rind, and season well.

3 Thoroughly drain the lentils and turn them into a bowl. Add most of the dressing and toss well, then set the lentils aside, stirring occasionally.

Cook's tip
Originally grown around the town of Puy in south-west France, these grey-green lentils have an excellent, earthy flavour and keep their shape on cooking. Do not add salt when cooking as it toughens the outer skin. Season when cooked.

4 Heat the oil in a deep frying pan and cook the onion or shallots over a low heat for about 4–5 minutes, until they are beginning to soften. Add the cumin and cook for 1 minute.

5 Add the spinach and season to taste, cover and cook for 2 minutes. Stir, then cook again briefly until wilted.

6 Stir the spinach into the lentils and leave the salad to cool. Bring back to room temperature if necessary. Stir in the remaining dressing and chopped parsley. Adjust the seasoning, adding extra red wine vinegar if necessary.

7 Turn the salad on to a serving platter and sprinkle over some parsley sprigs.

Energy 248kcal/1037kJ; Protein 11.2g; Carbohydrate 20.3g, of which sugars 2.1g; Fat 14.1g, of which saturates 2g; Cholesterol 0mg; Calcium 150mg; Fibre 5.1g; Sodium 102mg.

Moroccan carrot salad

Carrots have been renowned for hundreds of years for their health-giving properties and high vitamin A content. They are a very popular and versatile vegetable used in a wide variety of dishes such as this African salad, in which they are cooked before being tossed in a vinaigrette.

Serves 4–6

3–4 carrots, thinly sliced
5ml/1 tsp agave syrup
3–4 garlic cloves, chopped
1.5ml/¼ tsp ground cumin, or to taste
juice of ½ lemon
30–45ml/2–3 tbsp extra virgin olive oil
15–30ml/1–2 tbsp red wine vinegar or fruit
   vinegar, such as raspberry
30ml/2 tbsp chopped fresh coriander (cilantro)
   leaves or a mixture of coriander and parsley
salt and ground black pepper

1 Cook the carrots by either steaming or boiling in lightly salted water until they are just tender but not soft. Drain, leave for a few moments to dry, then put in a large bowl.

2 Add the agave syrup, garlic, cumin, lemon juice, olive oil and vinegar and toss together until all the carrots are evenly coated. Add the herbs and season. Serve warm or chilled.

Energy 53kcal/220kJ; Protein 0.6g; Carbohydrate 4.2g, of which sugars 3.9g; Fat 3.9g, of which saturates 0.6g; Cholesterol 0mg; Calcium 29mg; Fibre 1.6g; Sodium 15mg.

Beetroot and red onion salad

There is a wide range of beetroots available – most are an intense red colour but there are also pink and yellow varieties, which are well worth seeking out. This tangy and refreshing salad looks especially attractive when made with a mixture of the red and yellow types.

Serves 6

500g/1¼lb small red and yellow
   beetroot (beets)
75ml/5 tbsp water
60ml/4 tbsp olive oil
90g/3½oz/scant 1 cup walnut or
   pecan halves
10ml/2 tsp agave syrup
30ml/2 tbsp walnut oil
15ml/1 tbsp balsamic vinegar
5ml/1 tsp soy sauce
5ml/1 tsp grated orange rind
2.5ml/½ tsp ground roasted coriander seeds
5–10ml/1–2 tsp orange juice
1 red onion, halved and very thinly sliced
15–30ml/1–2 tbsp chopped fresh fennel
75g/3oz watercress or mizuna leaves
handful of baby red chard or beetroot
   leaves (optional)
sea salt and ground black pepper

3 Meanwhile, heat 15ml/1 tbsp of the olive oil in a small frying pan and cook the walnuts or pecans until they begin to brown.

4 Add 5ml/1 tsp of agave syrup to the pan and cook, stirring, until the nuts begin to caramelize. Season with salt and lots of black pepper, then turn the nuts out on to a plate and leave to cool.

5 In a jug (pitcher) or small bowl, whisk together the remaining olive oil, the walnut oil, vinegar, soy sauce, orange rind and ground roasted coriander seeds to make the dressing. Season with salt and pepper to taste and mix in the rest of the agave syrup. Whisk in orange juice to taste.

6 Separate the red onion slices into half-rings and add them to the strips of beetroot. Add the dressing and toss thoroughly to mix.

7 When ready to serve, toss the salad with the fennel, watercress or mizuna and red chard or beetroot leaves, if using. Transfer to individual bowls or plates and sprinkle with the caramelized nuts. Serve immediately.

1 Preheat the oven to 180°C/350°F/Gas 4. Place the beetroot in a shallow ovenproof dish just large enough to hold them in a single layer, and add the water. Cover the dish tightly with a close-fitting lid or foil and bake for about 1–1½ hours, or until the beetroot are just cooked and tender.

2 Allow the beetroot to cool. Once cooled, peel them, then slice them into roughly equal strips and place in a large bowl. Add about 15ml/1 tbsp of the olive oil to the bowl and mix thoroughly until the beetroot strips are well coated in oil.

Energy 239kcal/991kJ; Protein 3.3g; Carbohydrate 8.2g, of which sugars 7.2g; Fat 21.7g, of which saturates 2.3g; Cholesterol 0mg; Calcium 50mg; Fibre 2.6g; Sodium 121mg.

Sea vegetable salad

This salad is a fine example of the traditional Japanese idea of eating: look after your appetite and your health at the same time. Seaweed is a nutritious, alkaline food which is rich in fibre and iodine. Its unique flavours are a great complement to vegetable and tofu dishes.

Serves 4

5g/⅛oz each dried wakame, dried arame and
    dried hijiki seaweeds
130g/4½oz enokitake mushrooms
2 spring onions (scallions)
a few ice cubes
½ cucumber, cut lengthways
250g/9oz mixed salad leaves

For the marinade
15ml/1 tbsp rice vinegar
10ml/2 tsp soy sauce

For the dressing
60ml/4 tbsp rice vinegar
7.5ml/1½ tsp toasted sesame oil
15ml/1 tbsp shoyu
15ml/1 tbsp water with a pinch of dashi-no-
    moto (dashi stock granules)
2.5cm/1in piece fresh root ginger, grated

1 First rehydrate the seaweeds. Soak the dried wakame seaweed for about 10 minutes in one bowl of water and, in a separate bowl of water, soak the dried arame and hijiki seaweeds together for 30 minutes.

2 Using a sharp knife, trim off the hard end of the enokitake mushroom stalks and discard. Cut the bunch in half and separate the stems.

3 Make the spring onion curls for the garnish. Slice the spring onions into thin strips about 4cm/1½in long, then place the strips into a bowl of cold water with a few ice cubes added. This will cause the onion strips to curl up. Drain the onions thoroughly. Slice the cucumber into thin, half-moon shapes.

4 Cook the wakame and enokitake in boiling water for 2 minutes, then add the arame and hijiki for a few seconds. Immediately remove from the heat. Drain and sprinkle over the vinegar and soy sauce while still warm. Chill.

5 Mix the dressing ingredients in a bowl. Arrange the mixed salad leaves in a large bowl with the cucumber on top, then add the seaweed and enokitake mixture. Decorate the salad with spring onion curls and serve with the dressing.

Health benefit
The iodine in the seaweed helps to keep your thyroid gland in balance.

Energy 33kcal/139kJ; Protein 2.1g; Carbohydrate 2.2g, of which sugars 1.8g; Fat 1.9g, of which saturates 0.3g; Cholesterol 0mg; Calcium 48mg; Fibre 1.4g; Sodium 237mg.

Avocado and grapefruit salad

This is a light, refreshing lunchtime salad. The buttery texture of the avocados combines with the tanginess of the grapefruit to make the perfect summer dish. Serve it as an appetizer to a light main course of falafel or pakora, served with warm pitta bread.

Serves 4

90ml/6 tbsp olive oil
30ml/2 tbsp white wine vinegar
1 pink grapefruit
2 large ripe avocados
1 cos or romaine lettuce, separated
  into leaves
salt and ground black pepper

1 Using a balloon whisk or a fork, whisk the olive oil and white wine vinegar together in a large bowl, season to taste with salt and ground black pepper and vigorously whisk again.

2 Slice the top and bottom off the pink grapefruit. Peel the fruit by running a small knife all around it, between the peel and flesh. Make sure all the bitter pith is removed.

3 Hold the grapefruit over the bowl containing the dressing and cut carefully between the membranes, so that all the segments fall into the bowl. Squeeze the remaining pulp over the bowl to extract all the juice.

4 Run a knife around the length of the avocados. Twist the sides in opposite directions to separate the halves. Use a large spoon to remove the stone (pit), then peel the halves. Slice the flesh and cover the slices with the dressing, to stop them from discolouring.

5 Tear the lettuce into pieces and add them to the bowl. Toss gently until evenly coated in the dressing. Adjust the seasoning to taste and serve.

Variation

Try other fruit combinations. Mango and strawberries go well together, as do papaya and limes.

Energy 151kcal/625kJ; Protein 1.1g; Carbohydrate 5.6g, of which sugars 5.2g; Fat 13.9g, of which saturates 2.4g; Cholesterol 0mg; Calcium 24mg; Fibre 1.9g; Sodium 13mg.

Mayan pumpkin salad

In this Latin American salad, red wine vinegar brings out the sweetness of the pumpkin, which is then combined with plenty of fresh parsley, which is rich in iron and calcium.

Serves 4

1 large red onion, peeled and very
   thinly sliced
200ml/7fl oz/scant 1 cup olive oil
60ml/4 tbsp red wine vinegar
675g/1½lb pumpkin, peeled and cut into
   4cm/1½in pieces
40g/1½oz/¾ cup fresh flat leaf parsley
   leaves, chopped
salt and ground black pepper

Variation
Try replacing the pumpkin with sweet potatoes. Wild rocket (arugula) or coriander (cilantro) can be used instead of the parsley.

1 Mix the red onion, olive oil and red wine vinegar in a large bowl. Stir well until thoroughly combined.

2 Put the pumpkin pieces in a large pan of cold salted water. Bring to the boil, then lower the heat and simmer gently for 15–20 minutes or until the pumpkin is tender, then drain.

3 Immediately add the drained pumpkin to the bowl containing the dressing. Toss lightly with your hands until the pumpkin is well coated. Leave to cool.

4 Stir in the chopped parsley, cover with clear film (plastic wrap) and chill. Allow the salad to come back to room temperature before serving.

Energy 404kcal/1663kJ; Protein 1.7g; Carbohydrate 5.2g, of which sugars 4g; Fat 42g, of which saturates 6.1g; Cholesterol 0mg; Calcium 73mg; Fibre 2.4g; Sodium 4mg.

Asparagus and orange salad

A slightly unusual combination of ingredients with a simple dressing based on good quality fruity olive oil, tender spears of asparagus, juicy oranges and ripe tomatoes.

Serves 4

225g/8oz asparagus, trimmed
   and cut into 5cm/2in lengths
2 large oranges
2 ripe tomatoes, cut into eighths
50g/2oz cos or romaine lettuce leaves
30ml/2 tbsp extra virgin olive oil
2.5ml/½ tsp sherry vinegar
   or balsamic vinegar
ground black pepper

1 Cook the asparagus in boiling, lightly salted water for 3–4 minutes, until just tender. The cooking time may vary according to the size of the asparagus stems. Drain and refresh under cold water, then leave on one side to cool.

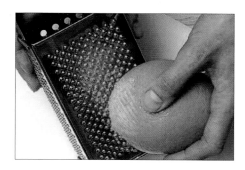

2 Finely grate the rind from half an orange and reserve. Peel both the oranges and cut them into segments. Squeeze the juice from the membrane and reserve.

3 Put the asparagus, orange segments, tomatoes and lettuce into a salad bowl.

4 Mix together the oil and vinegar, and add 15ml/1 tbsp of the reserved orange juice and 5ml/1 tsp of the grated rind. Season with salt and black pepper.

5 Just before serving, pour the dressing over the salad and mix gently to coat all the salad ingredients in the dressing.

Cook's tip
The bottom of the asparagus stalk is usually hard and woody – and becomes more so with age – so it will probably need to be cut off with a sharp knife. However, if you are using short, slender asparagus stems, sometimes called 'spruce', then it may not be necessary to trim them.

Energy 102kcal/424kJ; Protein 2.9g; Carbohydrate 9.3g, of which sugars 9.2g; Fat 6.1g, of which saturates 0.9g; Cholesterol 0mg; Calcium 58mg; Fibre 2.9g; Sodium 9mg.

Orange and olive salad

This is a refreshing salad to enjoy with a main course or it is equally good added to a selection of buffet or picnic dishes. It goes particularly well with home-made pizza.

Serves 6

5 large oranges
90g/3½oz/½ cup black olives
1 red onion, thinly sliced
1 large fennel bulb, thinly sliced,
    feathery tops reserved
15ml/1 tbsp chopped fresh mint,
    plus a few extra sprigs to garnish
15ml/1 tbsp chopped fresh coriander
    (cilantro), plus extra to garnish

For the dressing

60ml/4 tbsp olive oil
10ml/2 tsp lemon juice
2.5ml/½ tsp ground toasted
    coriander seeds
2.5ml/½ tsp orange flower water
salt and ground black pepper

1 Peel the oranges with a sharp knife, making sure you remove all the white pith, and cut them into 5mm/¼in slices. Remove any pips (seeds) and work over a bowl to catch all the orange juice. Set the juice aside for adding to the salad dressing.

2 Pit the olives, if you like. In a bowl, toss the orange slices, onion and fennel together with the olives, chopped fresh mint and coriander.

3 Make the dressing. In a bowl, whisk together the olive oil, 15ml/1 tbsp of the reserved orange juice and the lemon juice. Add the ground toasted coriander seeds and season to taste with salt and pepper. Mix thoroughly.

4 Toss the dressing into the salad, cover and leave to stand in a cool place for 30–60 minutes.

5 To serve, drain off any excess dressing and place the salad in a serving dish or bowl. Sprinkle with the chopped herbs and reserved fennel tops, and sprinkle with the orange flower water.

Energy 150kcal/629kJ; Protein 3g; Carbohydrate 18.9g, of which sugars 16.4g; Fat 7.6g, of which saturates 1.1g; Cholesterol 0mg; Calcium 102mg; Fibre 3.8g; Sodium 292mg.

Celery and coconut salad with lime

This salad is a delicious balance of the crunchy, slightly bitter celery with sweet and creamy coconut. The addition of lime juice makes this dish particularly refreshing.

Serves 3–4

45–60ml/3–4 tbsp coconut cream
2 garlic cloves, crushed
5ml/1 tsp grated lime rind
juice of 1 lime
8 long celery sticks, grated
  (leaves reserved for the garnish)
flesh of ½ fresh coconut, grated
salt and ground black pepper
a few sprigs of fresh flat leaf parsley,
  to garnish

1 Pour the coconut cream into a large bowl. Add the garlic and mix until well combined. Stir in the lime rind and juice and season with salt and plenty of ground black pepper.

2 Fold the grated celery and coconut into the bowl with the dressing, then set aside for 15–20 minutes to let the celery juices weep. Do not leave it for too long or it will become watery.

3 To serve, spoon the salad into a bowl and garnish with celery and parsley.

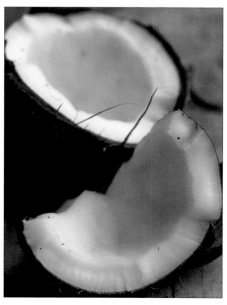

Energy 126kcal/521kJ; Protein 2.1g; Carbohydrate 2.9g, of which sugars 2.9g; Fat 11.9g, of which saturates 10.1g; Cholesterol 0mg; Calcium 63mg; Fibre 3.6g; Sodium 69mg.

Chopped vegetable salad

This classic summer salad lends itself to endless variety: try adding olives, diced beetroot or potatoes. You can also omit the chilli, vary the herbs, or use lime or lemon instead of vinegar.

Serves 4–6

1 each red, green and yellow (bell)
   pepper, seeded
1 carrot
1 cucumber
6 tomatoes
3 garlic cloves, finely chopped
3 spring onions (scallions), thinly sliced
30ml/2 tbsp chopped fresh coriander
   (cilantro) leaves
30ml/2 tbsp each chopped fresh dill,
   parsley and mint leaves
½–1 hot fresh chilli, seeds removed
   and chopped (optional)
45–60ml/3–4 tbsp extra virgin olive oil
juice of 1–1½ lemons
salt and ground black pepper

1 Using a sharp knife, finely dice the red, green and yellow peppers, carrot, cucumber and tomatoes. Place them in a large mixing bowl and toss gently with your hands to mix.

2 Add the garlic, spring onions, coriander, dill, parsley, mint and chilli, if using, to the chopped vegetables and toss together to combine.

3 Pour the olive oil and lemon juice over the vegetables, season with salt and pepper to taste and toss together. Chill before serving.

Variation
Try adding a handful of capers to the salad for extra piquancy.

Cucumber, potato and pepper salad

A great, refreshing and piquant salad for any time of year. It is hearty enough to enjoy on its own or as a side dish to a larger meal, such as part of a buffet selection. Try to use the best quality olives that are available. The black Kalamata style olives from Greece will be ideal.

Serves 4

1 large cucumber, thinly sliced
2 cold, boiled potatoes, sliced
1 each red, yellow and green (bell) pepper,
   seeded and thinly sliced
300g/11oz/1¼ cups pitted olives
½–1 hot fresh chilli, chopped, or
   2–3 shakes of cayenne pepper
3–5 garlic cloves, chopped
3 spring onions (scallions), sliced
   or 1 red onion, finely chopped
60–90ml/4–6 tbsp extra virgin olive oil
15–30ml/1–2 tbsp white wine vinegar
juice of ½ lemon, or to taste
15–30ml/1–2 tbsp chopped fresh
   mint leaves
15–30ml/1–2 tbsp chopped fresh
   coriander (cilantro) leaves
salt (optional)

1 Arrange the cucumber, potato and pepper slices and the pitted olives on a serving plate or in a dish.

2 Sprinkle the chopped fresh chilli or cayenne pepper over the salad and season with salt, if you like. (Bear in mind that olives tend to be very salty so you may not need to add any extra salt – taste before seasoning.)

3 Sprinkle the garlic, onions, olive oil, vinegar and lemon juice over the salad. Chill before serving, sprinkled with the chopped mint and coriander leaves.

Variation
Serve the salad garnished with sliced cooked beetroot (beet).

Energy 116kcal/485kJ; Protein 3g; Carbohydrate 12.2g, of which sugars 11.7g; Fat 6.5g, of which saturates 1.1g; Cholesterol 0mg; Calcium 43mg; Fibre 3.8g; Sodium 21mg.
Energy 159kcal/656kJ; Protein 1.9g; Carbohydrate 5.8g, of which sugars 5.6g; Fat 14.4g, of which saturates 2.1g; Cholesterol 0mg; Calcium 46mg; Fibre 2.4g; Sodium 13mg.

main courses

This chapter features dishes that take advantage of the huge variety of grains, beans, vegetables, pasta and rice that are available to those on a vegan diet. These deliciously diverse main courses are full of mouthwatering flavours, and bring together influences from cuisines across the world to create nourishing and satisfying meals for the whole family. From Black Bean Hotpot and Vegetable Moussaka with Tofu Topping, to Sweet Pumpkin and Peanut Curry and Couscous with Dried Fruit and Nuts, you will be spoilt for choice with the tempting range on offer.

Artichokes with beans and almonds

Globe artichokes are a variety of perennial thistle and have been a renowned epicurean delight for hundreds of years. Prized by the ancient Romans and grown in the garden of Henry VIII, they are still well deserving of a place in every vegan's kitchen. In this dish from Turkey, the tender bottoms are filled with fresh broad beans and flavoured with dill.

Serves 4

275g/10oz/2 cups shelled broad
  (fava) beans
4 large globe artichokes
120ml/4fl oz/½ cup olive oil
juice of 1 lemon
10ml/2 tsp sugar
75g/3oz/¾ cup blanched almonds
1 small bunch of fresh dill, chopped
2 tomatoes, skinned, seeded and diced
sea salt

1 Put the beans in a pan of water and bring to the boil. Lower the heat, then simmer for 10–15 minutes or until tender. Drain and refresh under cold running water, then peel off the skins.

2 Prepare the artichokes. Cut off the stalks and pull off all the leaves. Dig out the hairy choke from the middle using a teaspoon, then cut away any hard bits with a small sharp knife and trim into a neat cup shape. Rub the cup-shaped bases – called bottoms – with a mixture of lemon juice and salt to prevent them from discolouring.

3 Place the prepared artichokes in a large, heavy pan. Mix together the olive oil, lemon juice and 50ml/2fl oz/¼ cup water and pour the mixture over the artichokes.

4 Cover the pan with a tight-fitting lid and bring to a simmer. Cook the artichokes in the lemon juice and olive oil mixture gently for about 20 minutes.

5 Add the sugar, prepared broad beans and blanched almonds to the pan. Cover again with the lid and continue to simmer gently for a further 10 minutes, or until the artichokes are tender.

6 Toss half the chopped dill into the pan and season with sea salt. Mix all the ingredients together, then turn off the heat. Leave the artichokes to cool in the pan.

7 Lift the artichokes out of the pan and place them hollow-side up in a large serving dish. Mix the diced tomatoes with the beans and almonds in the pan.

8 Spoon the bean and vegetable mixture into the middle of the artichokes and all around them. Garnish with the remaining dill. Leave to cool to room temperature, then serve.

Energy 351kcal/1455kJ; Protein 8.2g; Carbohydrate 13.4g, of which sugars 8.3g; Fat 29.8g, of which saturates 3.6g; Cholesterol 0mg; Calcium 110mg; Fibre 5.5g; Sodium 29mg.

Lentils with mushrooms and anis

Rich in protein, iron, calcium and magnesium, lentils have been shown to be beneficial to the health of our hearts. Aniseed liqueur adds a delicious flavour to this nutritious dish.

Serves 4

30ml/2 tbsp olive oil
1 large onion, sliced
2 garlic cloves, finely chopped
250g/9oz/3 cups brown cap
  (cremini) mushrooms, sliced
150g/5oz/generous ½ cup brown
  or green lentils, soaked overnight
4 tomatoes, cut in eighths
1 bay leaf
175ml/6fl oz/¾ cup vegetable stock
25g/1oz/½ cup chopped fresh parsley
30ml/2 tbsp anis spirit or anisette
pinch of paprika
sea salt and ground black pepper

1 Heat the oil in a flameproof casserole. Add the onion and fry gently, with the garlic, until softened but not browned.

2 Add the sliced mushrooms and stir to combine with the onion and garlic. Continue cooking, stirring gently, for a couple of minutes.

3 Add the lentils, tomatoes, bay leaf and the stock. Simmer gently, covered, for 35 minutes until the lentils are soft, and the liquid has almost disappeared.

4 Stir in the parsley and anis. Season with salt, paprika and black pepper. Serve immediately in individual bowls.

Energy 216kcal/910kJ; Protein 12.4g; Carbohydrate 29.3g, of which sugars 9.6g; Fat 4.5g, of which saturates 0.7g; Cholesterol 0mg; Calcium 72mg; Fibre 6.9g; Sodium 26mg.

Curried leek and squash gratin

You can use virtually any kind of squash for this tasty gratin, which is perfect for a warming and hearty meal on a chilly day. Patty pans and acorn squash or pumpkins could all be used.

Serves 4–6

450g/1lb peeled and seeded squash,
    cut into 1cm/½in slices
60ml/4 tbsp olive oil
450g/1lb leeks, cut into thick, diagonal slices
675g/1½lb tomatoes, peeled and
    thickly sliced
2.5ml/½ tsp ground nutmeg
2.5ml/½ tsp ground toasted cumin seeds
300ml/½ pint/1¼ cups coconut mik
1 fresh red chilli, seeded and sliced
1 garlic clove, finely chopped
15ml/1 tbsp chopped fresh mint
30ml/2 tbsp chopped fresh parsley
60ml/4 tbsp rolled oats
salt and ground black pepper

1 Steam the squash over boiling salted water for 10 minutes.

2 Heat half the oil in a frying pan and cook the leeks gently for 5–6 minutes until lightly coloured. Try to keep the slices intact. Preheat the oven to 190°C/375°F/Gas 5.

3 Layer the squash, leeks and tomatoes in a 2 litre/3½ pint/8 cup gratin dish, arranging them in rows. Sprinkle with salt, pepper, nutmeg and cumin seeds.

Variation

For a curried version of this dish, use ground coriander as well as cumin. Use fresh coriander (cilantro) instead of the mint and parsley.

4 Pour the coconut milk into a small pan and add the sliced chilli, chopped garlic and mint. Bring to the boil over a low heat, then stir in the mint. Pour the mixture evenly over the layered vegetables, using a rubber spatula to scrape all the sauce out of the pan.

5 Cook for about 50–55 minutes, or until the gratin is bubbling and tinged brown. Sprinkle the parsley and oats on top and drizzle over the remaining oil. Bake for another 15–20 minutes until the oats have turned brown and crispy. Serve the gratin immediately.

Energy 248kcal/1032kJ; Protein 5.7g; Carbohydrate 16.7g, of which sugars 7.8g; Fat 18g, of which saturates 7.4g; Cholesterol 28mg; Calcium 126mg; Fibre 3.8g; Sodium 104mg.

Vegetable tarte tatin

This dish is a vegetable version of the classic upside-down pie, combining rice, garlic, onions and olives. You can experiment with as many different coloured vegetables as you like.

Serves 6

30ml/2 tbsp sunflower oil
25ml/1½ tbsp olive oil
1 aubergine (eggplant), sliced lengthways
1 large red (bell) pepper, seeded
 and cut into long strips
10 tomatoes
2 red shallots, finely chopped
1–2 garlic cloves, crushed
150ml/¼ pint/⅔ cup white wine
10ml/2 tsp chopped fresh basil
225g/8oz/2 cups cooked brown
 long grain rice
40g/1½oz/⅓ cup pitted black
 olives, chopped
350g/12oz vegan puff pastry
ground black pepper
salad leaves, to serve

1 Preheat the oven to 190°C/375°F/ Gas 5. Heat the sunflower oil with 15ml/1 tbsp of the olive oil in a frying pan and fry the aubergine slices, in batches if necessary, for 4–5 minutes on each side until golden brown. As each aubergine slice softens and browns, lift it out and drain on several sheets of kitchen paper to remove as much oil as possible.

Variations
• You can make individual tatins in ramekin dishes or in a muffin tray, if you prefer.
• Use a mixture of red, yellow and green (bell) peppers for extra colour.

2 Add the pepper strips to the oil remaining in the pan, turning them to coat. Cover the pan with a lid or foil and sweat the peppers over a medium-high heat for 5–6 minutes, stirring occasionally, until the pepper strips are soft and flecked with brown.

3 Slice two of the tomatoes using a sharp knife and set aside.

4 Plunge the remaining tomatoes into boiling water for 30 seconds, then drain. Peel off the skins, cut them into quarters and remove the core and seeds. Chop them roughly.

5 Heat the remaining oil in the frying pan and fry the shallots and garlic for 3–4 minutes until softened. Add the chopped tomatoes and cook for a few minutes until softened.

6 Stir in the white wine and fresh basil, with black pepper to taste. Bring the mixture to the boil, then remove from the heat and stir in the cooked rice and pitted black olives, making sure they are well distributed.

7 Arrange the tomato slices, cooked aubergine slices and peppers in a single layer over the base of a heavy, 30cm/12in shallow ovenproof dish. Spread the rice mixture on top.

8 Roll out the puff pastry to a circle slightly larger than the diameter of the dish and place it on top of the rice. Tuck the edges of the pastry circle down inside the dish.

9 Bake the tatin for 25–30 minutes, or until the pastry is golden and risen. Leave to cool slightly, then invert the tart on to a large, warmed serving plate. Serve in slices, accompanied by a leafy green salad or simply dressed lamb's lettuce or mâche.

Cook's tip
This tart would make a lovely lunch or supper dish. Serve it hot with new potatoes and a fresh green vegetable, such as mangetouts (snow peas), sugarsnap peas or green beans.

Energy 535kcal/2241kJ; Protein 8.2g; Carbohydrate 59.1g, of which sugars 8.8g; Fat 29.5g, of which saturates 1.2g; Cholesterol 0mg; Calcium 89mg; Fibre 2.6g; Sodium 521mg.

Grilled vegetable pizza

You really cannot go too far wrong with this classic mixture of grilled vegetables on home-made pizza dough. It is filling and healthy, and is a favourite with children.

Serves 6

4 plum tomatoes, skinned and chopped
60ml/4 tbsp olive oil
1 clove garlic, crushed
30ml/2 tbsp chopped fresh basil
1 courgette (zucchini), sliced
6 mushrooms, sliced
2 baby aubergines (eggplants)
    or 1 small aubergine, sliced
1 yellow (bell) pepper, seeded
    and sliced
50g/2oz/½ cup cornmeal
50g/2oz/½ cup buckwheat flour
50g/2oz/½ cup potato flour
50g/2oz/½ cup soya flour
5ml/1 tsp baking powder
2.5ml/½ tsp sea salt
50g/2oz/¼ cup non-hydrogenated vegan
    margarine or dairy-free spread
105ml/7 tbsp soya milk
salt and ground black pepper

For the cheesy topping
120ml/4fl oz rapeseed (canola) oil
120ml/4fl oz sweetened soya milk
15ml/1 tbsp tomato ketchup
5ml/1 tsp French mustard
5ml/1 tsp yeast extract or vegan
    bouillon powder

1 In a pan, place the chopped tomatoes, half the olive oil, garlic and the basil and season with salt and pepper. Simmer until reduced to a thick sauce.

2 Preheat the grill (broiler). Brush the courgette, mushrooms and aubergine slices with a little oil and place on a grill rack with the pepper slices. Cook under the grill until lightly browned, turning once.

3 Meanwhile, make the cheesy topping. With a hand blender or liquidizer, blend the oil and soya milk with the tomato ketchup, mustard and yeast extract or bouillon to form a mayonnaise consistency. If the sauce is too runny, add 15ml/1 tbsp of potato flour.

4 Meanwhile, preheat the oven to 200°C/400°F/Gas 6. Place the cornmeal, buckwheat flour, potato flour, soya flour, baking powder and salt in a large mixing bowl and stir until well combined. Lightly rub in the margarine or spread until the mixture resembles breadcrumbs, then stir in enough soya milk to make a soft dough.

5 Place the dough on a piece of baking parchment on a baking sheet and roll or gently press it out to form a 25cm/10in round, making the edges thicker than the centre.

6 Brush the dough with the remaining olive oil, then spread the thick tomato sauce evenly over the dough. Arrange the grilled vegetables on top of the tomato sauce and finish with the cheese topping. Bake for 25–30 minutes until crisp and golden brown, then serve in slices.

Energy 426kcal/1768kJ; Protein 9.2g; Carbohydrate 28.4g, of which sugars 7.1g; Fat 30.8g, of which saturates 5.9g; Cholesterol 1mg; Calcium 47mg; Fibre 4.2g; Sodium 139mg.

Vegetable moussaka with tofu topping

This vegan adaptation of the famous Greek dish is just as delicious as the traditional version made with lamb mince. An almond and tofu topping is used instead of the usual cheese sauce.

Serves 8

600g/1lb 6oz aubergines (eggplants), cut
   into 2.5cm/1in slices
30ml/2 tbsp olive oil
50ml/2fl oz/¼ cup vegetable stock
paprika and fresh basil leaves, to garnish
sea salt and ground black pepper

For the sauce
30ml/2 tbsp olive oil
2 large onions, coarsely chopped
2 garlic cloves, crushed
2 large carrots, finely chopped
4 courgettes (zucchini), sliced
200g/7oz mushrooms, sliced
2 x 400g/14oz cans chopped tomatoes
30ml/2 tbsp balsamic vinegar
15ml/1 tbsp agave syrup
5ml/1 tsp ground nutmeg

For the tofu topping
200g/7oz/1¾ cups ground almonds
350g/12oz tofu
15ml/1 tbsp soy sauce
15ml/1 tbsp lemon juice
2.5ml/½ tsp English (hot) mustard powder
30ml/2 tbsp tomato ketchup

1 Preheat the grill (broiler) to high. Place the aubergine slices in one layer on the rack. Drizzle with oil and grill (broil) for 2–3 minutes on each side until golden.

2 Make the sauce. Heat the oil in a large pan and fry the onions, garlic and carrots for 5–7 minutes. Add the remaining ingredients to the pan and season. Bring to the boil, then simmer for 20 minutes.

3 Meanwhile, make the topping. Toast the ground almonds in a heavy frying pan, without any oil, for 1–2 minutes, tossing occasionally until golden. Reserve 75g/3oz/¾ cup of the almonds. Place the remainder in a food processor or blender and add the rest of the ingredients. Process the mixture until smooth and well combined. Taste and adjust the seasoning.

4 Preheat the oven to 180°C/350°F/ Gas 4. Spread half the sauce in a 35 x 23cm/14 x 9in ovenproof dish. Add a layer of aubergine slices and spread over the remaining sauce. Finish with a layer of aubergine slices.

5 Spoon the tofu topping over the aubergine slices, ensuring it is spread evenly. Bake for about 20–25 minutes until the topping is set and has turned golden brown. Garnish with a sprinkling of paprika, fresh basil leaves and a little olive oil. Serve immediately.

Energy 768kcal/3255kJ; Protein 60.3g; Carbohydrate 109.6g, of which sugars 10.3g; Fat 13.1g, of which saturates 2.9g; Cholesterol 99mg; Calcium 357mg; Fibre 21.8g; Sodium 320mg.

Roasted courgettes and peaches with pine nuts

This distinctive dish is a colourful and delicious combination of succulent peaches and a medley of roasted vegetables. It makes a healthy dinner served with a tangy yogurt sauce, or even a tahini dressing if you prefer, and chunks of freshly baked crusty bread.

Serves 4

2 courgettes (zucchini)
2 yellow or red (bell) peppers, seeded
  and cut into wedges
100ml/3½fl oz/scant ½ cup olive oil
4–6 plum tomatoes
2 firm peaches, peeled, halved and stoned
  (pitted), then cut into wedges
30ml/2 tbsp pine nuts
salt and ground black pepper

For the yogurt sauce
500g/1¼lb/2¼ cups soya yogurt
2–3 garlic cloves, crushed
juice of ½ lemon

1 Preheat the oven to 200°C/400°F/ Gas 6. Using a vegetable peeler or a small, sharp knife, peel the courgettes lengthways in stripes like a zebra, then halve and slice them lengthways, or cut into wedges.

2 Place the courgettes and peppers in a baking dish, preferably an earthenware one. Drizzle the oil over them and sprinkle with salt, then bake in the oven for 20 minutes.

3 Take the dish out of the oven and turn the vegetables in the oil, then add the tomatoes and peaches. Bake for 20–25 minutes, until nicely browned.

4 Meanwhile, make the soya yogurt sauce. In a bowl, beat the yogurt with the garlic and lemon juice. Season with salt and pepper and set aside, or chill.

Variation
Instead of the yogurt sauce, try making a tahini dressing. Mix together 105ml/7 tbsp tahini, the juice of 1 lemon, 30ml/2 tbsp olive oil and 1 crushed garlic clove. Add water as needed to create your preferred consistency.

5 Dry-roast the pine nuts in a small, heavy pan until they turn golden brown and give off a nutty aroma. Remove from the heat.

6 When the roasted vegetables are ready, remove the dish from the oven and sprinkle the pine nuts over the top. Serve with the yogurt sauce.

Cook's tip
Try serving this dish with some pomegranate seeds for added colour and flavour.

Energy 362kcal/1507kJ; Protein 11.7g; Carbohydrate 26.7g, of which sugars 26.3g; Fat 24.1g, of which saturates 3.7g; Cholesterol 2mg; Calcium 284mg; Fibre 4.8g; Sodium 120mg.

Sweet pumpkin and peanut curry

A hearty, soothing curry perfect for autumn or winter evenings. Its cheerful colour alone will raise the spirits – and the combination of pumpkin and peanuts tastes great.

Serves 4

30ml/2 tbsp vegetable oil
4 garlic cloves, crushed
4 shallots, finely chopped
30ml/2 tbsp yellow curry paste
600ml/1 pint/2½ cups vegetable stock
2 kaffir lime leaves, torn
15ml/1 tbsp chopped fresh galangal
450g/1lb pumpkin, peeled, seeded and diced
225g/8oz sweet potatoes, diced
90g/3½oz/scant 1 cup unsalted, roasted peanuts, chopped
300ml/½ pint/1¼ cups coconut milk
90g/3½oz/1½ cups chestnut mushrooms, sliced
30ml/2 tbsp soy sauce
50g/2oz/⅓ cup pumpkin seeds, toasted, and fresh green chilli flowers, to garnish

1 Heat the oil in a wok. Add the garlic and shallots and cook over a medium heat, stirring occasionally, for 10 minutes, until softened and golden. Do not burn.

2 Add the yellow curry paste and stir-fry over medium heat for 30 seconds, until fragrant, then add the stock, lime leaves, galangal, pumpkin and sweet potatoes. Bring to the boil, stirring, then reduce the heat and simmer gently for 15 minutes.

3 Add the peanuts, coconut milk, mushrooms and soy sauce and simmer for 5 minutes more. Serve garnished with pumpkin seeds and chillies.

Variation
The well-drained vegetables from any of these curries would make a very tasty filling for a pastry or pie.

Energy 306kcal/1279kJ; Protein 9.6g; Carbohydrate 24.5g, of which sugars 11.4g; Fat 19.6g, of which saturates 3.3g; Cholesterol 0mg; Calcium 160mg; Fibre 6.4g; Sodium 409mg.

Parsnip and chickpea curry with roti

The sweet flavour of parsnips goes very well with the spices in this Indian-style vegetable stew. Serve it with dhal and Indian roti breads to mop up the delicious sauce.

Serves 4

200g/7oz/scant 1 cup dried chickpeas, soaked overnight, then drained
7 garlic cloves, finely chopped
1 small onion, chopped
5cm/2in piece fresh root ginger, chopped
2 fresh green chillies, such as jalapeños or Serranos, seeded and finely chopped
550ml/18fl oz/2½ cups water
60ml/4 tbsp groundnut (peanut) oil
5ml/1 tsp cumin seeds
10ml/2 tsp ground coriander seeds
5ml/1 tsp ground turmeric
2.5–5ml/½–1 tsp mild chilli powder
50g/2oz/½ cup cashew nuts, toasted and ground
250g/9oz tomatoes, peeled and chopped
900g/2lb parsnips, cut into chunks
5ml/1 tsp ground toasted cumin seeds
juice of ½–1 lime
salt and ground black pepper

To garnish
fresh coriander (cilantro) leaves
a few cashew nuts, toasted

1 Put the chickpeas in a pan, cover with cold water and bring to the boil. Boil vigorously for 10 minutes, then reduce the heat so that the water boils steadily and cook for 1–1½ hours, or until tender. The cooking time will depend on how long the chickpeas have been stored.

2 Meanwhile, make the sauce. Set 10ml/2 tsp of the garlic aside, and place the remainder in a food processor or blender. Add the onion, ginger and half the chillies. Pour in 75ml/5 tbsp of the water and process to a smooth paste.

Variation
You could substitute red kidney beans for chickpeas, or use carrots and butter (lima) beans.

3 Heat the oil in a large, deep frying pan and cook the cumin seeds for 30 seconds. Stir in the coriander seeds, turmeric, chilli powder and ground cashew nuts. Add the ginger and chilli paste and cook, stirring frequently, until the water begins to evaporate. Add the tomatoes and stir-fry until the mixture begins to turn red-brown in colour.

4 Drain the chickpeas and add to the pan with the parsnips and remaining water. Season with 5ml/1 tsp salt and black pepper. Bring to the boil, stir, then simmer, uncovered, for 15–20 minutes, until the parsnips are completely tender.

5 Thicken the liquid by boiling until the sauce is reduced. Add the toasted cumin seeds and lime juice to taste. Stir in the reserved garlic and chilli, and heat through. Sprinkle with the coriander leaves and cashew nuts and serve.

Cook's tip
For a milder, less spicy flavour, use paprika instead of chilli powder.

Energy 506kcal/2124kJ; Protein 18.4g; Carbohydrate 60.1g, of which sugars 18.2g; Fat 23.1g, of which saturates 3.4g; Cholesterol 0mg; Calcium 192mg; Fibre 17.1g; Sodium 86mg.

Tofu sausage popover

You can buy various delicious vegan tofu sausages to make this family favourite, but making them yourself is very easy and they taste simply wonderful. Serve with mashed potato.

Serves 4

For the sausages
150g/5oz/2½ cups wholemeal (whole-wheat) breadcrumbs
250g/9oz smoked tofu, drained
½ small onion, coarsely chopped
45ml/3 tbsp fresh parsley, thyme, sage or rosemary, finely chopped
10ml/2 tsp dried herbs
5ml/1 tsp Dijon mustard
5ml/1 tsp soy sauce
30ml/2 tbsp coconut oil

For the onion gravy
30ml/2 tbsp vegetable oil
1kg/2¼lb large onions, thinly sliced
105ml/7 tbsp red or dry white wine or balsamic vinegar
300ml/½ pint/1¼ cups vegetable stock
small bunch fresh thyme, woody stems removed, chopped (optional)
5ml/1 tsp yeast extract

For the batter
115g/4oz/1 cup self-raising (self-rising) flour
150ml/¼ pint/⅔ cup rapeseed (canola) oil
300ml/½ pint/1¼ cups soya milk
15ml/1 tbsp balsamic vinegar
sea salt and ground black pepper

1 Put all the sausage ingredients in a food processor, season and process until a thick paste forms. Divide the mixture into eight and roll to form sausage shapes with your hands. Arrange in a single layer on a plate, cover with clear film (plastic wrap) and chill until required.

2 Drizzle the sausages with olive oil and cook under a preheated grill (broiler) for 6–8 minutes or until pale golden brown, turning frequently.

3 To make the onion gravy, heat the oil in a large non-stick frying pan. Add the onion and cook over a medium heat for 5 minutes, until beginning to turn golden. Reduce the heat to low, then simmer for 10 minutes, stirring occasionally.

4 Add the wine or vinegar, stock, thyme and yeast extract and bring to the boil. Simmer, uncovered, for 10 minutes.

5 Make the batter. Sift the flour into a large mixing bowl and season with salt and black pepper.

6 Make a well in the middle, then add the rapeseed oil and balsamic vinegar. Mix the ingredients well. Gradually stir in the soya milk, mixing until fully incorporated, then beat until the batter is smooth.

7 Meanwhile, preheat the oven to 220°C/425°F/Gas 7. Oil a shallow ovenproof dish, then arrange the vegan sausages in the base in a single layer, leaving a little space between each.

8 Pour the batter into the dish, ensuring that it is spread evenly around the sausages. Bake in the oven for about 40–45 minutes, or until the batter is well risen and golden brown.

9 Serve the popover cut into portions with two sausages for each diner. Place the onion gravy in a jug (pitcher) and serve alongside the popover so diners can help themselves.

Variations
• The vegan sausages are also delicious cooked on their own. Grill (broil) them as in step 2 on a greased baking sheet until golden brown all over and heated through.
• Add a little finely chopped red (bell) pepper or onion, miso, or other fresh herbs to the sausage mixture.
• If you prefer wheat-free sausages, use rolled oats in place of the wholemeal breadcrumbs.

Energy 722kcal/3010kJ; Protein 17.8g; Carbohydrate 73.7g, of which sugars 17g; Fat 41.4g, of which saturates 8.5g; Cholesterol 0mg; Calcium 485mg; Fibre 5.4g; Sodium 535mg.

Tofu balls with spaghetti

This dish is popular with children and adults alike so will make a great vegan meal for the whole family. The delicious tofu balls are served with a rich and healthy vegetable sauce.

Serves 4

250g/9oz firm tofu, drained
1 onion, coarsely grated
2 garlic cloves, crushed
5ml/1 tsp Dijon mustard
15ml/1 tbsp ground cumin
1 small bunch of parsley, finely chopped
15ml/1 tbsp soy sauce
50g/2oz/½ cup ground almonds
30ml/2 tbsp olive oil
350g/12oz spaghetti
sea salt and ground black pepper
1 bunch of fresh basil, to garnish

For the sauce

15ml/1 tbsp olive oil
1 large onion, finely chopped
2 garlic cloves, chopped
1 large aubergine (eggplant), diced
2 courgettes (zucchini), diced
1 red (bell) pepper, seeded and finely chopped
15ml/1 tbsp agave syrup
400g/14oz can chopped tomatoes
200ml/7fl oz/scant 1 cup vegetable stock

1 Place the drained tofu, grated onion, crushed garlic, mustard, ground cumin, chopped parsley, soy sauce and ground almonds into a bowl. Season with sea salt and ground black pepper and mix thoroughly. Roll into about 20 walnut-sized balls, squashing the mixture together with your hands.

2 Heat the olive oil in a large frying pan, then add the tofu balls, in batches if necessary. Cook gently, turning them occasionally until brown all over. Remove the balls from the pan and set aside on a plate.

3 Heat the oil for the sauce in the same frying pan, add the onion and garlic and cook for 5 minutes, or until softened.

4 Add the aubergine, courgette, pepper and agave syrup and stir-fry for about 10 minutes until the vegetables are beginning to soften and have turned slightly brown. Season with salt and pepper.

5 Stir in the tomatoes and stock. Cover and simmer for 20 minutes, or until the sauce is rich and thickened. Just before the end of the cooking time, place the tofu balls on top of the sauce, cover and heat through for 2–3 minutes.

6 Meanwhile, cook the pasta in a large pan of salted, boiling water according to the manufacturer's instructions, then drain. Check the seasoning in the sauce before serving with the spaghetti, garnished with basil leaves.

Energy 576kcal/2422kJ; Protein 22.5g; Carbohydrate 79.4g, of which sugars 15.6g; Fat 21g, of which saturates 2.6g; Cholesterol 0mg; Calcium 425mg; Fibre 8g; Sodium 288mg.

Smoked tofu and vegetable fusilli

This quick and easy recipe is endlessly versatile. Feel free to change the ingredients to suit your own taste and what you have to hand. Try to find colourful and contrasting vegetables.

Serves 4

4 carrots, halved lengthways
    and thinly sliced diagonally
1 butternut squash, peeled, seeded
    and cut into small chunks
2 courgettes (zucchini),
    thinly sliced diagonally
1 red onion, cut into wedges
1 red (bell) pepper, seeded
    and sliced into thick strips
1 garlic bulb, cut in half horizontally
4 fresh rosemary or thyme sprigs,
    stalks removed (optional)
60ml/4 tbsp olive oil
60ml/4 tbsp balsamic vinegar
30ml/2 tbsp soy sauce
500g/1¼lb marinated deep-fried tofu
10–12 cherry tomatoes, halved
250g/9oz dried pasta, such as papardelle,
    fusilli or conchiglie
sea salt and ground black pepper

1 Preheat the oven to 220°C/425°F/ Gas 7. Place the carrots, butternut squash, courgettes, onion and pepper in a roasting pan. Add the garlic and herbs. Drizzle over the olive oil, balsamic vinegar and soy sauce.

2 Season to taste with salt and pepper and toss to coat evenly with the oil. Roast for 40–50 minutes, until the vegetables are tender and lightly browned. Toss the vegetables around once or twice during the cooking so that they all cook evenly. Add the tofu and tomatoes to the pan 10 minutes before the end of the roasting time.

3 Meanwhile, bring a large pan of lightly salted water to the boil. Add the pasta and bring the water back to the boil. Cook for about 10 minutes or until the pasta is al dente. Drain the pasta and return to the pan with a few tablespoons of the cooking water.

4 Remove the roasting pan from the oven and squeeze the garlic out of the baked skins. Toss the pasta with the vegetables, tofu and garlic. Taste and adjust the seasoning, if necessary, and serve immediately.

Cook's tip
When cooking pasta, start timing when the water returns to the boil – and boil fairly vigorously, do not simmer. Test shortly before the end of the cooking time by biting a small piece of pasta. It should feel tender, but still firm to the bite.

Energy 719kcal/3009kJ; Protein 41.2g; Carbohydrate 63.4g, of which sugars 15.4g; Fat 35.1g, of which saturates 2g; Cholesterol 0mg; Calcium 1958mg; Fibre 6.6g; Sodium 464mg.

Black bean hotpot

This dish is a nutritious and tasty mix of black beans, vibrant red and yellow peppers and orange butternut squash. The molasses imparts a rich treacly flavour to the spicy sauce.

2 Heat the oil in the pan and fry the onion and garlic for about 5 minutes until softened, stirring occasionally. Add the mustard powder, molasses, agave syrup, thyme and chilli flakes and cook for 1 minute, stirring. Stir in the black beans and spoon the mixture into a flameproof casserole.

3 Add enough water to the reserved cooking liquid to make 400ml/14fl oz/ 1⅔ cups, then mix in the bouillon powder and pour into the casserole. Bake for 25 minutes.

4 Add the peppers and squash or pumpkin and mix well. Cover, then bake for a further 45 minutes until the vegetables are tender. Serve immediately garnished with thyme.

Serves 4

225g/8oz/1¼ cups dried black beans
1 bay leaf
30ml/2 tbsp vegetable oil
1 large onion, chopped
1 garlic clove, chopped
5ml/1 tsp English (hot) mustard powder
15ml/1 tbsp blackstrap molasses
30ml/2 tbsp agave syrup
5ml/1 tsp dried thyme
2.5ml/½ tsp dried chilli flakes
5ml/1 tsp vegetable bouillon powder
1 red (bell) pepper, seeded and diced
1 yellow (bell) pepper, seeded and diced
675g/1½lb butternut squash or pumpkin,
   seeded and cut into 1cm/½in dice
salt and ground black pepper
sprigs of thyme, to garnish

1 Soak the beans overnight in plenty of water, then drain and rinse well. Place in a large pan, cover with fresh water and add the bay leaf. Bring to the boil, then boil rapidly for 10 minutes. Reduce the heat, cover, and simmer for about 30 minutes until tender. Drain, reserving the cooking water. Preheat the oven to 180°C/350°F/Gas 4.

Health benefit
Blackstrap molasses is a by-product of sugar processing and contains less sugar than treacle. It is a good source of iron, calcium, zinc, copper and chromium.

Energy 289kcal/1222kJ; Protein 15.5g; Carbohydrate 43.5g, of which sugars 13.2g; Fat 7.1g, of which saturates 1.1g; Cholesterol 0mg; Calcium 124mg; Fibre 7.9g; Sodium 17mg.

Aubergine, olive and bean tagine

Spiced with coriander, cumin, cinnamon, turmeric and chilli sauce, this Moroccan-style stew makes a filling and healthy supper dish when served with couscous or quinoa.

Serves 4

1 small aubergine (eggplant),
    cut into 1cm/½in dice
2 courgettes (zucchini), thickly sliced
60ml/4 tbsp olive oil
1 large onion, sliced
2 garlic cloves, chopped
150g/5oz/2 cups brown cap
    (cremini) mushrooms, halved
15ml/1 tbsp ground coriander
10ml/2 tsp cumin seeds
15ml/1 tbsp ground cinnamon
10ml/2 tsp ground turmeric
225g/8oz new potatoes, quartered
600ml/1 pint/2½ cups passata
    (bottled strained tomatoes)
15ml/1 tbsp tomato purée (paste)
15ml/1 tbsp chilli sauce
75g/3oz/scant ½ cup ready-to-eat
    unsulphured dried apricots
400g/14oz/scant 3 cups canned butter
    (lima) beans, drained and rinsed
salt and ground black pepper
15ml/1 tbsp chopped fresh coriander
    (cilantro), to garnish
couscous or quinoa, to serve (optional)

3 Meanwhile, heat the remaining oil in a large, heavy pan and cook the onion and garlic for about 5 minutes until softened, stirring occasionally. Add the mushrooms and cook for 3 minutes until just tender. Add the spices and cook for 1 minute more, stirring, to allow the flavours to mingle.

4 Add the potatoes and cook for about 3 minutes, stirring. Pour in the passata, tomato purée and 150ml/¼ pint/⅔ cup water, cover, and cook for 10 minutes or until the sauce begins to thicken.

5 Add the aubergine, courgettes, chilli sauce, apricots and butter beans. Season and cook, partially covered, for 10–15 minutes until the potatoes are tender. Add extra water if the tagine is too dry. Serve with couscous or quinoa, if using, and garnish with coriander.

Health benefit
Butter beans, like many pulses, contain a good amount of protein, potassium and iron.

1 Sprinkle salt over the aubergine and courgettes and leave for 30 minutes. Rinse and pat dry with a dish towel.

2 Heat the grill (broiler) to high. Arrange the courgettes and aubergine on a baking sheet and toss in 30ml/2 tbsp of the olive oil. Grill (broil) for about 20 minutes, turning the vegetables occasionally, until they are tender and evenly browned.

Energy 359kcal/1509kJ; Protein 13.9g; Carbohydrate 45g, of which sugars 19.3g; Fat 15g, of which saturates 2.1g; Cholesterol 0mg; Calcium 123mg; Fibre 9.7g; Sodium 597mg.

Carrot and nut biryani

This simple and wholesome rice dish, based on the traditional biryani from India, makes a great meal for the whole family. Try adding some wild or cultivated mushrooms, if you like.

Serves 4

15–30ml/1–2 tbsp rapeseed (canola) oil
1 onion, chopped
1 garlic clove, crushed
1 large carrot, coarsely grated
225g/8oz/generous 1 cup brown
   basmati rice, soaked
5ml/1 tsp cumin seeds
10ml/2 tsp ground coriander
10ml/2 tsp black mustard seeds (optional)
4 green cardamom pods
450ml/¾ pint/scant 2 cups vegetable stock
1 bay leaf
75g/3oz/¾ cup walnuts and cashew nuts
salt and ground black pepper
fresh parsley or coriander (cilantro),
   to garnish

1 Heat the rapeseed oil in a large, shallow frying pan and gently fry the onion for 3–4 minutes. Add the garlic and carrot and fry for 3 minutes. Drain the rice and then add to the pan along with the spices. Cook for a further 1–2 minutes, stirring to coat the grains in the oil.

2 Pour in the stock, add the bay leaf and season well. Bring to the boil, then lower the heat, cover and simmer very gently for 10–12 minutes.

3 Remove the pan from the heat without lifting the lid. Leave to stand for about 5 minutes, then check the rice. If it is cooked, there will be small steam holes on the surface of the rice. Remove and discard the bay leaf and the cardamom pods.

4 Stir in the nuts and check the seasoning. Spoon on to a platter, garnish with the parsley or coriander and serve immediately.

Variations
• Use whichever nuts you prefer in this dish – even unsalted peanuts taste good, although almonds, cashew nuts or pistachios are more exotic.
• If you use mushrooms, add them right at the beginning while frying the onions.

Energy 364kcal/1517kJ; Protein 8.9g; Carbohydrate 52.4g, of which sugars 3.3g; Fat 13.2g, of which saturates 2.3g; Cholesterol 0mg; Calcium 33mg; Fibre 1.3g; Sodium 61mg.

Tofu and wild rice salad

This dish tastes wonderful on its own. Tofu is rich in protein and low in fat and makes a nutritious addition to a vegan meal, while also providing a wide range of essential vitamins and minerals.

Serves 4

175g/6oz/scant 1 cup basmati rice
50g/2oz/generous ¼ cup wild rice
250g/9oz firm tofu, drained and cubed
25g/1oz preserved lemon, finely chopped
   (see Cook's tip)
20g/¾oz bunch of fresh parsley, chopped

For the dressing
1 garlic clove, crushed
10ml/2 tsp clear agave syrup
10ml/2 tsp of the preserved lemon juice
15ml/1 tbsp cider vinegar
15ml/1 tbsp olive oil
1 small fresh red chilli, seeded
   and finely chopped
5ml/1 tsp harissa paste (optional)
ground black pepper

1 Cook the basmati rice and the wild rice in separate pans until tender. The basmati will take about 10–15 minutes to cook, while the wild rice will take 45–50 minutes. (It is possible to buy packets of ready-mixed long grain and wild rice. This takes 25 minutes to cook because the tough outer skin of the wild rice has been broken.)

2 Meanwhile, whisk together all the dressing ingredients in a small bowl. Add the tofu, stir to coat and leave to marinate for about 20 minutes while the rice cooks.

3 Drain the two rices, rinse well under cold water and drain again. Place in a large mixing bowl.

4 Mix the tofu, dressing, lemon and parsley into the rice. Serve immediately.

Cook's tip
Preserved lemons are available from Middle Eastern delicatessens or from some supermarkets.

Energy 284kcal/1185kJ; Protein 9.6g; Carbohydrate 47.6g, of which sugars 2.4g; Fat 5.8g, of which saturates 0.7g; Cholesterol 0mg; Calcium 355mg; Fibre 0.6g; Sodium 7mg.

Vegetable paella

The success of a paella depends on two of the essential ingredients: the rice and the stock. Always taste the stock before adding it to rice – this is your chance to add some wine, a bit of a stock cube, or even miso or soy sauce to boost the flavour of the dish.

3 Add the remaining oil to the pan and cook the onion for 3–4 minutes until beginning to soften. Add the garlic and cook for a further 2 minutes.

4 Add the peppers, green beans and mushrooms to the pan. Cook, stirring occasionally, for about 3 minutes until just beginning to soften.

5 Add the drained rice and cook for 1–2 minutes, stirring to ensure it is coated in the oil. Add the aubergine slices and stir to combine. Add the chilli and season to taste. Pour in the stock and add the peas and parsley.

6 Bring to boiling point, cover and cook over a low heat for 20–25 minutes, checking the liquid level toward the end (the rice should absorb the liquid, but not burn).

7 When the rice is tender, turn off the heat, cover the pan and leave to stand for 10 minutes for the remaining liquid to be absorbed. Garnish with parsley or coriander and serve immediately.

Serves 4

1 large aubergine (eggplant)
45ml/3 tbsp olive oil
2 onions, quartered and sliced
2 garlic cloves, finely chopped
1 red (bell) pepper, halved, seeded and sliced
1 yellow (bell) pepper, halved, seeded and sliced
200g/7oz/ 1⅓ cup fine green beans, halved
115g/4oz/1½ cups brown cap (cremini) mushrooms, halved
300g/11oz/1½ cups paella rice, washed and drained
1 dried chilli, seeded and crumbled
1 litre/1¾ pints/4 cups vegetable stock
115g/4oz/1 cup peas
60ml/4 tbsp chopped fresh parsley
salt and ground black pepper
fresh parsley or coriander (cilantro) leaves, to garnish

1 Halve the aubergine lengthways, then cut it into slices. Spread them out in a large colander or on a draining board, sprinkle with salt and leave for about 30 minutes. Rinse under cold running water and pat dry with kitchen paper.

2 Heat 30ml/2 tbsp olive oil in a large pan over a high heat. Cook the aubergine until slightly golden, turning once. Transfer to kitchen paper to drain.

Variation

Almost any roughly chopped or sliced vegetables can be used in this dish. Broccoli, carrots, cauliflower, courgettes (zucchini) and okra are all suitable – or try using frozen corn.

Energy 388kcal/1646kJ; Protein 13.5g; Carbohydrate 78.8g, of which sugars 7.5g; Fat 3.6g, of which saturates 0.9g; Cholesterol 0mg; Calcium 57mg; Fibre 8.5g; Sodium 299mg.

Couscous with dried fruit and nuts

This dish of couscous mixed with dates, raisins and nuts would typically form part of a celebration meal in Morocco. It is delicious served on its own, but for a more substantial meal it is especially good served alongside a spicy tagine made with chunky vegetables.

Serves 6

500g/1¼lb/3 cups couscous
600ml/1 pint/2½ cups warm water
5ml/1 tsp salt
pinch of saffron threads
45ml/3 tbsp sunflower oil
30ml/2 tbsp olive oil
115g/4oz/½ cup ready-to-eat
   dried apricots, cut into slivers
75g/3oz/½ cup dried dates, chopped
75g/3oz/generous ½ cup
   seedless raisins
115g/4oz/⅔ cup blanched
   almonds, cut into slivers
75g/3oz/½ cup pistachio nuts
10ml/2 tsp ground cinnamon
45ml/3 tbsp caster (superfine) sugar

1 Preheat the oven to 180°C/350°F/ Gas 4. Put the couscous in a bowl. Mix together the water, salt and saffron and pour it over the couscous, stirring. Leave to stand for 10 minutes. Add the sunflower oil and, using your fingers, rub it through the grains. Set aside.

2 Heat the olive oil in a large pan and stir in the apricots, dates, raisins, most of the almonds (reserve some for the garnish) and pistachio nuts.

3 Cook until the raisins plump up, then transfer into the couscous and mix well. Spoon the couscous into an ovenproof dish and cover with foil. Bake in the oven for 20 minutes, until heated through.

4 Toast the reserved sliced almonds. Pile the couscous in a mound on a serving dish and sprinkle with the cinnamon and sugar in stripes down the mound. Sprinkle the toasted almonds over the top and serve.

Energy 576kcal/2403kJ; Protein 12.5g; Carbohydrate 73g, of which sugars 29.4g; Fat 27.8g, of which saturates 3.1g; Cholesterol 0mg; Calcium 102mg; Fibre 4.2g; Sodium 74mg.

Pumpkin stuffed with pistachio, saffron and apricot pilaff

Pumpkins are not just for Halloween or making a classic pumpkin pie. They also make ideal cooking vessels, to be filled with aromatic pilaffs, as in this recipe, or perhaps with a quinoa-based dish: either way, they make an interesting and unusual centrepiece. This sumptuous and wholesome fruit and nut pilaff is great for special occasions, such as part of a celebration feast or a vegan dinner party.

Serves 4–6

1 medium pumpkin, weighing about
   1.2kg/2½lb
225g/8oz/generous 1 cup long grain
   brown rice, well rinsed
30–45ml/2–3 tbsp olive oil
15ml/1 tbsp soya margarine
pinch of saffron threads
5ml/1 tsp coriander seeds
2–3 strips of orange rind, finely sliced
45–60ml/3–4 tbsp shelled pistachio nuts
30–45ml/2–3 tbsp dried cranberries
175g/6oz/¾ cup ready-to-eat
   dried apricots, chopped
1 bunch of fresh basil,
   leaves loosely torn
1 bunch each of fresh coriander
   (cilantro), mint and flat leaf parsley,
   coarsely chopped
salt and ground black pepper
lemon wedges and soya yogurt,
   to serve

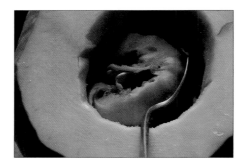

1 Preheat the oven to 200°C/400°F/ Gas 6. Wash the pumpkin and cut off the stalk end to use as a lid. Scoop all the seeds out of the middle with a metal spoon, and pull out the stringy bits. Replace the lid, put the pumpkin on a baking tray and bake for 1 hour.

2 Meanwhile, put the rice into a heavy pan and pour in just enough water to cover. Add a pinch of salt and bring the water to the boil, then lower the heat and partially cover the pan.

3 Simmer the rice for 10–12 minutes, until all the water has been absorbed and the grains of rice are cooked but still have a bite.

Cook's tip
You could use roasted pumpkin seeds instead of pistachio nuts.

4 Heat the oil and margarine in a wide, heavy pan. Stir in the saffron, coriander seeds, orange rind, pistachios, cranberries and apricots, then toss in the cooked rice and mix well. Season with salt and pepper.

5 Turn off the heat, cover the pan with a dish towel and press the lid tightly on top. Leave the pilaff to steam for about 10 minutes, then toss in the herbs.

6 Take the pumpkin out of the oven. Lift off the lid and spoon the pilaff into the cavity. Put the lid back on and pop it back in the oven for about 20 minutes.

7 To serve, remove the lid and slice a round off the top of the pumpkin. Place the ring on a plate and spoon some pilaff in the middle. Continue slicing and filling on individual plates until all the pumpkin and pilaff are used up. Serve with lemon wedges and soya yogurt.

Energy 345kcal/1443kJ; Protein 9.9g; Carbohydrate 50.1g, of which sugars 18.6g; Fat 12g, of which saturates 2.6g; Cholesterol 5mg; Calcium 299mg; Fibre 9.6g; Sodium 93mg.

side dishes

Separate side dishes enable you to add variety, colour and complementary nutrients to a vegan main dish and make it easier to get all the essential vitamins and minerals you need. This chapter features a delicious range of dishes that can be used as accompaniments or as light meals in themselves, such as Scalloped Potatoes with Garlic or Cauliflower with Tomatoes and Cumin. There are also great ways to enliven those important greens, such as Kale with Mustard Dressing or Spiced Greens with Hemp Seeds.

Avocado guacamole

Often served as a dip with corn chips, this highly nutritious salsa is also great served alongside a main course. It is made from avocados, onion and tomatoes spiked with fresh chilli, crushed garlic, toasted cumin seeds and fresh lime juice. Half mash and half dice the avocados for a more interesting, chunky texture.

Serves 4

2 large ripe avocados
1 small red onion, finely chopped
1 fresh red or green chilli, seeded and
    very finely chopped
1 garlic clove, crushed
finely shredded rind of ½ lime and juice
    of 1–1½ limes
225g/8oz tomatoes, seeded and chopped
30ml/2 tbsp roughly chopped fresh
    coriander (cilantro)
2.5–5ml/½–1 tsp ground toasted
    cumin seeds
15ml/1 tbsp olive oil
ground black pepper
lime wedges and fresh coriander (cilantro)
    sprigs, to garnish
lightly salted corn chips, to serve (optional)

1 Cut one of the avocados in half and lift out and discard the stone (pit). Scrape the flesh from both halves into a bowl and mash it roughly with a fork.

2 Add the onion, chilli, garlic, lime rind, tomatoes and coriander and stir well. Add the ground cumin seeds and pepper to taste, then stir in the olive oil.

3 Halve and stone the remaining avocado. Dice the flesh and stir it into the guacamole.

4 Squeeze in fresh lime juice to taste, mix well, then cover and leave to stand for 15 minutes so that the flavour develops. Serve with lime wedges and garnish with fresh coriander sprigs.

Energy 187kcal/771kJ; Protein 2.4g; Carbohydrate 4.7g, of which sugars 3.3g; Fat 17.6g, of which saturates 3.5g; Cholesterol 0mg; Calcium 41mg; Fibre 4g; Sodium 14mg.

Cactus salsa

Often seen lurking in the background of Hollywood western movies, nopales are the tender, fleshy leaves, or paddles, of an edible cactus known variously as the cactus pear or the prickly pear cactus. They grow wild in Mexico and some areas of North America, but they are also cultivated and can be bought from specialist food stores and some large supermarkets.

Serves 4

2 fresh red fresno chillies
250g/9oz nopales (cactus paddles)
3 spring onions (scallions)
3 garlic cloves, peeled
½ red onion
100g/3¾oz fresh tomatillos
2.5ml/½ tsp salt
150ml/¼ pint/⅔ cup cider vinegar

1 Spear the chillies on a long-handled metal skewer and roast them over the flame of a gas burner until the skins blister and darken. Do not let the flesh burn. Alternatively, dry fry them in a griddle pan until the skins are scorched. Place the roasted chillies in a strong plastic bag and tie the top to keep the steam in. Set aside for 20 minutes.

2 Remove the chillies from the bag and peel off the skins. Cut off the stalks, then slit the chillies and scrape out the seeds. Chop the chillies roughly and set them aside.

3 Carefully remove the thorns from the nopales. Wearing gloves or holding each cactus paddle in turn with kitchen tongs, cut off the bumps that contain the thorns with a sharp knife.

4 Cut off and discard the thick base from each cactus paddle. Rinse the paddles well and cut them into strips, then cut the strips into small pieces.

5 Bring a large pan of lightly salted water to the boil. Add the cactus paddle pieces, spring onions and garlic. Boil for 10–15 minutes, until the paddle pieces are just tender.

6 Drain the mixture in a colander, rinse under cold running water to remove any remaining stickiness, then drain again. Discard the spring onions and garlic.

7 Chop the red onion and the tomatillos finely. Place in a bowl and add the cactus and chillies.

8 Spoon the mixture into a preserving jar, add the salt, pour in the vinegar and seal. Chill for at least a day, turning the jar occasionally to ensure that the nopales are marinated. The salsa will keep in the refrigerator for 10 days.

Energy 18kcal/79kJ; Protein 1.5g; Carbohydrate 2.8g, of which sugars 2.4g; Fat 0.3g, of which saturates 0g; Cholesterol 0mg; Calcium 72mg; Fibre 1.5g; Sodium 6mg.

Black bean salsa

This salsa has a fabulously striking appearance. It is rare to find a predominantly black dish and it provides a wonderful contrast to the more common reds and greens on the plate. The pasado chillies add a subtle citrus flavour. Leave the salsa for a day or two after preparing it to allow all the wonderful flavours to develop and mingle fully.

3 Spear the fresno chillies on a long-handled metal skewer and roast them over the flame of a gas burner until the skins blister and darken. Do not let the flesh burn. Alternatively, dry fry them in a griddle pan until the skins are scorched. Then place the roasted chillies in a strong plastic bag and tie the top to keep the steam in. Set aside for 20 minutes.

4 Meanwhile, chop the red onion finely. Remove the chillies from the bag and peel off the skins. Slit them, remove the seeds and chop them finely.

5 Transfer the beans into a bowl and add the onion and both types of chilli. Stir in the lime rind and juice, beer, oil and coriander. Season with salt and mix well. Chill before serving.

Serves 4

175g/6oz/1 cup black beans, soaked overnight in water to cover
1 pasado chilli
2 fresh red fresno chillies
1 red onion
grated rind and juice of 1 lime
30ml/2 tbsp Mexican beer (optional)
15ml/1 tbsp olive oil
small bunch of fresh coriander (cilantro), finely chopped
salt

1 Drain the beans and place in a large pan. Pour in water to cover and place the lid on the pan. Bring to the boil, then simmer for 40 minutes or until tender. They should still have a little bite. Drain, rinse under cold water, then drain again and set aside until cold.

2 Soak the pasado chilli in hot water for about 10 minutes until softened. Drain, remove the stalk, then slit the chilli and scrape out the seeds with a small sharp knife. Chop the flesh finely.

Cook's tip

Mexican beer is a light beer; Sol and Tecate are popular varieties.

Energy 109kcal/461kJ; Protein 6.6g; Carbohydrate 14g, of which sugars 1.1g; Fat 3.4g, of which saturates 0.5g; Cholesterol 0mg; Calcium 49mg; Fibre 2.7g; Sodium 9mg.

Spinach and raisins with pine nuts

It is impossible to have too many vegan recipes that show new and delicious ways to prepare spinach. This makes a change from the classic creamy garlicky spinach dishes. It makes an excellent filling wrapped up in filo pastry to serve as finger food at a party. The combination of raisins, nuts and tangy onions make this a truly delectable accompaniment to a larger meal.

Serves 4

60ml/4 tbsp raisins
1kg/2¼lb fresh spinach leaves, washed
45ml/3 tbsp olive oil
6–8 spring onions (scallions), thinly sliced
 or 1–2 small yellow or white onions,
 finely chopped
60ml/4 tbsp pine nuts
salt and ground black pepper

1 Put the raisins into a small bowl and pour over boiling water to cover. Leave to stand for about 10 minutes until plumped up, then drain.

2 Steam or cook the spinach in a pan over a medium-high heat, with only the water that clings to the leaves after washing, for 1–2 minutes until the leaves are bright green and wilted. Remove from the heat and drain well. Leave to cool.

3 When the spinach has cooled, chop roughly with a sharp knife.

Variations
• Add goji berries instead of raisins.
• Try using apricot kernels instead of the pine nuts.

4 Heat the oil in a frying pan over a medium-low heat, then lower the heat further and add the spring onions or onions. Fry for about 5 minutes, or until soft, then add the spinach, raisins and pine nuts. Raise the heat and cook for 2–3 minutes to warm through. Season with salt and ground black pepper to taste and serve immediately.

Energy 206kcal/855kJ; Protein 5.8g; Carbohydrate 15.5g, of which sugars 11.1g; Fat 13.8g, of which saturates 1.6g; Cholesterol 0mg; Calcium 228mg; Fibre 3.4g; Sodium 218mg.

Charred artichokes with lemon oil

There is no reason why you have to miss out on summer barbecues as a vegan. Many vegetables make great kebabs, and these young artichokes are delicious cooked over charcoal. They are also good roasted in the oven, as here. Store any surplus in olive oil in the refrigerator.

Serves 2–4

15ml/1 tbsp lemon juice or white wine vinegar
2 globe artichokes
45ml/3 tbsp olive oil
sea salt
sprigs of fresh flat leaf parsley, to garnish

For the lemon oil dip
12 garlic cloves, unpeeled
1 lemon
45ml/3 tbsp extra virgin olive oil

Cook's tip
This is a perfect dish to have alongside a vegan pizza.

1 Preheat the oven to 200°C/400°F/ Gas 6. Stir the lemon juice or vinegar into a bowl of cold water.

2 Cut each artichoke lengthways into wedges. Pull the hairy choke out from the centre of each wedge and drop the pieces into the acidulated water.

3 Drain the artichokes and place in a roasting pan with the garlic cloves. Toss in the oil. Sprinkle with salt and roast for 40 minutes, stirring once or twice, until the artichokes are tender.

4 Meanwhile, make the dip. Pare away two strips of rind from the lemon and scrape away any pith. Place the rind in a pan with water to cover. Simmer for 5 minutes, then drain, refresh in cold water and chop roughly.

5 Arrange the artichokes on a plate and set aside to cool for 5 minutes. Flatten the garlic cloves so that the flesh pops out of the skins.

6 Transfer the garlic flesh to a bowl, mash to a purée, then add the lemon rind. Squeeze the lemon juice into the bowl. Stir in the extra virgin olive oil and, using a fork or whisk, stir until the mixture is well combined.

7 Serve the artichokes warm. Garnish them with the parsley and serve the lemon dip alongside.

Energy 165kcal/679kJ; Protein 1.3g; Carbohydrate 2.6g, of which sugars 0.8g; Fat 16.7g, of which saturates 2.4g; Cholesterol 0mg; Calcium 24mg; Fibre 1.1g; Sodium 31mg.

Marinated mushrooms

These succulent mushrooms make a fabulous alternative to traditional garlic mushrooms.
Experiment with different varieties of the many wild mushrooms now available in food stores.
Serve with plenty of home-made wholemeal bread to mop up the delicious juices.

Serves 4

30ml/2 tbsp olive oil
1 small onion, very finely chopped
1 garlic clove, finely chopped
15ml/1 tbsp tomato purée (paste)
50ml/2fl oz/¼ cup sherry
50ml/2fl oz/¼ cup vegetable stock
2 cloves
225g/8oz/3 cups button (white) mushrooms
salt and ground black pepper
chopped fresh parsley, to garnish

Cook's tip
In Spain, wild mushrooms, known
as setas, are served in this way.

1 Heat the oil in a pan. Add the onion
and garlic and cook until soft. Stir in the
tomato purée, sherry, stock and the
cloves and season with salt and pepper.

2 Bring to the boil, cover and simmer
gently for 45 minutes, adding more
water if it becomes too dry.

3 Add the mushrooms to the pan, then
cover and allow to simmer for about
5 minutes.

4 Remove from the heat and allow to
cool, still covered. Chill in the refrigerator
overnight. Serve the mushrooms cold,
sprinkled with fresh parsley.

Energy 80kcal/329kJ; Protein 1.4g; Carbohydrate 2.1g, of which sugars 1.7g; Fat 5.8g, of which saturates 0.9g; Cholesterol 0mg; Calcium 9mg; Fibre 0.9g; Sodium 14mg.

Cauliflower with tomatoes and cumin

This recipe makes an excellent side dish to serve alongside vegetable kebabs or tofu burgers. It is also a great addition to a buffet or served with other tapas dishes.

Serves 4

30ml/2 tbsp sunflower or olive oil
1 onion, chopped
1 garlic clove, crushed
1 small cauliflower, broken into florets
5ml/1 tsp cumin seeds
a good pinch of ground ginger
4 tomatoes, peeled, seeded and quartered
15–30ml/1–2 tbsp lemon juice (optional)
30ml/2 tbsp chopped fresh coriander
   (cilantro) (optional)
salt and ground black pepper

Variation
Whole cherry tomatoes can also be used in this dish instead of the tomato slices.

1 Heat the oil in a heavy pan, add the onion and garlic. Stir-fry for 2–3 minutes until the onion is softened. Add the cauliflower and stir-fry for 2–3 minutes until the cauliflower is flecked with brown.

2 Add the cumin seeds and ginger, fry briskly for 1 minute, and then add the tomato wedges, 175ml/6fl oz/¾ cup water and some salt and pepper.

3 Bring to the boil and then reduce the heat, cover with a plate or with foil and simmer for 6–7 minutes, until the cauliflower is just tender.

4 Stir in a little lemon juice, if using, to sharpen the flavour. Taste and adjust the seasoning if necessary. Sprinkle over the chopped coriander, if using, and serve immediately.

Roast vegetable salad

Roasting vegetables in the oven helps to concentrate all the delicious flavours and adds a lovely hint of smokiness. This versatile salad can be served hot with practically anything.

Serves 4

8 chestnut mushrooms
2–3 courgettes (zucchini)
1 Spanish (Bermuda) onion
2 red (bell) peppers
16 cherry tomatoes
2 garlic cloves, chopped
pinch of cumin seeds
5ml/1 tsp fresh thyme or 4–5 torn basil leaves
60ml/4 tbsp olive oil
juice of ½ lemon
5–10ml/1–2 tsp harissa or Tabasco sauce
fresh thyme sprigs, to garnish

Cook's tip
Try roasting the vegetables with added chunks of tofu for some extra protein.

1 Preheat the oven to 220°C/425°F/Gas 7. Halve the mushrooms. Top and tail the courgettes and cut into long strips. Cut the onion into thin wedges. Halve the peppers, discard the seeds and core, and cut into bitesize chunks.

2 Place the vegetables in a cast iron dish or roasting pan, add the tomatoes, garlic, cumin seeds and thyme or basil. Sprinkle with olive oil and toss to coat.

3 Place the pan in the oven and leave for 25–30 minutes until the vegetables are very soft and tender and slightly charred at the edges.

4 Put the lemon juice into a bowl and stir in the harissa or Tabasco sauce. Pour over the vegetables and gently toss to coat evenly. Serve immediately while still hot, garnished with the fresh thyme sprigs.

Energy 106kcal/441kJ; Protein 4.5g; Carbohydrate 7.3g, of which sugars 6.5g; Fat 6.7g, of which saturates 1g; Cholesterol 0mg; Calcium 32mg; Fibre 3g; Sodium 19mg.
Energy 319kcal/1343kJ; Protein 8.8g; Carbohydrate 49.6g, of which sugars 8g; Fat 10.8g, of which saturates 1.6g; Cholesterol 0mg; Calcium 34mg; Fibre 4g; Sodium 9mg.

Cauliflower with garlic crumbs

This dish makes a great appetizer served with chutney or a spicy fruit sauce. It also perfectly complements filo pastry dishes or can be eaten as a healthy lunch with a crisp green salad.

2 Heat 60–75ml/4–5 tbsp of the olive or vegetable oil in a frying pan. Add the breadcrumbs and cook over a medium heat, tossing and turning, until evenly browned and crisp.

3 Add the garlic to the pan. Stir once or twice for 2 minutes. Remove the breadcrumbs and garlic from the pan and set aside.

4 Heat the remaining oil in the pan, then add the cauliflower, mashing and breaking it up a little as it lightly browns in the oil. (Do not overcook, but just cook lightly in the oil.)

5 Add the garlic breadcrumbs to the pan and cook, stirring, until well combined and some of the cauliflower is still holding its shape. Season with salt and pepper and serve hot or warm.

Serves 4–6

600ml/1 pint/2½ cups vegetable stock
1 large cauliflower, cut into bitesize florets
90–120ml/6–8 tbsp olive or vegetable oil
130g/4½oz/2¼ cups dry white or wholemeal (whole-wheat) breadcrumbs
3–5 garlic cloves, thinly sliced or chopped
salt and ground black pepper

Variation
You can swap the breadcrumbs for rolled oats, if you prefer.

1 Pour the vegetable stock into a large pan and bring to the boil. Add a pinch of salt and the cauliflower florets. Simmer until just tender. Drain and leave to cool.

Cook's tip
Try serving this dish as they do in Italy: with cooked pasta such as spaghetti or rigatoni.

Energy 244kcal/1016kJ; Protein 8.9g; Carbohydrate 18.8g, of which sugars 2.2g; Fat 15.3g, of which saturates 3.8g; Cholesterol 10mg; Calcium 162mg; Fibre 1.7g; Sodium 280mg.

Spiced greens with hemp seeds

Here is a perfect way to enliven your greens. It works well with crunchy cabbages but is also good for kale and other purple sprouting leaves – even Brussels sprout tops can be used.

Serves 4

1 medium cabbage, or the equivalent in
  quantity of your chosen green vegetable
15ml/1 tbsp groundnut (peanut) oil
5ml/1 tsp grated fresh root ginger
2 garlic cloves, crushed
2 shallots, finely chopped
2 red chillies, seeded and finely sliced
30ml/2 tbsp hemp seeds
salt and ground black pepper

Cook's tip
This dish is the perfect way to encourage children to get their fill of nutritious leafy green vegetables.

1 Remove any tough outer leaves from the cabbage then quarter it and remove the core. Shred the leaves.

2 Pour the groundnut oil into a large pan and as it heats stir in the ginger and garlic. Add the shallots and as the pan becomes hotter add the chillies.

3 Add the greens and toss to mix thoroughly. Cover the pan and reduce the heat. Cook, shaking the pan occasionally, for about 3–5 minutes. Remove the lid and increase the heat to dry off the steam. Add the hemp seeds, season with salt and pepper and cook for a further minute. Serve immediately.

Energy 77kcal/322kJ; Protein 2.6g; Carbohydrate 9.9g, of which sugars 9.4g; Fat 3.1g, of which saturates 0.5g; Cholesterol 0mg; Calcium 90mg; Fibre 3.9g; Sodium 13mg.

Kale with mustard dressing

This is a winter dish from Ireland, where sea kale is a popular vegetable. Its pale green fronds have a slightly nutty taste. Use curly kale or a dark green cabbage if sea kale is unavailable, although you will need to boil it briefly for a few minutes before chilling and serving.

Serves 4

250g/9oz sea kale or curly kale
45ml/3 tbsp light olive oil
5ml/1 tsp wholegrain mustard
15ml/1 tbsp white wine vinegar
5ml/1 tsp agave syrup
salt and ground black pepper

1 Wash the kale, drain, then trim it and tear into pieces. Cook briefly if needed.

2 Whisk the oil into the mustard in a bowl. When it is blended completely, whisk in the white wine vinegar. It should begin to thicken.

3 Season the mustard dressing to taste with agave syrup, a little salt and plenty of ground black pepper.

4 Toss the sea kale in the dressing and serve immediately.

Energy 99kcal/409kJ; Protein 2.1g; Carbohydrate 1.9g, of which sugars 1.9g; Fat 9.3g, of which saturates 1.3g; Cholesterol 0mg; Calcium 82mg; Fibre 1.9g; Sodium 27mg.

Sweet potato and beetroot with coconut

This dish benefits from the wonderful sweetness that develops when the vegetables are oven roasted. The potatoes and beetroot are perfectly complemented by the savoury onions, and the aromatic coriander, coconut, ginger and garlic paste adds an irresistible spicy fragrance.

Serves 4–6

30ml/2 tbsp groundnut (peanut) oil
  or mild olive oil
450g/1lb sweet potatoes, peeled
  and cut into thick strips or chunks
4 beetroot (beets), cooked, peeled
  and cut into wedges
450g/1lb small red or yellow onions, halved
5ml/1 tsp coriander seeds, lightly crushed
3–4 small whole fresh red chillies
salt and ground black pepper
chopped fresh coriander (cilantro), to garnish

For the paste
2 large garlic cloves, chopped
1–2 green chillies, seeded and chopped
15ml/1 tbsp chopped fresh root ginger
45ml/3 tbsp chopped fresh coriander (cilantro)
75ml/5 tbsp coconut milk
30ml/2 tbsp groundnut (peanut) oil
  or mild olive oil
grated rind of ½ lime
5ml/1 tsp agave syrup

1 First make the spicy paste. Put the garlic, chillies, ginger, coriander and coconut milk in a food processor or blender. Process the mixture until it is thoroughly combined.

2 Transfer the paste into a small mixing bowl. Pour in the groundnut or olive oil, add the lime rind and the agave syrup. Whisk the mixture with a fork until all the ingredients are well combined. Meanwhile, preheat the oven to 200°C/ 400°F/Gas 6.

3 Heat the oil in a roasting pan in the oven for 5 minutes. Add the sweet potatoes, beetroot, onions and coriander seeds, tossing them in the hot oil. Roast for 10 minutes.

4 Stir the paste and the whole red chillies into the vegetables in the pan. Season well with salt and ground black pepper. Gently toss the vegetables to coat them thoroughly with the paste.

5 Roast the vegetables for a further 25–35 minutes, or until the sweet potatoes and onions are fully cooked and tender. Stir 2–3 times during cooking to prevent the paste from sticking to the pan.

6 Serve the vegetables immediately, garnished with fresh coriander.

Energy 272kcal/1143kJ; Protein 4.4g; Carbohydrate 39.8g, of which sugars 19.1g; Fat 11.8g, of which saturates 1.7g; Cholesterol 0mg; Calcium 98mg; Fibre 6.3g; Sodium 122mg.

Grilled leek and fennel salad with tomato dressing

This is an excellent salad to make when young leeks are in season and ripe tomatoes are full of flavour. It makes a fabulous accompaniment to a vegan pizza or grilled vegetable kebabs.

Serves 6

675g/1½lb leeks
2 large fennel bulbs
120ml/4fl oz/½ cup extra virgin olive oil
2 shallots, chopped
150ml/¼ pint/⅔ cup dry white wine
   or white vermouth
5ml/1 tsp fennel seeds, crushed
6 fresh thyme sprigs
2–3 bay leaves
good pinch of dried red chilli flakes
350g/12oz ripe tomatoes, peeled,
   seeded and diced
5ml/1 tsp sun-dried tomato paste (optional)
salt and ground black pepper
75g/3oz/¾ cup small black olives,
   to serve

2 Trim the fennel bulbs, reserving any tops for the garnish, if you like, and cut the bulbs either into thin slices or into thicker wedges, according to taste.

3 Cook the fennel in the reserved cooking water for about 5 minutes, then drain thoroughly and toss with 30ml/2 tbsp of the olive oil. Season to taste with black pepper.

6 Add the diced tomatoes to the pan and cook briskly for about 5–8 minutes, or until they have reduced and the consistency of the mixture has thickened slightly.

7 Add the sun-dried tomato paste, if using. Taste and adjust the seasoning if necessary.

1 Cook the leeks in boiling salted water for 4–5 minutes. Use a slotted spoon to remove them and place in a colander to drain thoroughly. Leave to cool. Reserve the cooking water in the pan. Squeeze out any excess water from the leeks and cut into 7.5cm/3in lengths.

Cook's tip
When buying fennel, look for rounded bulbs; they have a better shape for this dish. The flesh should be crisp and white, with no signs of bruising. Avoid specimens with broken leaves or with brown or dried-out patches.

4 Heat a ridged cast-iron griddle until very hot. Arrange the leeks and fennel on the griddle and cook, turning once or twice, until they have deep brown stripes across them. Remove the vegetables from the griddle, place them in a large shallow dish and set aside.

5 Place the remaining olive oil, the shallots, white wine or vermouth, crushed fennel seeds, thyme, bay leaves and chilli flakes in a large pan. Bring the mixture to the boil over a medium heat. Lower the heat and simmer for about 10 minutes.

8 Pour the tomato dressing over the leeks and fennel in the dish. Toss all the vegetables gently to mix in the tomato dressing, then set the dish aside to cool.

9 When ready to serve, stir the salad once more and then sprinkle over the fennel tops, if using. Serve with black olives.

Health benefit
Leeks provide useful levels of iron as well as the antioxidants carotene and vitamins E and C.

Energy 193kcal/801kJ; Protein 2.8g; Carbohydrate 6.7g, of which sugars 5.9g; Fat 14.7g, of which saturates 2.2g; Cholesterol 0mg; Calcium 53mg; Fibre 4.6g; Sodium 297mg.

Hot vegetable and tarragon salad

This delicious side dish contains a variety of tender young vegetables, which are just lightly cooked to bring out their different flavours and to retain as much nutrient value as possible. The tarragon adds a wonderful depth of flavour to this bright, fresh dish.

Serves 4

5 spring onions (scallions)
30ml/2 tbsp olive oil
1 garlic clove, crushed
115g/4oz asparagus tips
115g/4oz mangetouts (snow peas), trimmed
115g/4oz broad (fava) beans
2 Little Gem (Bibb) lettuces
5ml/1 tsp finely chopped fresh tarragon
ground black pepper

1 Cut the spring onions into quarters lengthways with a sharp knife. Heat the olive oil in a large frying pan, add the spring onions and the crushed garlic and fry gently over a medium-low heat for a few minutes, until softened.

2 Add the asparagus tips, mangetouts and broad beans to the pan and stir around. Mix well, covering all the vegetables with oil.

3 Just cover the base of the pan with water, season with pepper, and allow to simmer gently for a few minutes.

4 Cut the lettuce into quarters with a sharp knife and add to the frying pan. Cook for 3 minutes, then remove the pan from the heat.

5 Transfer the cooked vegetables to a warmed serving dish, add the chopped tarragon, and serve immediately.

Energy 124kcal/515kJ; Protein 5.1g; Carbohydrate 6.8g, of which sugars 3.5g; Fat 8.7g, of which saturates 3.8g; Cholesterol 13mg; Calcium 62mg; Fibre 3.9g; Sodium 44mg.

Garlic and potato mash

These creamy mashed potatoes are perfect with all kinds of roast or grilled vegetables – and although it seems a lot of garlic is used, the flavour is deliciously sweet and subtle when cooked in this way. Try adding some nori seaweed flakes for a tasty and nutritious twist.

Serves 6–8

2 garlic bulbs, separated into
  cloves, unpeeled
115g/4oz/½ cup soya margarine
1.3kg/3lb baking potatoes
120–175ml/4–6fl oz/½–¾ cup soya milk
salt and white pepper

1 Bring a small pan of water to the boil over a high heat. Add the garlic cloves and boil for about 2–3 minutes, then drain and peel.

2 In a heavy frying pan, melt half the margarine over a low heat. Add the blanched garlic cloves, then cover and cook gently for 20–25 minutes until very tender and just golden, shaking the pan and stirring occasionally. Do not allow the garlic to scorch or brown.

3 Remove the pan from the heat. Spoon the garlic and any margarine into a blender or a food processor and process until smooth. Transfer to a small bowl, cover the surface to prevent a skin forming and set aside.

4 Peel and quarter the potatoes, place in a large pan and add enough cold water to just cover them. Salt the water generously and bring to the boil over a high heat. Reduce the heat and simmer the potatoes until tender.

5 Drain the potatoes then work through a food mill or press through a sieve (strainer) back into the pan.

6 Return the pan to a medium heat and, using a wooden spoon, stir the potatoes for about 1–2 minutes to dry them out completely. Remove the pan from the heat.

7 Warm the milk over a medium-high heat until bubbles form. Gradually beat the soya milk, remaining margarine and reserved garlic purée into the potatoes, then season with salt, if needed, and white pepper. Serve immediately.

Energy 261kcal/1093kJ; Protein 5g; Carbohydrate 33.3g, of which sugars 3.8g; Fat 12.8g, of which saturates 7.9g; Cholesterol 32mg; Calcium 43mg; Fibre 2.4g; Sodium 118mg.

Roasted rosemary new potatoes

These new potatoes, flavoured with fresh rosemary and lots of garlic, are excellent with vegetable stews but equally perfect with a Sunday nut roast, pie or even a salad.

Serves 4

800g/1¾lb small new potatoes
5 garlic cloves, peeled and bruised
3 rosemary sprigs
30ml/2 tbsp olive oil
sea salt and ground black pepper

Health benefit
Garlic is particularly valued for its ability to boost the immune system.

1 Preheat the oven to 200°C/400°F/ Gas 6. Put the potatoes, garlic and rosemary in a roasting pan and drizzle with the oil to coat. Season well.

3 Discard the rosemary and garlic from the pan, if you wish, and serve.

Cook's tip
Garlic cloves lose their pungency when roasted, becoming sweeter.

2 Bake for 40–45 minutes, shaking halfway through cooking, until the potatoes are crisp on the outside and soft in the centre.

Variation
Shallots can be roasted in the same way. Cook for 35 minutes or until they are tender.

Orange-glazed carrots

Naturally sweet carrots, combined with a glossy sweet mustard glaze, make a healthy and delicious accompaniment to all sorts of vegan main courses.

Serves 4

450g/1lb carrots, cut into
  thick matchsticks
25g/1oz/2 tbsp soya margarine
15ml/1 tbsp olive oil
1 garlic clove, crushed
15ml/1 tbsp chopped fresh
  rosemary leaves
5ml/1 tsp Dijon mustard
10ml/2 tsp agave syrup

1 Steam the carrot matchsticks in a steamer over a pan of boiling water for 2–4 minutes.

2 Heat the soya margarine and oil in a heavy pan, add the garlic and rosemary and cook, stirring, for 1 minute or until the garlic is golden brown. Ensure that it does not burn, otherwise it will taste bitter and spoil the sweetness of the dish.

Health benefit
Carrots are a rich source of beta carotene, the plant form of vitamin A. One carrot can supply the body with enough of this vitamin for an entire day.

3 Add the carrots, Dijon mustard and agave syrup to the pan, and cook, stirring constantly, for 2–3 minutes or until the carrots are only just tender. Serve immediately.

Energy 691kcal/2900kJ; Protein 24.9g; Carbohydrate 85.3g, of which sugars 6.4g; Fat 30.2g, of which saturates 10.6g; Cholesterol 39mg; Calcium 410mg; Fibre 4.2g; Sodium 620mg.
Energy 122kcal/507kJ; Protein 1g; Carbohydrate 11.1g, of which sugars 10.4g; Fat 8.6g, of which saturates 2.8g; Cholesterol 1mg; Calcium 32mg; Fibre 2.7g; Sodium 85mg.

Stir-fried pineapple and ginger

This dish makes an interesting accompaniment to tofu dishes. If the idea seems strange, think of it as resembling a fresh mango chutney, but with pineapple as the principal ingredient.

Serves 4

1 pineapple
15ml/1 tbsp vegetable oil
2 garlic cloves, finely chopped
2 shallots, finely chopped
5cm/2in piece fresh root ginger, peeled and finely shredded
30ml/2 tbsp light soy sauce
juice of ½ lime
1 large fresh red chilli, seeded and finely shredded

Variation
Peaches or nectarines can be substituted for the diced pineapple.

1 Trim and peel the pineapple. Cut out the core and dice the flesh.

2 Heat the oil in a wok or frying pan. Stir-fry the garlic and shallots over a medium heat for 2–3 minutes, until golden. Do not let the garlic burn or the dish will taste bitter.

3 Add the pineapple. Stir-fry for about 2 minutes, or until the pineapple cubes start to turn golden on the edges.

4 Add the ginger, soy sauce, lime juice and shredded chilli. Toss together until well mixed. Cook over a low heat for a further 2 minutes, then serve.

Energy 89kcal/375kJ; Protein 0.7g; Carbohydrate 14.1g, of which sugars 13.7g; Fat 3.7g, of which saturates 0.4g; Cholesterol 0mg; Calcium 27mg; Fibre 1.8g; Sodium 3mg.

Scalloped potatoes with garlic

This tasty side dish goes perfectly with chunky vegetable stews or can be enjoyed as a light lunch on its own. Cooking the potatoes in stock gives them a deliciously rich flavour.

Serves 4–6

900g/2lb waxy potatoes, peeled and
  thinly sliced
450ml/¾ pint/scant 2 cups vegetable stock
15g/½oz/1 tbsp soya magarine or
  dairy-free spread
1 large onion, very finely sliced into rings
2–4 garlic cloves, finely chopped
2.5ml/½ tsp dried thyme
60ml/4 tbsp rolled oats
30ml/2 tbsp olive oil
sea salt and ground black pepper

3 Carefully arrange an overlapping layer of potato slices on top of the onion mixture. Continue to layer the ingredients in the dish in this way until all the onions, garlic, herbs and potatoes are used up, finishing with a layer of sliced potatoes.

Variation
To vary the flavour, try substituting chopped rosemary or sage in place of the dried thyme.

4 Sprinkle over the oats, drizzle with the oil and season with salt and pepper. Bake for about 30 minutes until crispy and golden on top. Serve immediately.

1 Preheat the oven to 180°C/350°F/ Gas 4. Bring the stock to the boil in a pan. Add the potatoes and simmer for 6–7 minutes until just tender but not breaking apart.

2 Grease a baking tray with the soya margarine or spread. Place a layer of onions in the tray, then sprinkle over a little of the chopped garlic, thyme, salt and pepper.

Energy 213kcal/898kJ; Protein 4.4g; Carbohydrate 34.8g, of which sugars 4.3g; Fat 7.2g, of which saturates 1.6g; Cholesterol 0mg; Calcium 25mg; Fibre 2.8g; Sodium 153mg.

Potatoes with chilli beans

East meets West in this delicious side dish, with potatoes and beans given a distinctly Chinese twist. It can also be enjoyed as a light meal on its own when you fancy a dish with a little kick.

Serves 4

4 medium firm or waxy potatoes,
    cut into thick chunks
30ml/2 tbsp sunflower or groundnut
    (peanut) oil
3 spring onions (scallions), sliced
1 large fresh red chilli, seeded
    and thinly sliced
2 garlic cloves, crushed
400g/14oz can red kidney beans, drained
30ml/2 tbsp soy sauce
15ml/1 tbsp sesame oil
salt and ground black pepper
15ml/1 tbsp sesame seeds,
    to garnish
chopped fresh coriander (cilantro)
    or parsley, to garnish

1 Cook the potatoes in boiling water until they are just tender. Take care not to overcook them. Drain and set aside.

2 Heat the oil in a large frying pan or wok over a medium-high heat. Add the spring onions and chilli and stir-fry for about 1 minute, then add the garlic and stir-fry for a few seconds longer.

3 Add the potatoes, stirring well, then the beans and finally the soy sauce and sesame oil.

4 Season to taste with salt and pepper and continue to cook the vegetables until they are heated through. Sprinkle with the sesame seeds and the coriander or parsley and serve immediately.

Tomato and potato bake

An adaptation of a classic Greek dish, which is usually cooked on top of the stove. This recipe has a richer, deeper flavour as it is stove cooked first before being baked in the oven.

Serves 4

120ml/4fl oz/½ cup olive oil
1 large onion, finely chopped
3 garlic cloves, crushed
4 large ripe tomatoes, peeled,
    deseeded and chopped
1kg/2¼lb firm or waxy potatoes
salt and ground black pepper
flat leaf parsley, to garnish

1 Preheat the oven to 180°C/350°F/ Gas 4. Heat the oil in a flameproof casserole. Fry the onion and garlic for 5 minutes until beginning to soften and just starting to brown.

Cook's tip
Make sure that the potatoes are completely coated in the oil for even cooking.

2 Add the tomatoes to the pan, season with salt and pepper and cook, stirring constantly, for 1 minute.

3 Cut the potatoes into wedges. Add to the pan. Cook, stirring, for 10 minutes. Season again and cover with a lid.

4 Place the casserole in the middle of the oven and bake for 45–50 minutes until the potatoes are tender. Serve immediately, garnished with parsley.

Energy 272kcal/1141kJ; Protein 9.7g; Carbohydrate 34.8g, of which sugars 5.7g; Fat 11.4g, of which saturates 1.6g; Cholesterol 0mg; Calcium 107mg; Fibre 7.6g; Sodium 936mg.
Energy 415kcal/1735kJ; Protein 6g; Carbohydrate 50.5g, of which sugars 11.2g; Fat 22.4g, of which saturates 3.3g; Cholesterol 0mg; Calcium 45mg; Fibre 4.7g; Sodium 37mg.

Escalivada

The Catalan name of this celebrated dish means 'baked over embers', but it can also be very successfully baked in the oven and is just as delicious. Cooking vegetables using this method is great for vegans as it helps to concentrate their flavours, resulting in an extremely tasty dish.

Serves 4

2–3 courgettes (zucchini)
1 large fennel bulb
1 Spanish (Bermuda) onion
2 large red (bell) peppers
450g/1lb butternut squash
6 garlic cloves, unpeeled
75ml/5 tbsp olive oil
juice of ½ lemon
pinch of cumin seeds, crushed
4 sprigs fresh thyme
4 medium tomatoes
salt and ground black pepper

1 Preheat the oven to 220°C/425°F/ Gas 7. Cut the courgettes lengthways into four pieces.

2 Cut the fennel into wedges of a similar size. Slice the onion lengthways into chunks. Halve and seed the peppers, and slice thickly lengthways.

3 Cut the squash into thick chunks. Smash the garlic cloves with the flat of a knife, but leave the skins on.

4 Choose a roasting pan into which all the vegetables will fit in roughly one layer. Put in all the vegetables except the tomatoes.

5 Mix together the oil and lemon juice. Pour over the vegetables and toss to coat. Sprinkle with the cumin seeds, season and add the thyme sprigs. Roast for 20 minutes.

6 Remove the pan and gently toss the vegetables. Cut the tomatoes into wedges and add to the pan. Cook for 15–20 minutes, or until the vegetables are tender and slightly charred around the edges. Serve immediately.

Variation
You can vary the vegetables according to what is in season. Baby vegetables are excellent roasted. Look out for tiny fennel and young leeks in season.

Energy 209kcal/864kJ; Protein 4.6g; Carbohydrate 14.3g, of which sugars 13g; Fat 15.1g, of which saturates 2.4g; Cholesterol 0mg; Calcium 86mg; Fibre 5.6g; Sodium 17mg.

Aubergines in red wine

Apparently it was the Arabs who introduced this strange looking vegetable to Spain, where it was cooked with the Arab flavourings of cumin and garlic. Later, dishes similar to French ratatouille became popular using aubergine as one of the main ingredients.

Serves 4

1 large aubergine (eggplant)
60–90ml/4–6 tbsp olive oil
2 shallots, thinly sliced
4 tomatoes, quartered
2 garlic cloves, thinly sliced
60ml/4 tbsp red wine
30ml/2 tbsp chopped fresh parsley,
  plus extra to garnish
30–45ml/2–3 tbsp extra virgin
  olive oil (if serving cold)
salt and ground black pepper

1 Slice the aubergine into 1cm/½in rounds. Place them in a large colander and sprinkle with 5–10ml/1–2 tsp salt. Leave to drain for 30 minutes.

2 Rinse the aubergine slices well, then press between several layers of kitchen paper to remove any excess liquid.

3 Heat 30ml/2 tbsp of the oil in a large frying pan until smoking. Add one layer of aubergine slices and fry, turning once, until golden brown. Transfer to a plate covered with kitchen paper. Heat more oil in the pan and fry the second batch in the same way.

4 Heat 15ml/1 tbsp of oil in the pan and cook the shallots for 5 minutes until golden.

5 Cut the aubergine slices into strips. Add these to the shallots with the tomatoes, garlic and wine. Cover the pan and simmer for 30 minutes, stirring from time to time.

6 Stir in the parsley, and check the seasonings, adjusting if necessary. Garnish with a little more parsley and serve immediately if you want it hot. To serve cold, drizzle a little extra virgin olive oil over the dish and bring it to room temperature before serving.

Energy 137kcal/569kJ; Protein 1.6g; Carbohydrate 4.8g, of which sugars 4.6g; Fat 11.7g, of which saturates 1.7g; Cholesterol 0mg; Calcium 34mg; Fibre 2.8g; Sodium 15mg.

Sichuan spiced aubergine

This straightforward yet versatile vegan dish is based on the style of cooking in the Chinese province of Sichuan. It can be served hot, warm or cold, as the occasion demands. Topped with a sprinkling of toasted sesame seeds, it is easy to prepare and tastes absolutely wonderful.

Serves 4–6

2 aubergines (eggplants), total weight
  about 600g/1lb 6oz, cut into
  large chunks
15ml/1 tbsp salt
5ml/1 tsp chilli powder, or to taste
75–90ml/5–6 tbsp sunflower oil
15ml/1 tbsp rice wine
100ml/3½fl oz/scant ½ cup water
salt and ground black pepper
a few toasted sesame seeds,
  to garnish

For the chilli sauce
15–30ml/1–2 tbsp chilli paste
2 garlic cloves, crushed
15ml/1 tbsp dark soy sauce
15ml/1 tbsp rice vinegar
10ml/2 tsp light soy sauce

1 Put all the chilli sauce ingredients in a jug (pitcher) and mix well. Set aside.

2 Place the aubergine chunks on a plate, sprinkle them with the salt and leave to stand for 15–20 minutes.

3 Rinse well, drain and dry thoroughly on kitchen paper. Toss the aubergine cubes in the chilli powder.

4 Heat the oil in a wok. Add the aubergine chunks and the rice wine. Cook, stirring constantly, until the aubergine chunks start to brown. Stir in the water, cover the wok and steam for 2–3 minutes. Add the chilli sauce and cook for 2 minutes. Season to taste, then transfer to a serving dish, garnish with sesame seeds and serve.

Kan Shao green beans

This is a delicious Sichuan-inspired dish suitable for vegans. Kan Shao means 'dry-cooked' – meaning no stock or water is used. The slim green beans, usually available all the year round, are ideal in this quick and easy recipe. Other long green beans can be substituted.

Serves 6

175ml/6fl oz/¾ cup sunflower oil
450/1lb fresh green beans, topped,
  tailed and cut in half
1cm/½in piece fresh root ginger,
  peeled and cut into matchsticks
5ml/1 tsp agave syrup
10ml/2 tsp light soy sauce
salt and ground black pepper

Variation
This simple recipe works just as well with various other fresh green vegetables. Try replacing the green beans with baby asparagus spears or okra, cut into chunks.

1 Heat the oil in a wok. When the oil is just beginning to smoke, carefully add the beans and fry them for about 1–2 minutes until just tender.

2 Lift out the green beans on to a plate lined with kitchen paper. Using a ladle carefully remove all but 30ml/2 tbsp of oil from the wok.

3 Reheat the remaining oil, add the ginger and stir-fry for a minute or two to flavour the oil.

4 Return the green beans to the wok, stir in the agave syrup and soy sauce and season with salt and pepper. Toss together quickly to ensure the beans are well coated. Serve immediately.

Energy 108kcal/448kJ; Protein 1.5g; Carbohydrate 3.7g, of which sugars 2.2g; Fat 9.6g, of which saturates 1.2g; Cholesterol 0mg; Calcium 13mg; Fibre 2.5g; Sodium 3mg.
Energy 170kcal/698kJ; Protein 1.5g; Carbohydrate 3.2g, of which sugars 2.6g; Fat 16.9g, of which saturates 2.1g; Cholesterol 0mg; Calcium 28mg; Fibre 1.7g; Sodium 119mg.

desserts

There is a wide variety of tempting desserts that can be enjoyed while following a vegan lifestyle. This chapter features delicious ideas that provide a great opportunity to include plenty of vitamin-packed fruit in your diet, from the exotic Piquant Fruit Salad to the refreshing Pineapple with Coconut Rum. There are also more indulgent treats that many people believe vegans have to go without, such as Tofu Berry Cheesecake, Plum Charlottes with Calvados Cream and Baked Pumpkin with Coconut Custard. In addition, you will find you are spoilt for choice with the delectable ice creams and sorbets.

Date and tofu ice

Generously spiced with cinnamon and full of dried fruit, this delicious and unusual ice cream is also packed with plenty of soya protein. It also contains omega 3 fats and no added sugar.

Serves 4

250g/9oz/1½ cups stoned (pitted) dates
600ml/1 pint/2½ cups apple juice
5ml/1 tsp ground cinnamon
285g/10½oz pack chilled fresh tofu, cubed
150ml/¼ pint/⅔ cup unsweetened soya milk
60ml/4 tbsp hemp or flax oil
8 walnut halves, to decorate

1 Put the dates in a pan. Pour in 300ml/½ pint/1¼ cups of the apple juice and set aside to let the dates soak in the juice for 2 hours.

2 Bring the mixture to the boil and then simmer gently for 10 minutes. Set aside to cool then, using a slotted spoon, lift out about one-quarter of the dates. Chop them roughly and set aside.

3 Blend the remaining dates in a food processor or blender to a smooth purée. Add the cinnamon and process with enough of the remaining apple juice to make a smooth paste.

4 Add the tofu to the food processor, a few at a time, processing after each addition. Pour in the remaining apple juice and the soya milk and mix well.

5 Churn the mixture in an ice cream maker until very thick, but not thick enough to scoop. Scrape the ice cream into a plastic tub.

6 Stir in most of the chopped dates, retaining a few pieces for decorating, and freeze for 2–3 hours until firm.

7 Scoop into dessert glasses and decorate with the remaining chopped dates and the walnut halves.

Variation
You could make this tasty ice cream with any soft dried fruits; dried figs, apricots or peaches would be especially good. Alternatively, you could use a combination for a vitamin- and fibre-packed feast.

Energy 290kcal/1232kJ; Protein 9.1g; Carbohydrate 58.2g, of which sugars 57.9g; Fat 3.9g, of which saturates 0.5g; Cholesterol 0mg; Calcium 407mg; Fibre 2.5g; Sodium 24mg.

Coconut sorbet

You may have already had a few sorbets in your time if you have been avoiding dairy. This tropical version from South-east Asia proves they do not have to be restricted to orange or lemon.

Serves 6

250ml/8fl oz/1 cup agave syrup
120ml/4fl oz/½ cup coconut milk
50g/2oz/⅔ cup grated or desiccated
   (dry unsweetened shredded) coconut
a squeeze of lime juice

1 Place the agave syrup in a heavy pan and add 200ml/7fl oz/scant 1 cup water. Bring to the boil, stirring the mixture constantly.

2 Stir the coconut milk into the syrup, along with most of the grated or desiccated coconut and the lime juice. Pour the mixture into a bowl or freezer container and freeze for 2 hours.

3 Take the sorbet out of the freezer and beat it with a fork, or blend it in a food processor, until smooth and creamy. Return it to the freezer for 30 minutes.

Cook's tip
If using fresh coconut, serve the sorbet in the shells.

4 Remove the sorbet from the freezer again and beat it with a fork, or blend it in a food processor, until it is smooth and creamy. Then return it to the freezer and leave until completely frozen.

5 Before serving, allow the sorbet to stand at room temperature for about 10–15 minutes to allow it to soften slightly. Serve in small bowls and decorate with the remaining grated or desiccated coconut.

Energy 170kcal/717kJ; Protein 0.7g; Carbohydrate 32g, of which sugars 32g; Fat 5.2g, of which saturates 4.5g; Cholesterol 0mg; Calcium 23mg; Fibre 1.2g; Sodium 26mg.

Iced clementines

These pretty, sorbet-filled fruits store well in the freezer, and will prove perfect for an impromptu summer party, a picnic or simply a refreshing treat on a hot summer's afternoon.

3 Put the sugar and water in a heavy pan and heat gently, stirring until the sugar has completely dissolved. Boil for about 3 minutes without stirring, then leave the syrup to cool. Stir in the lemon juice.

4 Finely grate the rind from the remaining whole clementines. Squeeze the fruits and stir the juice and grated rind into the syrup.

5 Process the clementine flesh in a food processor or blender, then press it through a sieve (strainer) placed over a bowl to extract as much juice as possible. Add the juice to the syrup, discarding the pulp from the sieve. You need about 900ml/1½ pints/3¾ cups of liquid. Add extra fresh orange juice if necessary.

6 To make by hand: pour the mixture into a shallow container and freeze for 3–4 hours, beating twice as the sorbet thickens. If using an ice cream maker: churn the mixture in the machine until it holds its shape.

Serves 12

16 large clementines
175g/6oz/scant 1 cup caster
   (superfine) sugar
105ml/7 tbsp water
juice of 2 lemons
a little fresh orange juice
   (if necessary)
fresh mint or lemon balm
   leaves, to decorate

1 Slice the tops off 12 of the large clementines to make lids. Set aside the lids on a baking sheet.

2 Loosen the clementine flesh with a sharp knife then carefully scoop it out into a bowl, keeping the shells intact. Scrape out as much of the membrane from the shells as possible. Add the shells to the baking sheet with the lids and place in the freezer.

7 Pack the sorbet into the clementine shells, mounding them up slightly in the centre. Position the lids on top and return the filled clementines to the freezer for several hours or overnight.

8 Transfer the clementines to the refrigerator 30 minutes before serving, to soften slightly. Serve on individual plates and decorate with lemon balm leaves.

Energy 77kcal/329kJ; Protein 0.6g; Carbohydrate 19.9g, of which sugars 19.9g; Fat 0.1g, of which saturates 0g; Cholesterol 0mg; Calcium 24mg; Fibre 0.6g; Sodium 3mg.

Spiced sorbet pears

Pears poached in wine make an elegant dessert at any time of the year. In this recipe the pears are hollowed out and filled with a delicious sorbet flavoured with red wine and pears.

Serves 6

175ml/6fl oz/¾ cup red wine
2 cinnamon sticks, halved
250ml/8fl oz/1 cup agave syrup
6 plump pears

1 Put the wine, cinnamon sticks and agave syrup in a heavy pan that is big enough to hold all the pears. Simmer for 2 minutes.

2 Peel the pears, leaving the stalks attached. Stand them upright in the syrup in the pan, taking care not to pack them too tightly.

3 Cover and simmer very gently for 10–20 minutes until just tender, turning so they colour evenly. (The cooking time varies depending on the softness of the pears.)

4 Lift out the pears with a slotted spoon and set them aside to cool. Boil the juices briefly until reduced to 350ml/12fl oz/1½ cups. Set aside and leave to cool.

5 Cut a deep 2.5cm/1in slice off the top of each pear and reserve. Use an apple corer to remove the cores.

6 Using a teaspoon, scoop out the centre of each pear, leaving a thick shell. Put the pear shells and their lids in the freezer.

7 Strain the poaching juices from the pan. Reserve about 90ml/6 tbsp and add the rest to a food processor or blender with the pear flesh. Process until smooth.

8 Pour the mixture into a container and freeze for 3–4 hours, beating twice as it thickens, or use an ice cream maker.

9 Using a teaspoon, pack the sorbet into the frozen pears, piling it up high. Add the lids and return to the freezer overnight.

10 Remove the pears from the freezer and leave them to stand at room temperature for about 30 minutes before serving. The pears should have softened but the sorbet remain icy. Transfer to serving plates and spoon a little of the reserved syrup around each one before serving.

Energy 198kcal/835kJ; Protein 0.6g; Carbohydrate 35.2g, of which sugars 35.2g; Fat 0.2g, of which saturates 0g; Cholesterol 0mg; Calcium 33mg; Fibre 3.3g; Sodium 12mg.

Oranges with caramel wigs

These attractive oranges make the perfect dessert to serve at a dinner party as you can prepare them beforehand. The slightly bitter, caramelized orange rind and syrup has a wonderful flavour and texture that sits in perfect contrast to the sweet, juicy oranges.

Serves 6

6 oranges
120g/4oz/generous ½ cup soft light
  brown sugar
120ml/4fl oz/½ cup boiling water
cocktail sticks (toothpicks)

1 Using a vegetable peeler, thinly pare the rind off a few of the oranges to make 12 long strips.

2 Using a sharp knife, peel all the oranges, reserving the rind and discarding the pith. Reserve the juice and freeze the oranges separately for 30 minutes.

3 Slice the oranges, reform and secure with cocktail sticks. Chill.

4 Put half the sugar into a pan and add 15ml/1 tbsp water. Heat gently until the mixture caramelizes, shaking the pan a little if one side starts to brown too fast.

5 As soon as the mixture colours, dip the bottom of the pan into cold water. Add 30ml/2 tbsp hot water and the orange rind to the caramel, then stir until the caramel dissolves. Turn the rind on to a plate, to cool.

6 Make a caramel syrup for serving. Put the remaining sugar in a small pan with 15ml/1 tbsp water, and make caramel as before. When it has coloured nicely, stand well back, pour in the boiling water and stir with a wooden spoon to dissolve. Add the reserved juices and pour into a serving jug (pitcher).

7 To serve, arrange the orange strips in a criss-cross pattern on top of each orange. Remove the cocktail sticks and pour a little caramel syrup round the base of each orange.

Energy 122kcal/521kJ; Protein 1.4g; Carbohydrate 30.8g, of which sugars 30.8g; Fat 0.1g, of which saturates 0g; Cholesterol 0mg; Calcium 66mg; Fibre 2g; Sodium 7mg.

Vanilla, date and saffron pears

These sweet juicy pears, poached in agave syrup infused with vanilla, saffron and lime, make a truly elegant dessert. For a low-fat version you can eat them on their own, but for a really luxurious, indulgent treat, serve with soya, cashew or coconut ice cream.

Serves 4

2 vanilla pods (beans)
250ml/8fl oz/1 cup agave syrup
5ml/1 tsp finely grated lime rind
a large pinch of saffron
475ml/16fl oz/2 cups apple juice
4 large, firm ripe dessert pears
vegan ice cream, to serve

1 Using a small sharp knife, carefully split the vanilla pods in half. Scrape the seeds into a heavy pan large enough to hold all the pears, then add the vanilla pods as well.

2 Pour the agave syrup into the pan with the vanilla, then add the lime rind and the saffron. Pour the apple juice into the pan and bring the mixture to the boil. Reduce the heat to low and simmer, stirring occasionally, while you prepare the pears.

3 Peel the pears, then add to the pan and gently turn in the syrup to coat evenly. Cover the pan and simmer gently for about 12–15 minutes, turning the pears halfway through cooking, until they are just tender.

4 Lift the pears from the syrup using a slotted spoon and transfer to four serving bowls. Set aside.

5 Bring the syrup back to the boil and cook gently for about 10 minutes, or until the liquid has reduced slightly and thickened. Spoon the syrup over the pears and serve either warm or chilled with ice cream.

Cook's tip

For the best results use firm varieties of dessert pears, such as comice or conference, that are well ripened.

Variation

Try using different flavourings in the syrup. Use 10ml/2 tsp chopped fresh root ginger and 1 or 2 star anise in place of the saffron and vanilla, or 1 cinnamon stick, 3 cloves and 105ml/7tbsp maple syrup in place of the agave syrup.

Energy 283kcal/1207kJ; Protein 0.8g; Carbohydrate 74.3g, of which sugars 74.3g; Fat 0.2g, of which saturates 0g; Cholesterol 0mg; Calcium 38mg; Fibre 3.3g; Sodium 10mg.

Pineapple with coconut rum

The tropical flavour of pineapple is enhanced by the addition of coconut rum. For a really special treat, serve topped with coconut cream and grated vegan chocolate.

4 Add the remaining agave syrup to the pan and boil for about 10 minutes, stirring frequently, until the syrup has thickened. Remove from the heat and set aside to cool slightly, then stir in the coconut rum.

5 Pack the drained pineapple loosely in warmed sterilized jars. Pour in the syrup until the fruit is covered, tapping and twisting the jars to release any air bubbles. Store in the refrigerator and eat within 2 weeks.

Cook's tip
Choose plump pineapples that feel heavy for their size, with fresh, stiff plumes. To test for ripeness, gently pull out one of the bottom leaves; it should come away easily.

Variation
This dessert is delicious served with a coconut ice cream mixture. Blend equal quantities of bananas and coconut ice cream with 30ml/ 2 tbsp maple syrup and freeze.

Makes about 900g/2lb

1 orange
1.2 litres/2 pints/5 cups apple juice
475ml/16fl oz/2 cups agave syrup
2 pineapples, peeled, cored and cut into small chunks
300ml/½ pint/1¼ cups coconut rum

1 Using a vegetable peeler, thinly pare strips of rind from the orange, then slice into thin matchsticks.

2 Put the apple juice and half the agave syrup in a large pan with the rind and boil for 5–10 minutes until reduced slightly.

3 Carefully add the pineapple pieces to the syrup and return to the boil. Reduce the heat and simmer gently for 10 minutes. Using a slotted spoon, remove the pineapple from the pan and set aside to drain.

Energy 4660kcal/19834kJ; Protein 7.7g; Carbohydrate 1119.7g, of which sugars 1119.7g; Fat 1.6g, of which saturates 0g; Cholesterol 0mg; Calcium 636mg; Fibre 9.6g; Sodium 106mg.

Piquant fruit salad

Organic summer fruits make a delicious seasonal fruit salad. Any combination of fruits can be used although this exotic choice and the added brandy is particularly suitable for a dinner party.

Serves 6

175ml/6fl oz/¾ cup agave syrup
thinly pared rind of 1 lime
150ml/¼ pint/⅔ cup apple juice
juice of 1 lime
60ml/4 tbsp brandy
5ml/1 tsp decaffeinated coffee granules or
  powder dissolved in 30ml/2 tbsp boiling water
1 small pineapple
1 papaya
2 pomegranates
1 medium mango
2 passion fruits or kiwi fruit
fine strips of lime rind, to decorate

3 Halve the papaya and scoop out the seeds. Cut away the skin, then slice the flesh. Halve the pomegranates and scoop out the seeds. Add to the bowl.

Cook's tip
Allow the salad to stand in the refrigerator for an hour before serving so the flavours can blend.

4 Cut the mango lengthways into three pieces, along each side of the stone (pit). Peel the skin off the flesh. Cut into chunks and add to the bowl.

5 Halve the passion fruits, if using, and scoop out the flesh using a teaspoon. If using kiwi fruits, peel then chop the flesh into pieces and add to the bowl. Chill until ready to serve. Decorate with strips of lime rind before serving.

1 Put the agave syrup and lime rind in a small pan with the apple juice. Bring to the boil and simmer for 5 minutes. Leave to cool, then strain into a large serving bowl, discarding the lime rind. Stir in the lime juice, brandy and dissolved coffee.

2 Using a sharp knife, cut the plume and stalk ends from the pineapple. Slice off the peel and cut the flesh into bitesize pieces. Add to the bowl. Discard the central core.

Energy 186kcal/790kJ; Protein 1.1g; Carbohydrate 42.1g, of which sugars 42g; Fat 0.3g, of which saturates 0g; Cholesterol 0mg; Calcium 41mg; Fibre 3.2g; Sodium 86mg.

Raw Key lime pie

The classic lime dessert originated in the Florida Keys and is now an American favourite. Here it enjoys a raw healthy makeover for vegans with the usual eggs and condensed milk replaced with a mix of avocado and coconut to give a creamy dessert that is packed with vitamin E.

Serves 6

For the filling
75g/3oz/6 tbsp extra virgin cold-pressed coconut oil
250g/9oz avocado flesh, roughly 2 medium avocados with skin and stones (pits) removed
75g/3oz/scant ½ cup ready-to-eat dried apricots
10ml/2 tsp pumpkin seed oil
finely grated rind of 2 limes
juice of 1 lime
15ml/1 tbsp agave syrup

For the base
50g/2oz/½ cup ground pumpkin seeds
50g/2oz/½ cup ground almonds
75g/3oz/½ cup medjool dates, chopped
15ml/1 tbsp agave syrup

1 Blend together all the ingredients for the base in a food processor or blender until you have a nice firm dough.

2 Lightly oil a 20cm/8in pie dish. Scrape the dough from the processor or blender and press the dough into the base of dish, ensuring it is evenly distributed.

3 Melt the coconut oil in a heatproof bowl resting in a pan of hot water.

4 Blend together the avocados, dried apricots, pumpkin oil, and lime rind and juice in a food processor or blender. Gradually stir in the melted coconut oil.

5 Spread the mixture evenly on to the pie base using a palette knife or metal spatula. Chill for about 2 hours.

6 Serve decorated with thinly sliced lime twists, if you like.

Energy 360kcal/1494kJ; Protein 4.9g; Carbohydrate 15.4g, of which sugars 13.1g; Fat 31.4g, of which saturates 12.4g; Cholesterol 0mg; Calcium 48mg; Fibre 3.6g; Sodium 20mg.

Tofu berry cheesecake

This is a relatively low-sugar dessert, considering how delightful it tastes. Natural sugars in the fruit and apple juice sweeten the cheesecake, while the low-fat tofu and soya yogurt make it deliciously creamy – a perfect foil to the delicious summer fruits.

Serves 6

425g/15oz firm tofu
300g/11oz/scant 2 cups soya yogurt
1 sachet powdered vegetarian jelly crystals
90ml/6 tbsp apple juice
175g/6oz soft fruits, such as raspberries,
  strawberries and blueberries
30ml/2 tbsp redcurrant jelly
30ml/2 tbsp lemon juice, heated

For the base
50g/2oz/¼ cup dairy-free spread or
  soya margarine
30ml/2 tbsp apple juice
115g/4oz/6 cups bran flakes

1 To make the base, place the dairy-free spread or soya margarine and apple juice in a pan and heat them gently until the spread or margarine has melted. Crush the cereal and stir it into the apple juice mixture.

2 Transfer the mixture into a 23cm/9in loose-based round flan tin (pan) and press down firmly with your fingers. Leave the base to cool. Chill until set.

3 To make the filling, place the tofu and yogurt in a food processor and process them until smooth. Heat the apple juice, then add the jelly crystals until dissolved, and blend into the tofu mixture.

4 Spread the tofu mixture over the base, smoothing it evenly. Chill for 1–2 hours, until the filling has set.

5 Carefully remove the flan tin and place the cheesecake on a serving plate.

6 Arrange the fruits on top of the cake. Place the redcurrant jelly in a small bowl and add the heated lemon juice.

7 Stir the mixture well until the jelly has completely melted. Leave it to cool slightly and then spoon or lightly brush it over the fruit. Chill until required and then serve.

Health benefit

Made from soya beans, tofu is an excellent source of protein and it is low in fat, making this dessert a well-balanced dish. It is packed with vitamins and health-giving nutrients in the fruit and fibre in the bran-flake base.

Energy 175kcal/735kJ; Protein 8.1g; Carbohydrate 23.2g, of which sugars 13.7g; Fat 6g, of which saturates 1.4g; Cholesterol 1mg; Calcium 314mg; Fibre 2.8g; Sodium 241mg.

Baked figs with hazelnut and maple syrup tofu ice cream

Figs have been cultivated for thousands of years, and with their deliciously intense flavour it is easy to see why. The nutty tofu ice cream is the perfect complement to these ancient fruits.

Serves 4

1 lemon grass stalk, finely chopped
1 cinnamon stick, roughly broken
60ml/4 tbsp maple syrup
200ml/7fl oz/scant 1 cup apple juice
8 large or 12 small figs

For the hazelnut soya ice cream
450ml/¾ pint/scant 2 cups soya cream
30ml/2 tbsp soya margarine
50ml/2fl oz/¼ cup maple syrup
45ml/3 tbsp silken tofu
1.5ml/¼ tsp vanilla extract
75g/3oz/¾ cup hazelnuts

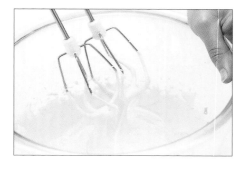

1 In a bowl, blend together the ice cream ingredients, except for the hazelnuts, using an electric or hand whisk.

2 Transfer the ice cream mixture to a metal or plastic freezer container and freeze for 2 hours, or until the mixture feels firm around the edge.

3 Preheat the oven to 180°C/350°F/ Gas 4. Place the hazelnuts on a baking sheet and roast for 10–12 minutes, or until they are golden brown. Leave the nuts to cool, then place them in a food processor or blender and process until they are coarsely ground.

4 Remove the container from the freezer and whisk the ice cream to break down the ice crystals. Stir in the ground hazelnuts and freeze the mixture again until half-frozen. Whisk again, then freeze until firm.

Cook's tips
• If you prefer, rather than whisking the semi-frozen ice cream, transfer it into a food processor and process until smooth.
• There are several types of figs available and they can all be used in this recipe. Choose from the green-skinned figs that have an amber-coloured flesh, dark purple-skinned fruit with a deep red flesh or green/yellow-skinned figs with a pinky-coloured flesh.

Variation
This recipe also works well with halved, stoned (pitted) nectarines or peaches, baked in the same way.

5 Place the lemon grass, cinnamon stick, maple syrup and apple juice in a small pan and heat slowly until boiling. Lower the heat and simmer the mixture for 5 minutes, then leave the syrup to stand for 15 minutes.

6 Preheat the oven to 200°C/400°F/ Gas 6. Meanwhile, carefully cut the figs into quarters, leaving them intact at the bases. Place the figs in an ovenproof baking dish and pour over the maple-flavoured syrup.

7 Cover the dish tightly with foil and bake the figs for about 15 minutes, or until they are tender.

8 Take the ice cream from the freezer about 10 minutes before serving, to allow it to soften slightly. While still warm, transfer the baked figs to individual serving plates.

9 Drizzle a little of the spiced syrup over the figs. Serve them with a scoop or two of hazelnut ice cream.

Energy 500kcal/2098kJ; Protein 12.5g; Carbohydrate 62.8g, of which sugars 62.4g; Fat 23.2g, of which saturates 4.3g; Cholesterol 1mg; Calcium 280mg; Fibre 5.9g; Sodium 248mg.

Fried bananas

This dish makes a delicious change from the usual banana split. The bananas are coated in a beer batter and then fried. Eat them hot, straight from the pan, as a quick and tasty snack or make this a more indulgent treat by serving with vanilla or chocolate soya ice cream.

3 Dip each one into the beer batter, making sure it is well coated, and carefully slip it into the hot oil. Cook the bananas in batches, so they do not stick together in the pan. Use tongs or chopsticks for turning and make sure each piece is crisp and golden all over.

4 Drain the fried bananas on kitchen paper and sprinkle them with sugar. Serve immediately and eat hot.

Serves 4

4 ripe but firm bananas
vegetable oil, for deep-frying
caster (superfine) sugar, for sprinkling

For the batter
115g/4oz/1 cup rice flour or plain
   (all-purpose) flour
2.5ml/½ tsp baking powder
45ml/3 tbsp agave syrup
150ml/¼ pint/⅔ cup rice milk
150ml/¼ pint/⅔ cup beer

1 To make the batter, sift the flour with the baking powder into a bowl. Add the syrup and beat in a little of the rice milk and beer to make a smooth paste. Gradually beat in the rest of the rice milk and beer to form a thick batter. Leave to stand for 20 minutes.

2 Peel the bananas and cut them in half crossways, then cut in half again lengthways. Heat enough of the vegetable oil for deep-frying in a large, heavy pan.

Energy 385kcal/1616kJ; Protein 5.9g; Carbohydrate 53.9g, of which sugars 29.7g; Fat 17.7g, of which saturates 5.8g; Cholesterol 48mg; Calcium 59mg; Fibre 3g; Sodium 22mg.

Deep-fried mung bean dumplings

While many European desserts rely heavily on eggs and dairy, these vegan sweet rice dumplings are popular snacks in the Far East. In this dish, potato and rice-flour dumplings are stuffed with a delicious filling of sweetened mung bean paste and rolled in sesame seeds.

Serves 6

100g/3½oz/scant ½ cup split mung beans, soaked for 6 hours and drained
120ml/4fl oz/½ cup agave syrup
300g/11oz/1¼ cups glutinous rice flour
50g/2oz/¼ cup rice flour
1 medium potato, boiled in its skin, peeled and mashed
250ml/8fl oz/1 cup rice milk
75g/3oz/6 tbsp sesame seeds
vegetable oil, for deep-frying

1 Put the mung beans in a large pan with half the agave syrup and pour in 450ml/¾ pint/scant 2 cups water. Bring to the boil, stirring constantly until blended. Reduce the heat and simmer gently for 15–20 minutes until the mung beans are soft. You may need to add more water if the beans are becoming dry, otherwise they will burn on the bottom of the pan.

2 Once the mung beans are soft and all the water has been absorbed, reduce the beans to a smooth paste in a mortar and pestle or food processor and leave to cool.

3 In a large bowl, beat the flours and syrup into the mashed potato. Add about 200ml/7fl oz/scant 1 cup rice milk to bind the mixture into a moist dough. Divide the dough into 24 pieces, roll each one into a small ball, then flatten with the heel of your hand to make a disc and lay it out on a lightly floured board.

Variation
These little fried dumplings may also be filled with a sweetened red bean paste, sweetened taro root or a lotus paste. Alternatively, the dumplings can be steamed.

4 Divide the bean paste into 24 small portions. Place a portion of the paste in the centre of each dough disc. Fold over the edges of the dough and then shape into a ball. Repeat the process with the remaining pieces of dough.

5 Spread the sesame seeds on a plate and roll the dumplings in them until evenly coated. Heat enough oil for deep-frying in a large, heavy pan. Fry the balls in batches until golden. Drain on kitchen paper and serve warm.

Energy 514kcal/2151kJ; Protein 10.4g; Carbohydrate 79.6g, of which sugars 20.9g; Fat 17.2g, of which saturates 2.2g; Cholesterol 0mg; Calcium 127mg; Fibre 5.1g; Sodium 13mg.

Pumpkin with vodka and cinnamon syrup

This unusual dish is based on a traditional dessert from the Far East. Pumpkin wedges are
baked in the oven with brown sugar and plenty of vodka, which results in a delicious syrup.

Serves 6

1 small pumpkin, about 800g/1¾lb
350g/12oz/1½ cups soft dark brown sugar
120ml/4fl oz/½ cup vodka
5ml/1 tsp ground cloves
12 cinnamon sticks, each about 10cm/4in
  in length
fresh mint sprigs, to decorate
soya yogurt, to serve

1 Preheat the oven to 190°C/375°F/
Gas 5. Halve the pumpkin, remove the
seeds and fibres and cut into wedges.
Arrange in a shallow, flameproof
casserole or heavy ovenproof dish.
Fill the hollows with the sugar.

2 Pour the vodka carefully into the pan,
taking care not to wash all the sugar to
the bottom. Make sure that some of the
vodka trickles down to the bottom to
prevent the pumpkin from burning.
Sprinkle on the ground cloves and add
two of the cinnamon sticks.

3 Cover the pan tightly and bake in the
oven for about 30 minutes, or until
the pumpkin is tender. Check the
casserole or pan occasionally to make
sure that the pumpkin does not dry out
or catch on the bottom.

4 Transfer the pumpkin to a platter
and pour the hot syrup over. Decorate
each portion with mint and cinnamon
sticks and serve with soya yogurt.

Variation
Try using sweet potato or papaya,
in place of the pumpkin, if you like.

Energy 247kcal/1054kJ; Protein 1.2g; Carbohydrate 63.9g, of which sugars 63.2g; Fat 0.3g, of which saturates 0.1g; Cholesterol 0mg; Calcium 70mg; Fibre 1.3g; Sodium 4mg.

Caramelized pineapple with lemon grass

This stunning dessert, garnished with jewel-like pomegranate seeds, is superb for entertaining. The tangy, zesty flavours of lemon grass and mint bring out the exquisite sweetness of the fruit.

Serves 4

30ml/2 tbsp very finely chopped lemon
   grass, and 2 lemon grass stalks,
   halved lengthways
450ml/¾ pint/scant 2 cups agave syrup
10ml/2 tsp chopped fresh mint leaves
150ml/¼ pint/⅔ cup pineapple juice
2 small, ripe pineapples
15ml/1 tbsp sunflower oil
60ml/4 tbsp pomegranate seeds
coconut cream, to serve

1 Place the chopped lemon grass, lemon grass stalks, 300ml/½ pint/1¼ cups of the agave syrup and the chopped mint leaves in a non-stick wok or large pan. Pour over the pineapple juice and bring to the boil over medium heat.

2 Reduce the heat and simmer the mixture for about 10–15 minutes, until thickened and reduced. Leave to cool slightly, then strain into a glass bowl, reserving the halved lemon grass stalks, then set aside.

3 Using a sharp knife, peel and core the pineapples and cut into 1cm/½in slices, then sprinkle the slices with the remaining agave syrup.

4 Brush a large non-stick wok or pan with the oil and place over a medium heat. Working in batches, cook the pineapple slices for 2–3 minutes on one side until they are just beginning to turn brown. Turn the slices over and cook the other side for another 2–3 minutes.

5 Transfer the pineapple slices to a flat serving dish and sprinkle over the pomegranate seeds.

6 Pour the lemon grass syrup over the fruit and garnish with the reserved stalks. Serve hot or at room temperature with coconut cream.

Cook's tip
To remove pomegranate seeds, halve the fruit and hold it over a bowl, cut side down. Tap all over with a wooden spoon or turn it completely inside out.

Energy 493kcal/2101kJ; Protein 1.7g; Carbohydrate 121.8g, of which sugars 121.8g; Fat 3.4g, of which saturates 0.3g; Cholesterol 0mg; Calcium 101mg; Fibre 3.6g; Sodium 11mg.

Plum charlottes with Calvados cream

There is a wide variety of plums and they can be used for much more than making into jam or turning into prunes. For this dish try seeking out and experimenting with the many different types – from tangy yellow greengages to sweet and juicy Victorias.

Serves 4

115g/4oz/½ cup soya margarine, melted
30ml/2 tbsp demerara (raw) sugar
450g/1lb ripe plums, stoned (pitted)
  and thickly sliced
50ml/2fl oz/¼ cup agave syrup
30ml/2 tbsp orange juice
1.5ml/¼ tsp ground cinnamon
25g/1oz/¼ cup ground almonds
8–10 large slices of wholemeal
  (whole-wheat) bread

For the Calvados sauce
5ml/1 tsp silken tofu
60ml/4 tbsp maple syrup
30ml/2 tbsp Calvados

1 Preheat the oven to 190°C/375°F/ Gas 5. Line the bases of four individual 10cm-/4in-diameter, deep, earthenware ramekin dishes with baking parchment. Brush evenly and thoroughly with a little of the melted soya margarine, then sprinkle each dish with a little of the demerara sugar, rotating the dish in your hands to make sure you coat each dish evenly.

Variations
• Slices of peeled pear or eating apples can be used in this recipe instead of the stoned, sliced plums.
• If you cannot find organic Calvados any organic fruit-based spirit will work in this dish.

2 Place the stoned plum slices in a pan with the agave syrup, orange juice and ground cinnamon and cook gently for 5 minutes, or until the plums have softened slightly. Leave the plums to cool, then stir in the ground almonds.

3 Cut the crusts off the bread and then use a plain pastry cutter to cut out four rounds to fit the bases of the ramekins. Dip the bread rounds into melted margarine and fit them into the dishes. Cut four more rounds to fit the tops of the dishes and set aside.

4 Cut the remaining bread into strips, dip into the melted margarine and use to line the sides of the ramekins.

5 Divide the plum mixture among the lined ramekins and level the tops. Place the bread rounds on top and brush with margarine. Place the ramekins on a baking sheet and bake for 25 minutes.

6 Make the sauce just before the charlottes are ready. Place the tofu and maple syrup in a large bowl, and blend them together until pale. Whisk in the Calvados. Continue whisking until the mixture is very light and frothy.

7 Remove the charlottes from the oven and turn out on to warm serving plates. Pour a little sauce over and around the charlottes and serve immediately.

Energy 600kcal/2513kJ; Protein 9.1g; Carbohydrate 69.6g, of which sugars 44.2g; Fat 32.5g, of which saturates 16.5g; Cholesterol 218mg; Calcium 128mg; Fibre 3.1g; Sodium 467mg.

Rice pudding with almonds

Rice is a popular dessert in many parts of the world. This delicious and healthy version of rice pudding is light and easy to make. The raisins benefit from pre-soaking in dry sherry before being added to the pudding. Top with orange segments or another tangy fruit of your choice.

Serves 4

75g/3oz/generous ½ cup raisins
75ml/5 tbsp dry sherry
90g/3½oz/½ cup short grain (pudding) rice
3 or 4 strips of pared lemon rind
250ml/8fl oz/1 cup rice milk
475ml/16fl oz/2 cups soya milk
1 cinnamon stick, about 7.5cm/3in in length,
    plus 3 more, to decorate
120ml/4fl oz/½ cup agave syrup
pinch of salt
5ml/1 tsp ground almonds
15g/½ oz/1 tbsp soya margarine
toasted flaked (sliced) almonds, to decorate
chilled orange segments, to serve

Cook's tip
Try drizzling with agave or maple syrup and sprinkle with nutmeg.

1 Put the raisins and dry sherry in a small pan. Heat gently until warm, then set the pan aside, which will allow the raisins to swell.

2 Mix the rice, lemon rind and rice milk in a heavy pan and bring the mixture gently to the boil. Lower the heat, cover the pan and simmer for approximately 20 minutes. Remove the lemon rind pieces from the pan with a slotted spoon and discard.

3 Add the soya milk and the cinnamon stick to the pan, then stir until the rice has absorbed the milk. Stir in the syrup and salt. Add the ground almonds and soya margarine. Stir until blended.

4 Drain the raisins and stir into the rice mixture. Cook for 2–3 minutes until heated through. Serve in individual bowls, topped with the toasted flaked almonds and orange segments, and decorate with a cinnamon stick.

Energy 325kcal/1365kJ; Protein 6.7g; Carbohydrate 56.2g, of which sugars 38.2g; Fat 6.3g, of which saturates 1.9g; Cholesterol 1mg; Calcium 44mg; Fibre 0.5g; Sodium 171mg.

Baked pumpkin with coconut custard

A vegan recipe based on a traditional dessert from Thailand. Once the custard-filled pumpkin is baked, the flesh is scooped out with the custard and a hot coconut sauce is drizzled over the top. Sweet and fragrant, this delicious dish is sheer indulgence and a real crowd pleaser.

Serves 4–6

1 small pumpkin, about 1.3kg/3lb, halved,
 seeded and fibres removed
400ml/14fl oz/1⅔ cups coconut milk
45ml/3 tbsp silken tofu
45ml/3 tbsp agave syrup, plus a little
 extra for drizzling
salt

For the sauce
250ml/8fl oz/1 cup coconut cream
30ml/2 tbsp agave syrup

1 Preheat the oven to 180°C/350°F/ Gas 4. Place the pumpkin halves, skin side down, in a baking dish.

2 In a large bowl, blend the coconut milk with a pinch of salt, the tofu and agave syrup, until the mixture is thick and smooth.

3 Pour the custard into each pumpkin half. Sprinkle a little extra agave syrup over the top of the custard and the rim of the pumpkin.

Variation
This recipe can also be made with butternut or acorn squash and, interestingly, with halved avocados, mangoes and papayas. Bear in mind that the quantity of custard and the cooking times may have to be adjusted.

4 Bake in the oven for 35–40 minutes. The pumpkin should feel tender when a skewer is inserted in it, and the custard should feel firm when lightly touched. If you like, you can brown the top further under the grill (broiler).

5 Just before serving, heat the coconut cream in a pan with a pinch of salt and the syrup. Scoop out pieces of pumpkin flesh with the custard and place in bowls. Pour a little sweetened coconut cream over the top to serve.

Energy 217kcal/906kJ; Protein 4.5g; Carbohydrate 16.3g, of which sugars 15.7g; Fat 15.4g, of which saturates 11.9g; Cholesterol 71mg; Calcium 71mg; Fibre 1.3g; Sodium 88mg.

cakes, bakes and breads

Vegans need not feel that they are missing out on life's little luxuries thanks to the heavenly cakes, flans, tarts and pies in this chapter. You can amaze your guests when you reveal the vegan ingredients in Chocolate and Orange Gateau, Pumpkin Pie or Chocolate Brownies. There are plenty more baked treats to enjoy, including cookies, muffins and various breads, such as Three Seed Loaf, Crumpets and Tandoori Rotis.

Parsnip cake with orange icing

This fabulous vegan cake is similar to the ever-popular carrot cake, and a perfect way to prove to your friends and family that vegan cake is just as delicious as any other.

Serves 10

250g/9oz/2¼ cups self-raising (self-rising)
    wholemeal (whole-wheat) flour
15ml/1 tbsp baking powder
5ml/1 tsp ground cinnamon
5ml/1 tsp freshly ground nutmeg
130g/4½oz/ generous ½ cup
    soya margarine
130g/4½oz/generous ½ cup
    soft light brown sugar
250g/9oz parsnips, coarsely grated
1 banana, mashed
finely grated rind and juice of 1 orange

For the topping

225g/8oz/1 cup soya cream cheese
45ml/3 tbsp icing (confectioners') sugar
juice of 1 small orange
fine strips of orange rind

1 Preheat the oven to 180°C/350°F/ Gas 4. Lightly grease the base of a 900g/2lb loaf tin (pan) with some soya margarine. Line the tin with a piece of baking parchment.

2 Sift the self-raising flour, baking powder, cinnamon and nutmeg into a large mixing bowl. Mix the ingredients together until thoroughly combined.

3 Gently melt the margarine in a pan. Add the sugar and stir until completely dissolved. Make a well in the flour mixture, then add the melted margarine and sugar, mixing to combine.

4 Add the parsnips, banana and the orange rind and juice to the bowl. Stir until the ingredients are thoroughly mixed. Spoon the mixture into the prepared tin and level the top with the back of a spoon.

5 Bake in the oven for 45–50 minutes until a skewer inserted into the centre of the cake comes out clean. Allow the cake to cool slightly before removing from the tin, then transfer to a wire rack to cool completely.

6 Meanwhile, make the topping. Beat together the soya cream cheese, icing sugar, orange juice and strips of orange rind until smooth.

7 Spread the topping evenly over the cake using a palette knife or metal spatula, ensuring it is spread to the edges. Run a fork lightly over the topping to create a pattern and leave to set. Store in an airtight container.

Variation
This cake goes really well with cashew nut cream or coconut ice cream. Sprinkle with hundreds and thousands sugar strands, if you like.

Energy 282kcal/1187kJ; Protein 5g; Carbohydrate 40.3g, of which sugars 22.9g; Fat 11.9g, of which saturates 4.9g; Cholesterol 2mg; Calcium 30mg; Fibre 3.5g; Sodium 108mg.

Celebration cake

This makes an ideal cake for a Christmas feast or a wedding or birthday celebration. You can decorate the cake with a layer of marzipan and icing, if you want to make it extra special.

Makes a 20cm/8in cake

1 large orange, quartered
  and seeded, but not peeled
1 large lemon, quartered
  and seeded, but not peeled
1 large cooking apple, cored
  and quartered, but not peeled
90g/3½ oz/generous ½ cup pitted dates
75g/3oz/6 tbsp soya margarine
75g/3oz/6 tbsp hazelnut butter
90g/3½oz/⅔ cup raisins
90g/3½oz/scant ½ cup currants
90g/3½oz/scant ½ cup dried apricots
90g/3½oz/scant ½ cup ready-to-eat
  pitted prunes, chopped
50g/2oz/⅔ cup broken walnuts
5ml/1 tsp ground cinnamon
5ml/1 tsp grated nutmeg
2.5ml/½ tsp mace
2.5ml/½ tsp ground cloves
115g/4oz/1 cup wholemeal
  (whole-wheat) flour
7.5ml/1½ tsp baking powder
60g/2oz/generous ½ cup rolled oats
60g/2oz/½ cup ground almonds
150g/5oz silken tofu
45–60ml/3–4 tbsp soya or rice milk

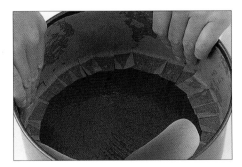

1 Preheat the oven to 150°F/300°C/ Gas 2. Oil and line a deep 20cm/8in round cake tin (pan).

2 Combine the orange, lemon and apple pieces in a food processor or blender. Add the dates, the soya margarine and hazelnut butter. Process the mixture until it forms a rough purée, taking care not to overprocess it.

3 Scrape the mixture into a bowl and stir in the dried fruit, nuts and spices.

4 Stir in the flour, baking powder, rolled oats, almonds and tofu. Stir in the soya or rice milk, and mix thoroughly.

5 Spoon the cake mixture into the prepared tin and bake for 1 hour or until a fine skewer inserted in the centre comes out clean. When ready, turn it out on to a wire rack and leave to cool before decorating or serving.

Energy 3378kcal/14144kJ; Protein 81.9g; Carbohydrate 358.3g, of which sugars 240.6g; Fat 189.7g, of which saturates 40.1g; Cholesterol 11mg; Calcium 1811mg; Fibre 45.8g; Sodium 813mg.

Chocolate and orange gateau

This indulgent cake is proof that vegans need not miss out on the luscious treats enjoyed by those who eat dairy products. Enjoy the look on diners' faces when you reveal it is a vegan cake.

Serves 8

250g/9oz/2¼ cups self-raising (self-rising) wholemeal (whole-wheat) flour
225g/8oz/1 cup soft light brown sugar
30ml/2 tbsp of unsweetened cocoa powder
10ml/2 tsp carob powder
120ml/4fl oz/½ cup rapeseed (canola) oil
150ml/¼ pint/⅔ cup soya milk
115g/4oz/1 cup broken walnuts
rind of 2 oranges
15ml/1 tbsp vegan yogurt or tofu
15ml/1 tbsp balsamic vinegar
salt

For the filling
60ml/4 tbsp vegan cream cheese
5ml/1 tsp finely grated lime rind
60ml/4 tbsp marmalade or apricot jam

For the chocolate sauce
115g/4oz dairy-free dark (bittersweet) chocolate
15ml/1 tbsp agave syrup
15ml/1 tbsp orange liqueur (optional)
250ml/8fl oz/1 cup soya cream

1 Place all the ingredients for the cake mixture in a large bowl. Mix thoroughly with a wooden spoon until they are thoroughly combined.

2 Coarsely grate or chop up 25g/1oz of the dairy-free chocolate from the chocolate sauce ingredients. Stir it into the cake mixture.

3 Preheat the oven to 180°C/350°F/ Gas 4. Lightly oil two 20cm/8in deep cake tins (pans) and line the bases with baking parchment. Spoon in the cake mixture evenly between the two tins.

4 Bake the cakes in the oven for about 20–30 minutes or until a metal skewer inserted in the centre comes out clean.

5 Meanwhile, prepare the filling. Put the cream cheese into a bowl and mix in the grated lime rind. Set aside until ready to use.

6 When the cakes are baked turn them out on to a wire rack. Leave them to cool completely.

7 When the cakes are cool, spread the lime cream cheese evenly over the top of one of the cakes. Spread the other with marmalade or jam. Sandwich them together with the two fillings facing each other and place on a plate.

8 Make the chocolate sauce. Break the chocolate into chunks and melt in a bowl set over a pan of boiling water. Mix in the agave syrup, liqueur, if using, and then the soya cream a little at a time while continuously stirring. Pour over the cake.

9 Leave to cool slightly, then serve with extra sauce, if you like.

Energy 536kcal/2245kJ; Protein 8.1g; Carbohydrate 68.9g, of which sugars 43.6g; Fat 26.9g, of which saturates 5.2g; Cholesterol 1mg; Calcium 99mg; Fibre 2.1g; Sodium 62mg.

Figgy pudding

This dessert is a delicious treat for grown-ups that will be the perfect end to a vegan meal.
The fruits are soaked in brandy and orange juice overnight to make them extremely succulent.

Serves 4

225g/8oz/2 cups self-raising (self-rising)
   wholemeal (whole-wheat) flour
115g/4oz/½ cup coconut fat (chilled)
300ml/½ pint/1¼ cups soya milk

For the filling
175g/6oz/1 cup dried figs
115g/4oz/½ cup prunes
75g/3oz/generous ½ cup raisins
   or sultanas (golden raisins)
50g/2oz/¼ cup ready-to-eat dried apricots
50g/2oz/⅓ cup dates
25g/1oz chopped apple
150ml/¼ pint/⅔ cup brandy
60ml/4 tbsp fresh orange juice
15ml/1 tbsp agave syrup
1.5ml/¼ tsp ground ginger
1.5ml/¼ tsp ground cinnamon

1 The night before making the pudding,
place the dried figs, prunes, raisins or
sultanas, apricots, dates and apple in a
large bowl. Pour in the brandy and the
orange juice and set aside to soak.

2 Next day remove any pits from the
soaked dates and prunes. Sift the flour
into a large bowl. Grate in the coconut
fat and mix together with your fingers.
Gradually add the soya milk, mixing
until a soft dough forms.

3 Turn out the dough on to a floured
surface and lightly knead until smooth.
Roll out two-thirds of the dough into a
round and use to line a well-oiled
1.2 litre/2 pint heatproof bowl.

4 Add the agave syrup, ginger and
cinnamon to the soaked fruits and
brandy mixture. Mix well and spoon the
fruits into the pastry-lined bowl.

5 Moisten the edges of the pastry with
soya milk. Cover with a lid rolled from
the remaining dough. Press the edges
together to seal.

6 Cover securely with oiled baking
parchment tied with string. Place the
bowl in a pan of simmering water that
comes about halfway up the bowl.
Simmer in the pan for about 2 hours.
Ensure that the water does not
evaporate, topping it up from time to
time with boiling water.

7 Carefully turn the pudding out on to
a plate, and serve immediately with
cashew nut cream, oat milk custard
or vegan ice cream, if you like.

Cook's tip
You can finely chop the dried fruit
for a less chunky filling.

Energy 773kcal/3238kJ; Protein 13.2g; Carbohydrate 92.2g, of which sugars 56.2g; Fat 32.6g, of which saturates 25g; Cholesterol 0mg; Calcium 171mg; Fibre 11.2g; Sodium 71mg.

Bakewell tart

This traditional sweet almond tart is always the first to go at vegan food festivals. It is often attributed to Mrs Greaves, landlady of a pub in the English Peak District town of Bakewell in 1820. References have, however, been found to similar tarts dating back to medieval times.

3 Spread a layer of raspberry jam in the base of the pastry case (pie shell).

4 In a bowl, mix together the flour, ground almonds, sugar, lemon rind and baking powder. Add the oil, soya milk and extracts and mix again.

5 Pour the mixture over the jammy pastry base. Sprinkle with flaked almonds on top. Bake for 35 minutes.

6 Serve the tart warm with hot oat milk custard or soya ice cream.

Serves 8

60ml/4 tbsp raspberry jam
225g/8oz/2 cups wholemeal
   (whole-wheat) flour
50g/2oz/½ cup ground almonds
175g/6oz/¾ cup soft light brown sugar
5ml/1 tsp finely grated lemon rind
10ml/2 tsp baking powder
150ml/¼ pint/⅔ cup vegetable oil
200ml/7fl oz/scant 1 cup soya milk
5ml/1 tsp vanilla extract
5ml/1 tsp almond extract
25g/1oz flaked (sliced) almonds

For the pastry

250g/9oz/2¼ cups wholemeal
   (whole-wheat) flour
75ml/2½fl oz/⅓ cup rapeseed
   (canola) oil
15ml/1 tbsp sesame tahini
75ml/2½fl oz/⅓ cup sweetened soya milk

1 Preheat the oven to 190°C/375°F/ Gas 5. Make the pastry. Rub together the flour, oil and tahini until it resembles breadcrumbs. Gradually add the soya milk and mix to form a soft dough.

2 Roll out the dough on a floured surface into a circle that will line a 20cm/8in oiled pie dish. Prick the dough all over with a fork and bake it in the oven for about 10–15 minutes. Set aside to cool.

Energy 538kcal/2257kJ; Protein 11g; Carbohydrate 66.9g, of which sugars 30g; Fat 26.9g, of which saturates 2.8g; Cholesterol 0mg; Calcium 76mg; Fibre 6.2g; Sodium 17mg.

Pumpkin pie

The colonists who settled in North America in the 17th century saw the Native Americans growing and eating pumpkins and they soon embraced this new food. This version of the classic dessert will be an essential part of any American Thanksgiving vegan feast.

Serves 6–8

350g/12oz silken tofu
450g/1lb stewed mashed pumpkin
7.5ml/1½ tsp ground cinnamon
2.5ml/½ tsp ground ginger
2.5ml/½ tsp ground nutmeg
5ml/1 tsp sea salt
5ml/1 tsp vanilla extract
15ml/1 tbsp carob molasses or agave syrup
260g/9½oz/generous 1 cup soft light
  brown sugar
75ml/2½fl oz/⅓ cup rapeseed (canola) oil

For the pastry
250g/9oz/2¼ cups wholemeal
  (whole-wheat) flour
7.5ml/1½ tsp ground cinnamon
75ml/2½fl oz/⅓ cup pumpkin seed oil
  or rapeseed (canola) oil
15ml/1 tbsp pumpkin seed or peanut butter
75ml/2½fl oz/⅓ cup sweetened soya milk

1 Make the pastry. Rub together the flour, cinnamon, oil and butter until it resembles breadcrumbs. Add soya milk to form a soft dough.

2 Roll out dough and line an oiled 20cm/8in pie dish. Preheat the oven to 180°C/350°F/Gas 4.

3 Mix all the ingredients for the filling in a food processor or blender until smooth and creamy.

4 Pour the filling into the unbaked pastry case (pie shell), and bake in the oven for 50 minutes to 1 hour until golden brown.

5 Carefully transfer the pie on to a plate. Chill in the refrigerator before serving.

Energy 434kcal/1809kJ; Protein 6.2g; Carbohydrate 35.3g, of which sugars 19.4g; Fat 30.8g, of which saturates 13.8g; Cholesterol 94mg; Calcium 108mg; Fibre 1.2g; Sodium 60mg.

Crunchy pear and apricot flan

Do not be tempted to add any sugar with the fruit, as this will cause them to produce too much liquid. All the sweetness that you will need is in the pastry and the delicious crunchy topping.

Serves 8

75g/3oz/6 tbsp soya margarine
175g/6oz/1½ cups wholemeal
   (whole-wheat) flour
25g/1oz/¼ cup ground almonds
15ml/1 tbsp soya milk
30ml/2 tbsp agave syrup
1.5ml/¼ tsp almond extract
sifted icing (confectioners') sugar, for dusting

For the crunchy topping

115g/4oz/1 cup wholemeal
   (whole-wheat) flour
1.5ml/¼ tsp mixed (pumpkin pie) spice
50g/2oz/¼ cup soya margarine
60ml/4 tbsp agave syrup
50g/2oz/½ cup flaked (sliced) almonds

For the filling

450g/1lb pears
30ml/2 tbsp raisins or sultanas (golden raisins)
225g/8oz ready-to-eat dried apricots, chopped

1 To make the pastry, rub the soya margarine into the flour, either with your fingertips in a large mixing bowl or in a food processor, until the mixture resembles fine breadcrumbs.

2 Mix the soya milk with the agave syrup and almond extract and stir into the dry ingredients to form a soft, pliable dough. Knead the dough lightly on a floured surface until smooth, wrap in clear film (plastic wrap) and set aside until ready to roll out.

3 Meanwhile, make the crunchy topping. Sift the flour and mixed spice into a bowl and rub in the margarine. Stir in the agave syrup and almonds.

4 Roll out the dough on a lightly floured surface and use it to line a 23cm/9in loose-based flan tin (pan), taking care to press it neatly into the edges and to make a lip around the top edge.

5 Roll off the excess pastry to neaten the edge. Leave to chill in the refrigerator for about 15 minutes.

6 Preheat the oven to 190°C/375°F/ Gas 5. Place a baking sheet in the oven to preheat. Peel, core and slice the pears thinly. Arrange the slices on top of the pastry in overlapping, concentric circles, doming the centre. Sprinkle over the raisins or sultanas and apricots. The flan will seem too full at this stage, but the pears will reduce down during cooking and the filling will drop slightly.

7 Cover the apples with the crunchy topping mixture, pressing it down lightly. Bake on the hot baking sheet for 25–30 minutes, or until the top is golden brown. Test to make sure the pears are tender by inserting a metal skewer into them.

8 Leave the flan to cool in the tin for 10 minutes before turning out. Dust the top of the flan with icing sugar. The flan can be served either warm or cool.

Energy 397kcal/1664kJ; Protein 8.1g; Carbohydrate 51.4g, of which sugars 28.7g; Fat 19.1g, of which saturates 6.2g; Cholesterol 2mg; Calcium 69mg; Fibre 7g; Sodium 166mg.

Raspberry and almond tart

This is a beautifully rich tart, ideal for serving at the end of a special celebratory feast or at a dinner party. The raspberries and ground almonds are perfect partners.

Serves 4

200g/7oz sweet shortcrust pastry
125g/4¼oz silken tofu
75ml/2½fl oz/⅓ cup soya cream
50ml/2fl oz/¼ cup agave syrup
50g/2oz/½ cup ground almonds
20g/¾oz/1½ tbsp soya margarine
350g/12oz/2 cups raspberries

1 Roll out the sweet shortcrust pastry and use it to line a 20cm/8in flan tin (pan). Prick the base all over with a fork and leave it to rest for at least 30 minutes. Preheat the oven to 200°C/400°F/Gas 6.

2 Put the tofu, soya cream, agave syrup and ground almonds into a large bowl and whisk together briskly. Melt the margarine gently in a pan and pour into the mixture, stirring until the ingredients are well combined.

5 Bake the tart in the preheated oven for 25 minutes. Leave to cool for 5 minutes. Serve warm or cold.

3 Sprinkle the raspberries over the pastry case (pie shell). The ones at the top will appear through the surface, so space them evenly or in a pattern.

4 Pour the tofu and almond mixture on top of the raspberries. Ensure that it is spread evenly over the tart and some fruits are poking out of the top.

Variation
Peaches will also make a very attractive and tasty tart. Use six large, ripe peaches and remove the skin and stone (pit). Cut into slices and use in the same way as the raspberries above. You could also use mulberries if you can get them.

Energy 432kcal/1804kJ; Protein 10.4g; Carbohydrate 38.7g, of which sugars 15.3g; Fat 27.2g, of which saturates 7.8g; Cholesterol 19mg; Calcium 262mg; Fibre 4.1g; Sodium 297mg.

Apple and walnut strudel

This crisp pastry roll, filled with a delicious mix of fruit and jam, is the perfect sweet treat to accompany a cup of tea. No one can resist a slice of strudel served with a glass of lemon tea.

3 Preheat the oven to 180°C/350°F/ Gas 4. To make the filling, core and finely chop the apples but do not peel. Put the apples in a bowl, add the sultanas or raisins, syrup, walnuts, cinnamon and apricot jam or conserve and mix together until well combined.

4 Divide the pastry into three equal pieces. Place one piece on a sheet of lightly floured baking parchment and roll out to a rectangle measuring about 45 x 30cm/18 x 12in.

5 Spread one-third of the filling over the pastry, leaving a 1–2cm/½–¾in border. Roll up the pastry to enclose the filling and place, seam side down, on a non-stick baking sheet.

6 Repeat with the remaining pastry and filling. Bake the strudels for 25–30 minutes until golden brown all over.

7 Remove the strudels from the oven and leave to rest for 5 minutes to allow them to firm up slightly. Dust them liberally with icing sugar. Serve either warm or cold.

Makes 3, each serves 4–6

250g/9oz/generous 1 cup soya margarine
250g/9oz/generous 1 cup silken tofu
60ml/4 tbsp agave syrup
5ml/1 tsp vanilla extract
large pinch of salt
250g/9oz/2¼ cups wholemeal
   (whole-wheat) flour
icing (confectioners') sugar, sifted,
   for dusting

For the filling

2–3 cooking apples
45–60ml/3–4 tbsp sultanas
   (golden raisins) or raisins
45ml/3 tbsp agave syrup
115g/4oz/1 cup walnuts, roughly chopped
5–10ml/1–2 tsp ground cinnamon
60ml/4 tbsp apricot jam or conserve

1 To make the pastry, beat the margarine until light and fluffy, then add the tofu, agave syrup, vanilla extract and salt, and beat together.

2 Sift the flour into the mixture and stir until a soft dough forms. Wrap the dough in clear film (plastic wrap) and chill in the refrigerator overnight or until needed.

Energy 232kcal/967kJ; Protein 4g; Carbohydrate 17.7g, of which sugars 9g; Fat 16.6g, of which saturates 5.5g; Cholesterol 2mg; Calcium 87mg; Fibre 1.8g; Sodium 129mg.

German stollen

This German Christmas treat originally symbolized baby Jesus in swaddling clothes. German miners renamed it stollen, meaning 'entrance to a mine', as it reminded them of the tunnel entrance.

Serves 8

50g/2oz fresh yeast
100g/4oz/scant ½ cup soft light brown sugar
250ml/8fl oz/1 cup soya milk
500g/1¼lb/4¼ cups wholemeal
   (whole-wheat) flour
pinch of ground nutmeg
pinch of ground cloves
pinch of salt
5ml/1 tsp vanilla extract
5ml/1 tsp almond extract
200g/7oz/scant 1 cup soya margarine
50g/2oz/½ cup finely chopped almonds
200g/7oz/scant 1½ cups raisins
100g/3½ oz/scant ¾ cup currants
130g/11oz/1¾ cups chopped mixed
   orange and lemon peel
225g/8oz/1 cup good quality vegan marzipan
olive oil and icing (confectioners') sugar,
   for dusting

1 Break up the fresh yeast and place in a bowl with 5ml/1 tsp of sugar. Very gently warm the soya milk in a pan. Add the milk to the yeast mixture, stir and leave it to rise.

2 Sift the flour into a large bowl. Add the sugar, ground nutmeg, ground cloves, salt, vanilla and almond extracts and mix it all together. Add the soya margarine and the risen yeast and knead it well.

3 Spread out the dough on a floured surface. Mix together the almonds, raisins, currants and peel. Sprinkle over the dough and knead again.

4 Place the dough back in the bowl and cover with clear film (plastic wrap) or a clean dish towel. Leave the bowl in a warm place for 1–2 hours or more to allow the dough to rise.

5 Knead the dough again and roll it out to a rectangle measuring about 45 x 30cm/18 x 12in. Roll out the marzipan to the same size and place in the centre of the dough.

6 Roll up the dough with the marzipan inside. Place on an oiled baking sheet and leave to rise for 1–2 hours or more.

7 Preheat the oven to 190°C/375°F/ Gas 5. Cover the stollen with baking parchment and bake for 50–55 minutes.

8 While hot, brush lightly with oil and dust with icing sugar. Leave to cool on a wire rack. Serve in slices.

Energy 731kcal/3077kJ; Protein 12.6g; Carbohydrate 109.1g, of which sugars 70.3g; Fat 29.6g, of which saturates 9.9g; Cholesterol 4mg; Calcium 115mg; Fibre 8.2g; Sodium 285mg.

Gingerbread

This deliciously moist cake is flavoured with ginger and has been popular for two centuries. There is no reason why vegans should be excluded from enjoying this delectable treat.

Makes one 900g/2lb loaf

115g/4oz/½ cup soft light brown sugar
75g/3oz/6 tbsp soft dairy-free margarine
75g/3oz/¼ cup agave syrup
75g/3oz/¼ cup black treacle (molasses)
105ml/7 tbsp soya milk
1 small banana, mashed
175g/6oz/1½ cups wholemeal
  (whole-wheat) flour
50g/2oz/½ cup gram flour
pinch of salt
10ml/2 tsp ground ginger
5ml/1 tsp ground cinnamon
7.5ml/1½ tsp baking powder

1 Preheat the oven to 160°C/325°F/ Gas 3. Lightly oil a 900g/2lb loaf tin (pan) and line with baking parchment. Melt the sugar, margarine, syrup and treacle in a pan, stirring occasionally.

2 Remove the pan from the heat, leave to cool slightly, then mix in the soya milk and mashed banana.

3 Sift the flours, salt, spices and baking powder into a large mixing bowl, and mix until well combined.

4 Make a well in the centre, pour in the liquid mixture and beat well.

5 Pour the mixture into the prepared tin and bake for 1–1¼ hours until firm to the touch and lightly browned.

6 Allow to cool in the tin for a few minutes, then turn out on to a wire rack to cool completely. Store it in an airtight container or wrapped in foil.

Variation
For a more gingery flavour fold 50g/2oz finely chopped preserved stem ginger into the raw cake mixture and add 5–10ml/1–2 tsp extra ground ginger.

Energy 2274kcal/9594kJ; Protein 36.6g; Carbohydrate 399g, of which sugars 252.9g; Fat 70g, of which saturates 28.3g; Cholesterol 11mg; Calcium 589mg; Fibre 21.1g; Sodium 928mg.

Chocolate brownies

Dark and full of flavour, these brownies are irresistible. They are a perfect after-dinner treat or an ideal accompaniment to a cup of herbal tea. They also make a fabulous gift for a vegan friend.

Makes 20

150g/5oz/⅔ cup soya margarine
150g/5oz/scant 1 cup pitted dates,
   softened in boiling water,
   then drained and finely chopped
150g/5oz/1¼ cups self-raising (self-rising)
   wholemeal (whole-wheat) flour
10ml/2 tsp baking powder
60ml/4 tbsp unsweetened cocoa powder
   dissolved in 30ml/2 tbsp hot water
60ml/4 tbsp apple and pear fruit spread
90ml/6 tbsp soya milk
50g/2oz/½ cup pecan nuts, roughly broken

1 Preheat the oven to 160°C/325°F/ Gas 3. Lightly grease a shallow baking tin (pan), measuring approximately 28 x 18cm/11 x 7in.

2 Cream the soya margarine with the chopped dates in a large bowl until the mixture is well combined.

3 Sift the flour with the baking powder into the margarine and date mixture and mix thoroughly.

4 In a separate bowl, whisk together the dissolved cocoa powder with the apple and pear fruit spread.

5 Gradually pour the soya milk into the cocoa and spread mixture, whisking constantly to combine the ingredients. Pour into the flour mixture, stirring with a wooden spoon until everything is well mixed. Stir the pecan nuts into the bowl.

6 Spoon the mixture into the prepared tin, smooth the surface and bake for about 45–50 minutes or until a metal skewer inserted in the centre comes out clean.

7 Cool for a few minutes in the tin, then cut into bars or squares. Transfer to a wire rack and leave to cool.

Cook's tip
Apple and pear fruit spread is made from concentrated fruit juice. Look for the additive-free versions available in health-food stores and larger supermarkets.

Variation
You can use other nuts in the brownies if you prefer. Try using walnuts or hazelnuts, or a mixture.

Energy 135kcal/563kJ; Protein 2.2g; Carbohydrate 12.6g, of which sugars 7.5g; Fat 8.8g, of which saturates 3.3g; Cholesterol 1mg; Calcium 13mg; Fibre 1.5g; Sodium 91mg.

Spicy sultana muffins

Relaxed Sunday breakfasts will never be the same again once you have tried these delicious muffins. They are quick and easy to prepare and take only a short time to bake.

Makes 6

75g/3oz/6 tbsp soya margarine
50g/2oz silken tofu
120ml/4fl oz/½ cup soya milk
150g/5oz/1¼ cups wholemeal
  (whole-wheat) flour
7.5ml/1½ tsp baking powder
5ml/1 tsp ground cinnamon
pinch of salt
115g/4oz/scant 1 cup sultanas
  (golden raisins) or raisins

1 Preheat the oven to 190°C/375°F/ Gas 5. Grease six muffin or deep bun tins (pans). Beat the margarine, tofu and soya milk together in a bowl.

2 Sift the flour, baking powder, cinnamon and salt over the beaten mixture. Fold in, then beat well. Add the sultanas or raisins and stir until the mixture is thoroughly combined. Spoon into the prepared tins, ensuring that there is an even amount in each one.

3 Bake for about 20 minutes, or until the muffins have risen well and are firm to the touch with an even golden brown colour. Transfer to a wire rack to cool slighty before serving.

Cook's tip
These muffins taste equally delicious served cold. They also freeze well – pack them into freezer bags when they have cooled completely. To serve, leave them to thaw overnight or for a couple of hours, or defrost in a microwave, then warm them briefly in the oven.

Energy 235kcal/986kJ; Protein 5g; Carbohydrate 29.6g, of which sugars 14.1g; Fat 11.5g, of which saturates 4.7g; Cholesterol 2mg; Calcium 67mg; Fibre 2.6g; Sodium 111mg.

Scottish shortbread

These melt-in-the-mouth biscuits were traditionally eaten during Christmas or Hogmanay – the Scottish New Year. These vegan versions will no doubt be enjoyed all year round.

Makes 16

225g/8oz/2 cups plain (all-purpose) flour
115g/4oz/1 cup cornflour (cornstarch)
115g/4oz/1 cup icing (confectioners') sugar
115g/4oz/½ cup soya margarine
caster (superfine) sugar, for dusting

1 Lightly oil a baking tin (pan). It should be approximtely 30 x 20cm/12 x 8in, and at least 2.5cm/1in deep.

2 Sift the flour, cornflour and icing sugar into a large mixing bowl. Lightly rub in the margarine until the mixture resembles breadcrumbs. Then knead until it forms a stiff dough.

3 Preheat the oven to 180°C/350°F/ Gas 4. Place the dough in the tin and press it down, ensuring that it fills the corners. Smooth the surface with a metal spatula or palette knife.

4 Bake in the oven for approximately 25–30 minutes until the biscuits are a light golden brown colour. While still warm cut into 16 slices.

5 Leave the shortbread to cool slightly in the tin and then transfer to a wire rack to cool completely.

Variation

If you want to be really indulgent you can make a vegan version of millionaire's shortbread. First coat the shortbread with a layer of stewed dates mixed with tahini or pear and apple spread. Then top with some melted vegan chocolate.

Energy 155kcal/652kJ; Protein 1.4g; Carbohydrate 25.1g, of which sugars 7.8g; Fat 6.1g, of which saturates 2.6g; Cholesterol 1mg; Calcium 25mg; Fibre 0.4g; Sodium 62mg.

Apricot and pecan flapjacks

These tasty and nutritious flapjacks are perfect to make for children, and they are tasty snacks for the lunch box. The coconut oil and oats provide an excellent source of energy.

Makes 10

150ml/¼ pint/⅔ cup coconut oil
150g/5oz/⅔ cup light muscovado (brown) sugar
30ml/2 tbsp maple syrup
200g/7oz/2 cups rolled oats
50g/2oz/½ cup pecan nuts, chopped
50g/2oz/¼ cup ready-to-eat dried apricots, finely chopped

Variations
• You can substitute walnuts for the pecan nuts if you prefer, though the nutty flavour will not be as intense.
• Use different dried fruits instead of the apricots, if you like.

1 Preheat the oven to 160°C/325°F/ Gas 3. Lightly grease an 18cm/7in square shallow baking tin (pan).

2 Put the oil, sugar and maple syrup in a large heavy pan and heat gently, stirring until the sugar has dissolved. Remove from the heat and stir in the oats, nuts and apricots until well mixed.

3 Spread evenly in the prepared tin and, using a knife, score the mixture into ten bars. Bake in the oven for about 25–30 minutes, or until golden.

4 Remove from the oven and cut through the scored lines with a sharp knife. Leave until completely cold before removing from the tin.

Energy 240kcal/1000kJ; Protein 3.2g; Carbohydrate 18.3g, of which sugars 3.7g; Fat 17.6g, of which saturates 8.1g; Cholesterol 32mg; Calcium 21mg; Fibre 1.9g; Sodium 98mg.

Millet and almond treacle cookies

These little vegan cookies are quick to make, and will no doubt disappear just as fast. They are great treats for children, who will also love assisting in the preparation.

Makes about 25–30

90g/3½oz/7 tbsp soya margarine
150g/5oz/⅔ cup light muscovado (brown) sugar
30ml/2 tbsp black treacle (molasses)
50g/2oz silken tofu
150g/5oz/1¼ cups plain (all-purpose) flour
50g/2oz/½ cup millet flakes
50g/2oz/½ cup almonds, chopped
200g/7oz/generous 1 cup mixed dried fruit

Variations
• Add in some crushed walnuts or some grated vegan chocolate for a change.
• Works well with wholemeal (whole-wheat) flour too.

1 Preheat the oven to 190°C/375°F/ Gas 5. Line two large baking sheets with baking parchment.

2 Put the margarine, muscovado sugar, treacle and silken tofu in a large mixing bowl and beat together until well combined. The mixture should be light and fluffy.

3 Stir in the flour and millet flakes, the almonds and dried fruit. Place tablespoonfuls of the mixture on to the prepared baking sheets.

4 Bake for about 15 minutes until brown. Leave on the baking sheets for a few minutes, then transfer to a wire rack to cool completely.

Energy 97kcal/411kJ; Protein 1.4g; Carbohydrate 15.7g, of which sugars 10.6g; Fat 3.7g, of which saturates 1.2g; Cholesterol 0mg; Calcium 33mg; Fibre 0.5g; Sodium 29mg.

Nut brittle

If you are craving a sugary treat then it is a good idea to choose a recipe with lots of nuts in it. This sweet recipe combines toasted nuts and caramel to produce a crisp nut brittle.

Makes about 24

115g/4oz/1 cup almonds,
   half blanched, half unblanched
115g/4oz/1 cup hazelnuts,
   half blanched, half unblanched
5ml/1 tsp almond oil or a flavourless oil
225g/8oz/1 cup soft light brown sugar
15ml/1 tbsp lemon juice

Cook's tip

This nut brittle is perfect as an after-dinner treat with a coffee. It is also good pulverized and used as a topping for vegan ice cream.

1 Preheat the oven to 150°C/300°F/ Gas 2. Sprinkle the nuts on a baking sheet and toast for about 30 minutes, shaking the sheet occasionally. The nuts should smell pleasant and have turned brown and be very dry.

2 Coarsely chop the toasted nuts or crush them roughly with a rolling pin. Cover another baking tray with foil and grease it generously with the oil.

3 Put the sugar into a small pan and pour the lemon juice over. Cook over a high heat, shaking the pan, until the sugar melts and becomes a coffee colour and turns into caramel.

4 Immediately add the nuts and stir once, then pour the mixture on to the foil and spread out into a thin, even layer. Leave the mixture to harden.

5 Once set, break up the caramel into pieces and store in an airtight container.

Energy 99kcal/412kJ; Protein 1.7g; Carbohydrate 10.4g, of which sugars 10.2g; Fat 5.8g, of which saturates 0.5g; Cholesterol 0mg; Calcium 23mg; Fibre 0.7g; Sodium 2mg.

Seeded herby oatcakes

Adding thyme and sunflower seeds to these delicious oatcakes makes them especially good for dipping into a bowl of hummus – or try them spread with avocado and Marmite.

Makes 32

175g/6oz/1½ cups wholemeal
 (whole-wheat) flour
175g/6oz/1½ cups fine oatmeal
5ml/1 tsp salt
1.5ml/¼ tsp bicarbonate of soda
 (baking soda)
90ml/6 tbsp coconut oil
15ml/1 tbsp fresh thyme leaves, chopped
30ml/2 tbsp sunflower seeds
rolled oats, for sprinkling

1 Preheat the oven to 150°C/300°F/ Gas 2. Sprinkle two ungreased, non-stick baking sheets with rolled oats and set aside.

2 Put the flour, oatmeal, salt and bicarbonate of soda in a large bowl and rub in the coconut oil until the mixture resembles fine breadcrumbs. Stir in the thyme leaves.

3 Add just enough cold water (about 90–105ml/6–7 tbsp) to the dry ingredients and mix to form a stiff but not sticky dough.

4 Gently knead the dough on a lightly floured surface until it becomes smooth, then cut it roughly in half. Roll out one piece on a lightly floured surface to make a 23–25cm/9–10in round, about 1cm/½in in thickness.

5 Sprinkle the sunflower seeds over the dough and press them in with the rolling pin. Cut into triangles and arrange on one of the baking sheets. Repeat with the remaining dough. Bake for 45–60 minutes until crisp but not brown. Cool on wire racks.

Energy 63kcal/264kJ; Protein 1.6g; Carbohydrate 7.7g, of which sugars 0.1g; Fat 3.1g, of which saturates 1.8g; Cholesterol 0mg; Calcium 6mg; Fibre 0.9g; Sodium 2mg.

Crumpets

These quintessentially British breads are made with a yeast batter and cooked in metal rings on top of the stove. They are delicious served freshly toasted, spread with soya margarine.

Makes about 10

225g/8oz/2 cups plain (all-purpose) flour
2.5ml/½ tsp salt
2.5ml/½ tsp bicarbonate of soda
    (baking soda)
5ml/1 tsp fast-action yeast granules
350ml/12fl oz/1½ cup soya milk
oil, for greasing

1 Sift the flour, salt and bicarbonate of soda into a bowl and stir in the yeast. Make a well in the centre. Heat the milk until lukewarm and pour into the well.

2 Mix well with a whisk or wooden spoon, beating vigorously to make a thick smooth batter. Cover and leave in a warm place for about 1 hour until the mixture has a spongy texture.

Cook's tip
Crumpets make a great base for a mini vegan pizza. Top with some chopped herbs, tomatoes and vegan cheese and cook under the grill (broiler) until the cheese bubbles.

3 Heat a griddle or heavy frying pan. Lightly oil the hot surface and the inside of three or four metal rings, each measuring about 8cm/3½in in diameter. Place the oiled rings on the hot surface and leave for 1–2 minutes until they have become hot.

4 Spoon the batter into the rings to a depth of about 1cm/½in. Cook over a medium-high heat for about 6 minutes until the top surface is set and bubbles have burst open to make holes.

5 When set, carefully lift off the metal rings and flip the crumpets over. Cook on the second side for just 1 minute until lightly browned.

6 Remove from the pan and leave to cool completely on a wire rack. Repeat with the remaining crumpet mixture. Just before serving, toast the crumpets on both sides and serve spread with soya margarine, jam or marmite.

Energy 88kcal/373kJ; Protein 3.1g; Carbohydrate 17.8g, of which sugars 0.6g; Fat 0.9g, of which saturates 0.2g; Cholesterol 0mg; Calcium 36mg; Fibre 0.7g; Sodium 110mg.

Rosemary focaccia

If you do not need both loaves, freeze one for another time and warm it in the oven before
serving. Sprinkle the loaves with finely chopped garlic, if you prefer.

Makes 2 loaves

675g/1½lb/6 cups strong white
   bread flour
15ml/1 tbsp easy-blend (rapid-rise)
   dried yeast
75ml/5 tbsp olive oil
45ml/3 tbsp chopped fresh rosemary

Cook's tip

Put a bowl of water in the oven
with the focaccia to prevent it
from drying out too much as
it bakes.

1 Put the flour and yeast in a large bowl
with 5ml/1 tsp salt. Stir in 45ml/3 tbsp
of the oil and 450ml/¾ pint/scant
2 cups lukewarm water. Mix with a
round-bladed knife, then by hand to
a soft dough, adding a little more
lukewarm water if the dough feels dry.

2 Turn the dough out on to a lightly
floured surface and knead for 10
minutes, until it is smooth and elastic.
Put it in a lightly oiled bowl and cover
with oiled clear film (plastic wrap).
Leave in a warm place for about 1 hour,
until the dough has doubled in size.

3 Preheat the oven to 200°C/400°F/
Gas 6. Turn out the dough on to
a floured surface and cut it in half.
Roll out each half into a 25cm/10in
round. Transfer the rounds to greased
baking sheets, cover with lightly oiled
clear film and leave for 20 minutes,
until risen.

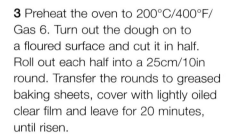

4 Press your fingers into the dough to
make deep holes all over it about
3cm/1¼ in apart. Leave for a further
5 minutes.

5 Sprinkle with the rosemary and plenty
of sea salt. Sprinkle with water to
keep the crust moist and bake for
25 minutes, until pale golden. Remove
from the oven and drizzle with the
remaining olive oil. Transfer to a wire
rack to cool.

Energy 1436kcal/6068kJ; Protein 34.8g; Carbohydrate 266g, of which sugars 5.1g; Fat 33.1g, of which saturates 4.6g; Cholesterol 0mg; Calcium 575mg; Fibre 10.5g; Sodium 18mg.

Three seed loaf

Cornmeal and a cornucopia of seeds give this superb loaf a delicious flavour and unique texture. It is perfect served with a hummus dip.

3 Turn out the dough on to a lightly floured surface and knead for about 5 minutes until smooth and elastic.

4 Place in a lightly oiled bowl, cover with lightly oiled clear film (plastic wrap) and leave to rise, in a warm place, for about 1 hour, or until doubled in size.

5 Turn out the dough on to a lightly floured surface and knock back (punch down). Gently knead the pumpkin and sesame seeds into the dough. Shape into a round ball and flatten slightly.

6 Place on the prepared baking sheet, cover with lightly oiled clear film or slide into a large, lightly oiled plastic bag and leave to rise in a warm place again for 45 minutes, or until doubled in size.

7 Meanwhile, preheat the oven to 200°C/400°F/Gas 6. Brush the top of the loaf with water and sprinkle evenly with the sunflower seeds. Bake the loaf for 30–35 minutes, or until it is golden and sounds hollow when tapped on the base. Transfer the loaf to a wire rack to cool completely.

Makes 1 Loaf

275g/10oz/2½ cups unbleached
  white bread flour
50g/2oz/½ cup cornmeal
5ml/1 tsp salt
20g/¾oz fresh yeast
120ml/4fl oz/½ cup lukewarm water
120ml/4fl oz/½ cup soya milk
15ml/1 tbsp pumpkin seeds
15ml/1 tbsp sesame seeds
30ml/2 tbsp sunflower seeds

1 Lightly grease a baking sheet. Sift the flours and salt into a large bowl.

2 Cream the yeast with a little of the water in a jug (pitcher). Stir in the remainder of the water and the soya milk. Pour this into the centre of the flour and mix to a fairly soft dough.

Energy 1511kcal/6371kJ; Protein 45.7g; Carbohydrate 259.7g, of which sugars 5.9g; Fat 37.2g, of which saturates 4.2g; Cholesterol 0mg; Calcium 553mg; Fibre 13.5g; Sodium 2016mg.

Tandoori rotis

These unleavened rotis are one of the many delicious breads from India. They would normally be baked in a clay oven called a tandoor but are easily cooked in a traditional oven, as here.

Makes 6

350g/12oz/3 cups wholemeal
   (whole-wheat) flour
5ml/1 tsp salt
250ml/8fl oz/1 cup water
30–45ml/2–3 tbsp coconut oil for brushing

1 Sift the flour and salt into a large bowl. Add the water and mix to a soft dough. Knead the dough on a lightly floured surface for 3–4 minutes until smooth.

2 Place the dough in a lightly oiled bowl, cover with lightly oiled clear film (plastic wrap). Leave to rest for 1 hour.

3 Turn out on to a lightly floured surface. Divide the dough into six pieces and shape each into a ball. Press out into a larger round with your hand, cover with lightly oiled clear film and leave to rest for 10 minutes.

4 Meanwhile, preheat the oven to 230°C/450°F/Gas 8. Place three baking sheets in the oven to heat. Roll the rotis into 15cm/6in rounds, place two on each baking sheet and bake in the oven for about 8–10 minutes. Lightly brush each roti with oil and serve warm.

Cook's tips
• The rotis are ready when light brown bubbles appear on the surface and they puff up slightly.
• Add in extra spices such as cumin or cardamom, if you like.

Energy 244kcal/1030kJ; Protein 5.5g; Carbohydrate 45.3g, of which sugars 0.9g; Fat 5.8g, of which saturates 2.5g; Cholesterol 0mg; Calcium 82mg; Fibre 1.8g; Sodium 329mg.

Societies and shopping

There are many vegan societies around the world. They provide information and advice on ways of living a life that is free from animal products. There are also plenty of stores selling a range of vegan products, from food and drink to clothing, shoes and toiletries.

United Kingdom

The Vegan Society,
Donald Watson House,
21 Hylton Street,
Hockley,
Birmingham
B18 6HJ
Tel: 0121 523 1730
www.vegansociety.com

Vegan Village
www.veganvillage.co.uk

Beyond Skin
34 Westbourne Gardens
Hove, East Sussex
BN3 5PP
Tel: 0845 373 3648
www.beyondskin.co.uk

Bourgeois Boheme
Hydrex House,
Garden Road
Richmond
TW9 4NR
Tel: 0208 878 8388
www.bboheme.com

Essential Trading Co-operative Ltd
Unit 3
Lodge Causeway Trading Estate
Fishponds, Bristol
BS16 3JB
Tel: 0117 958 3550
www.essential-trading.co.uk

Ethical Junction CIC
112 Lyndhurst Road
Ashurst, Southampton
Hampshire
SO40 7AU
Tel: 023 8029 3763
www.ethical-junction.org/directory

Foods for Life Nutritionists
96-98 High Street,
Croydon
CR0 1ND
Tel: 0871 288 4642
www.optimumnutritionists.com

GoodnessDirect
South March, Daventry
NN11 4PH
Tel: 0871 871 6611
www.GoodnessDirect.co.uk

The Health Store
Unit 10, Blenheim Park Road
Nottingham
NG6 8YP
Tel: 0115 976 7200
www.thehealthstore.co.uk

Highland Wholefoods Workers
Cooperative Ltd
Unit 6, 13 Harbour Road
Inverness
IV1 1SY
Tel: 01463 712393
www.highlandwholefoods.co.uk

Holland and Barrett
Samuel Ryder House, Townsend Drive
Nuneaton
CV11 6XW
Tel: 0870 606 6605
www.hollandandbarrett.com

Lush Cosmetics
Unit 3, 19 Willis Way,
Fleets Industrial Estate,
Poole,
BH15 3SS
Tel: 01202 668545
www.lush.co.uk

National Association of Health Stores
PO Box 14177,
Tranent,
EH34 5WX
Tel: 01875-341 408
www.nahs.co.uk

Plamil Foods Ltd
Folkestone
Kent
CT19 6PQ
Tel: 01303 850588
www.plamilfoods.co.uk

The Redwood Wholefood Co. Ltd
Redwood House, Burkitt Road
Earlstrees Industrial Estate,
Corby
NN17 4DT
Tel: 01536 400557
www.redwoodfoods.co.uk

Suma Wholefoods
Lacy Way,
Lowfields Business Park,
Elland
HX5 9DB
Tel: 01422 313845
www.suma.co.uk

Traidcraft Plc
Kingsway
Gateshead
Tyne and Wear
NE11 0NE
Tel: 0845 330 8900
www.traidcraftshop.co.uk

Vegan Store Ltd
PO Box 110
Rottingdean
Brighton
BN51 9AZ
www.veganstore.co.uk

Yaoh
PO Box 333
Bristol
BS99 1NF
Tel: 0117 9239053
www.yaoh.co.uk

USA

American Vegan Society
56 Dinshah Lane
P.O. Box 369
Malaga NJ 08328
Tel: (856) 694-2887
www.americanvegan.org

Earth Save
http://www.earthsave.org/

Alternative Outfitters
Suite 1, 408 S. Pasadena Ave
Pasadena, CA 91105
Tel: (626) 396-4972
www.alternativeoutfitters.com

Different Daisy
515 Second Street
Portsmouth OH 45662
Tel: (740) 935-3146
www.differentdaisy.com

Flora Inc.
Post Office Box 73
805 E. Badger Road
Lynden
Washington 98264
Tel: 1-800-446-2110
www.florahealth.com

Green People
Suite #206
41 Highland Ave
Highland Park NJ 08904
Tel: (732) 514-1066
www.greenpeople.org

The Hain Celestial Group 4600
Sleepytime Dr.
Boulder, CO 80301
Tel: 1-800-434-4246
www.hain-celestial.com

Organic Consumers Association
6771 South Silver Hill Drive
Finland MN 55603
Tel: (218) 226-4164
www.organicconsumers.org

Whole Foods Market, Inc.
550 Bowie Street
Austin TX 78703-4644
Tel: (512) 477-4455
www.wholefoodsmarket.com

Vegan Store
2381 Lewis Ave
Rockville MD 20851
1-800-340-1200
www.veganstore.com

Vegan essentials
Unit 8, 1701 Pearl St
Waukesha WI 53186
Tel: (262) 574-7761
www.veganessentials.com

Australia

The Vegan Society of Australia
PO Box 85
Seaford
VIC 3198
Tel: (03) 9776 4425
www.veganaustralia.net

Vegetarian/Vegan Society
of Queensland
1086 Waterworks Road
The Gap QLD 4061
Tel: (07) 3300 9320
www.vegsoc.org.au

Vegan Society NSW
PO Box 467
Broadway NSW 2007
Tel: (02) 9544 3328
www.vegansocietynsw.com

The Cruelty Free Shop
76 Waratah St
Haberfield NSW 2045
Tel: (02) 9799 4776
www.crueltyfreeshop.com.au

Fundamental food store
140 Keen Street
Lismore NSW 2480
Tel: (02) 6622 2199
www.fundies.com.au

Only Australian Groceries
1/ 37 Queens Rd, Everton Hills
Brisbane QLD 4053
Tel: (07) 3353 5782
www.onlyoz.com.au

Vegan Perfection
59 Queen St
Altona VIC 3018
Tel: (03) 9398 6302
www.veganperfection.com.au

Vegan Wares (shoes)
78 Smith Street
Collingwood 3066
Tel: (03) 9417 0230
www.veganwares.com

New Zealand

Porphyry's People
www.vegan.org.nz

Green Peace
Private Bag 92507
Wellesley Street, Auckland 1141
Tel: (09) 630 6317
www.gefreefood.org.nz/outlets.asp

Sanitarium Health Food Company
Private Bag 92127
Auckland 1142
Tel: 0800 100 257
www.sanitarium.co.nz

Wrights Vegan Wines
Tel: (06) 868 0967
www.wrightswines.co.nz

World Vegan Day

www.wvd.org.au
www.worldveganday.org.uk
www.vegansworldnetwork.org

Index

Acknowledgements

Picture acknowledgements:
Alamy p15t & b, p32b, p41bl & br; American Vegan Society p11br; Corbis p10t; Foods for Life p10b; Istock p6t, p11t, p13t, p20b, p30b, p31t & b, p35t; OKÉ/Pete Stephens p29t; Plamil Foods Ltd p11bl; Spirit of Nature Ltd/Ecolution Srl p30t.

Photographers: Karl Adamson; Edward Allwright; Peter Anderson; Caroline Arber; David Armstrong; Tim Auty; Steve Baxter; Martin Brigdale; Louisa Dare; Nicki Dowey; Micki Dowie; James Duncan; Gus Filgate; John Freeman; Ian Garlick; Michelle Garrett; Will Heap; Peter Henley; John Heseltine; Amanda Heywood; Ferguson Hill; Janine Hosegood; Becky Johnson; David Jordan; Maris Kelly; Dave King; Don Last; William Lingwood; Patrick McLeavey; Michael Michaels; Steve

Moss; Roisin Neild; Thomas Odulate; Spike Powell; Craig Robertson; Bridget Sargeson; Simon Smith; Sam Stowell; Polly Wreford.

Recipe writers: Pepita Aris; Catherine Atkinson; Josephine Bacon; Mridula Baljekar; Jane Bamforth; Mary Banks; Alex Barker; Valerie Barrett; Ghillie Başan; Judy Bastyra; Steve Baxter; Michelle Berridale-Johnson; Susannah Blake; Angela Boggiano; Janet Brinkworth; Kathy Brown; Carla Capalbo; Kit Chan; Jacqueline Clark; Maxine Clark; Carole Clements; Andi Clevely; Trish Davies; Roz Denny; Patrizia Diemling; Matthew Drennan; Tessa Evelegh; Joanna Farrow; Rafi Fernandez; Marina Filippelli; Jenni Fleetwood; Christine France; Silvana Franco; Yasuko Fukuoka; Sarah Gates; Shirley Gill; Brian Glover;

Nicola Graimes; Rosamund Grant; Carole Handslip; Juliet Harbutt; Rebekah Hassan; Shehzad Husain; Deh-Ta Hsuing; Christine Ingram; Judy Jackson; Becky Johnson; Bridget Jones; Peter Jordan; Manisha Kanani; Soheila Kimberley; Lucy Knox; Masaki Ko; Elisabeth Lambert Ortiz; Ruby Le Bois; Clare Lewis; Sara Lewis; Lesley Mackley; Norma MacMillan; Sue Maggs; Kathy Man; Sally Mansfield; Elizabeth Martin; Maggie Mayhew; Christine McFadden; Norma Miller; Jane Milton; Sallie Morris; Annie Nichols; Suzannah Olivier; Maggie Pannell; Katherine Richmond; Keith Richmond; Rena Salaman; Jennie Shapter; Anne Sheasby; Ysanne Spevack; Marlene Spieler; Jenny Stacey; Liz Trigg; Christopher Trotter; Linda Tubby; Oona van den Berg; Sunil Vijayaker; Hilaire

Walden; Laura Washburn; Steven Wheeler; Jenny White; Kate Whiteman; Lucy Whiteman; Rosemary Wilkinson; Carol Wilson; Elizabeth Wolf-Cohen; Jeni Wright.

Food stylists and home economists: Eliza Baird; Alex Barker; Caroline Barty; Angela Boggiano; Fergal Connolly; Joanne Craig; Nicki Dowey; Tonia George; Joanna Farrow; Christine France; Silvana Franco; Annabel Ford; Carole Handslip; Jo Harris; Amanda Heywood; Claire Louise Hunt; Kate Jay; Becky Johnson; Jill Jones; Emma MacIntosh; Penny Markham; Lucy McKelvie; Sarah O'Brien; Marion Price; Bridget Sargeson; Jennie Shapter; Carol Tennant; Helen Trent; Linda Tubby; Sunil Vijayaker; Jenny White; Elizabeth Wolf-Cohen.